POWERING PLACES *Santa Monica*

Land Art Generator Initiative

POWERING PLACES *Santa Monica*

Land Art Generator Initiative

PRESTEL
MUNICH · LONDON · NEW YORK

CONTENTS

"Art always reflects society—whether past, present, or future—and serves a function by showing us ourselves as we are (and as who we might become)."

—Elizabeth Monoian and Robert Ferry
Founding Directors, Land Art Generator Initiative

The Ocean Still:
Lagrimas de Santa Monica
Nuith Morales, Stephanie Hsia, Courtney A. Goode,
Michelle Arevalos Franco, Helen E. Kongsgaard

See page 206

FOREWORD

Craig Watson
Director, California Arts Council

The Land Art Generator Initiative is devoted to bringing deep imagination and hard science to bear on a complex problem tailored to a specific location. Many a viewer of the results might be tempted to identify these projects as a form of "alchemy" or magic. That was admittedly my first reaction as I gazed upon the cover image, *The Solar Hourglass*, for the publication documenting the Copenhagen 2014 LAGI competition. That transcendental feeling was reinforced by countless other images as I leafed through the book. And strangely, the feeling was familiar, rather than wholly new. It took me back to 1976.

That year I had the good fortune to find myself in Sonoma County, California, just as Christo and Jeanne-Claude were preparing the final installation of their genre-bending project, *Running Fence*. As a recent studio art graduate in sculpture and having fallen in love with Christo and Jeanne-Claude's previous bold, physical interventions in the landscape, I was fortunate to get hired on with several hundred other young "locals" to complete this project. As the reader should know, *Running Fence* was composed of a continuous set of 18-foot, glistening white fabric panels tracing the rolling Sonoma County hills for 24.5 miles until sinking at its terminus in the Pacific Ocean at Bodega Bay. Anyone fortunate to witness this project firsthand, particularly over the course of a full day or more, recalls that *Running Fence* immediately changed your view of the stunning beauty that are the gold and green and brown coastal California hills it traversed. Like the experience of visually following a cattle fence as it tucks and turns and disappears as if a real-time 3-D topographical map, *Running Fence* amplified and focused our eyes to truly see the land, appreciate its contours, relish its peaks, and imagine its hollows. Though *Running Fence*, along with Christo and Jeanne-Claude's previous and subsequent work, were not designed to generate clean water or clean energy, they sit lightly on the land or the water, utilize state-of-the-art technology, and leave us asking important questions about how we interact with our planet.

For me, what LAGI demands is a similar respect for a specific place. It forces us to merge a robust, place-based understanding with something that enhances the depth of our experience of environment and, ideally, fills us with new wonder. After all, what can be more magnificent than the alchemy of art and science helping us to reimagine a world where our creations add to our abundance, not deplete it.

The Solar Hourglass
The first place winner of LAGI 2014
Copenhagen was designed by Santiago
Muros Cortés. The artwork utilizes
concentrated solar power (thermal
beam-down tower with heliostats).

INTRODUCTION

The Power of the Arts to Address Climate Change

Shannon Daut
City of Santa Monica Cultural Affairs Manager

Climate change is the biggest issue of our time. As the effects of climate change become more and more pronounced with each passing year, citizens across the globe are becoming increasingly aware of the need to do something . . . *anything* . . . to address this issue. The enormity of the problem cannot be overstated, and we will need all hands on deck to stem the tide of climate change. Artists and the arts can play a significant role in helping us meet this challenge head-on by humanizing global issues, deepening community engagement, and stimulating creative solutions to seemingly intractable problems.

Art helps us see things in new ways; it can transform our understanding of our relationship to issues, both within ourselves and in our communities. From Chris Jordan's *Running the Numbers* project, which visualizes large-scale statistics in ways that help people comprehend the enormity of global consumption, to *CURRENT:LA*, a public art biennial produced by the City of Los Angeles that featured temporary art installations exploring the theme of water, the arts are a powerful tool to help people grasp the severity of our environmental challenges. Art is able to create meaning in a way that speeches and public policy briefings cannot—it is a powerful clarion call to environmental issues because it can make the abstract personal, real.

The arts can serve as a powerful platform to promote community dialogue around critical social issues. By providing a space for people to gather, share stories, and participate in active discussion, artistic experiences can generate new forums through which people are empowered to make a meaningful difference in their communities. Alaska is often seen as the "canary in the coal mine" for climate change in the United States. In 2016, the Island Institute, based in Sitka, Alaska, organized a unique artist residency program, Tidelines, which featured Alaska Native and international artists whose work addressed climate change. The group toured Southeast Alaska on the ferry system, stopping in nine cities over the course of a month to host performances, workshops, and community conversations about the impacts of climate change on their communities, their livelihoods, and their way of life. Further, by engaging Indigenous communities in an exploration of ways that traditional practices can inspire innovation, new possibilities are unleashed. This is just one of a myriad of examples of artists and arts organizations working with and in communities to create spaces for people to gather and have meaningful conversations about issues that matter in their lives and for our planet.

Wake Up
A submission to LAGI 2016 by Henry
Moll and Mary Carroll-Coelho

Finally, artists can help foster the development and implementation of creative approaches to solve our most pressing problems. Working alongside scientists and engineers, artists provide unique perspectives that can lead to new discoveries. Plus, they make the final product much more aesthetically pleasing! Whether it is playful swan floats that generate energy through the waves at the ocean's wake, or weightless balloons that float above the coastal horizon while capturing energy from the wind and sea, the lens through which artists view the world contains untold potential to find new models and approaches for this work. The Land Art Generator Initiative is a pioneer in this important work, providing a platform for artists, scientists, and engineers to work together to address climate change. The projects included in this book illustrate the dynamic possibilities that are created when artists are involved in helping to imagine new possibilities for our planet.

POWERING PLACES

Elizabeth Monoian and Robert Ferry

We may look back on the year 2016 as a turning point for the climate and our cultural and social responses to it.

The effects of a very strong El Niño event gave us a glimpse into the new normal for twenty-first-century temperatures. Atmospheric scientist Ed Hawkins gave us the *Climate Spiral* visualization that shows the earth's average temperature spinning quickly out of control toward a 2°C average global shift,[1] highlighting how the COP 21 Paris aspirations of maintaining a 1.5-degree cap may be overly optimistic.

Attorneys General in twenty states launched climate fraud investigations against Exxon, accused of acting intentionally to confuse the public on the issue of climate change, after the Center for International Environmental Law and *InsideClimate News* uncovered internal Exxon documents proving that the company has understood the science of atmospheric CO_2 levels since the 1960s,[2] pointing then to the year 2000 as the point when catastrophic changes would begin to set in. The similarity between Big Oil's subsequent funding of climate denial campaigns and Big Tobacco's war on health science earlier in the century are becoming quickly apparent.

The year brought good news as well, with the International Renewable Energy Agency (IRENA) reporting that 2015 was another record year for added renewable energy infrastructure capacity, adding 152 gigawatts, or 8.3% more than the previous year, bringing the total online capacity to nearly 2,000 gigawatts globally. Renewable energy accounted for 68% of added United States power plant capacity added in 2015, putting the squeeze on natural gas (only 25% of new capacity in 2015), while the percentage of electricity generated from coal in the U.S. continues to decline year after year (14 gigawatts were shuttered in 2015).[3]

North America (United States, Canada, Mexico) jointly committed to 50% zero-carbon electricity by 2050. California has promised to meet that same goal 20 years earlier in 2030 (of course, Denmark shows us all what real goals are with their target of 100% carbon-free electricity by 2035).[4]

What all of this means is that everything is about to change. The tipping point has occurred, and the path to a postcarbon future is coming into focus. While it is important that we act quickly and decisively,[5] it is also important that we don't make mistakes along the way. We need the path to our postcarbon future to be an equitable one that empowers people everywhere to improve their lives on their own terms and in harmony with nature. We must be careful to not add to the cost of living regressively, or to introduce new externalities as we build the renewable energy economy by maintaining strict standards of economic justice, regenerative design,[6] and circular economies.[7] We must look to solutions outside of the synthetic industrial engineering paradigm of the twentieth century, and avoid the emergence of a "renewable energy resource curse" for those who live in regions rich in solar, wind, geothermal, and water resources.[8]

In her final memorial project, *What Is Missing*, which is dedicated to expanding awareness of species and habitat loss within the context of climate change, Maya Lin points out the fact that deforestation accounts for 10–20% of global carbon emissions and that new forest biomass can contribute to carbon sequestration. By protecting forests through reforestation projects we can save species habitats while also slowing the rate of carbon dioxide increase in the atmosphere. As Maya Lin puts it so wonderfully, we can "save two birds with one tree."[9]

1. E. Hawkins, IPCC AR5 Contributing Author (National Centre for Atmospheric Science, University of Reading, May 9, 2016), http://www.climate-lab-book.ac.uk/2016/spiralling-global-temperatures.

2. Neela Banerjee, John H. Cushman Jr., David Hasemyer, and Lisa Song, "CO_2's Role in Global Warming Has Been on the Oil Industry's Radar Since the 1960s," *InsideClimate News*, April 13, 2016. See also online at https://insideclimatenews.org/news/13042016/climate-change-global-warming-oil-industry-radar-1960s-exxon-api-co2-fossil-fuels.

3. http://www.eia.gov, accessed on July 15, 2016.

4. These measures do not account for heat energy, transportation, and other energy uses, which Denmark includes in its 100% goal for 2050. These are unfortunately left out of some strategic plans, which focus only on electricity. Electricity accounted for 40% of energy used globally in 2012.

5. NASA's Jet Propulsion Laboratory says we are already "locked into" one meter of additional sea level rise this century, and Robert M. DeConto and David Pollard writing in the journal *Nature* (10.1038/nature17145) offer evidence to support the fragility of the Antarctic ice sheet, which itself could add 15 meters to sea level by 2500 if emissions continue unabated this century.

6. The Product-Life Institute in Geneva was founded in 1982 by Walter R. Stahel and Orio Giarini, http://www.product-life.org/. See also: John Lyle, *Regenerative Design for Sustainable Development and Design for Human Ecosystems* (New York: Wiley, 1994).

We love the inherent optimism of the phrase and the notion that the climate challenge, while the most complex and intractable of problems that humanity has ever had to face, also presents opportunities for collective action and public policy changes that can have positive effects within many aspects of our lives that may seem less obviously related to climate.

This is a sentiment that is also echoed in Naomi Klein's 2014 book.[10] The "two birds" that are saved in the context of *This Changes Everything* are: (1) environmental systems are allowed to heal following aggressive climate action; and (2) social systems are also allowed to heal as a consequence of effective climate action that necessarily involves an expansion of communitarian and egalitarian public policy.

The realization that the most direct path to climate change mitigation is paved with regulations and policies that will empower people, communities, and civic institutions is increasingly informing Land Art Generator Initiative projects. In 2015–2016 we launched four new projects, all with a focus on community-oriented approaches to both public art and renewable energy.[11]

Social and cultural benefits of climate action have been a part of LAGI's mission since its founding in 2008. Specifically we have been advocating for the design of renewable energy infrastructure that communities can embrace. The world that we would like to see emerge in the next decade is one in which the mass proliferation of clean energy systems will also lead to some of the twenty-first century's greatest works of art and social projects.

The two (or three) birds that we wish to save, so to speak, are the natural environment (climate), our visual environment (the aesthetics of public space and the design of cities), and access to clean energy without externalities (energy justice).

Naomi Klein points to another way in which climate action can have positive effects beyond the most obvious one in which generations hence get to live on a planet that is still habitable. The steps that we must take to reduce carbon emissions are the same steps that we must take if we are serious about alleviating social and economic inequity. Addressing the issue of global equity is indispensably a part of closing the climate policy gap.[12] Acting together in our most pressing common interest requires a new sense of communitarianism and empathy, and a turning away from the seductions of rugged individualism and mindless consumerism.

We typically refer to a global development divide by speaking in terms of the "developed world" and the "developing world." While this is a welcome improvement on "first world" and "third world" we would like to propose a new frame: "high-carbon world" and "low-carbon world." The reason is that it flips the value set inherent in the language that we use, and it reminds inhabitants of the high-carbon world (we count ourselves in that number) that the responsibility lies with us to move toward the low-carbon world—those who have already succeeded in maintaining a more balanced relationship with nature with regard to the resources that are used on a daily basis to support average lifestyles. Let's celebrate those who maintain that balance, rather than disparage sustainable cultures as somehow in need of "development."

This new framing also questions the assumption that "development" as it is defined by the United Nations Development Program and the World Bank (a classification of nations determined by per capita gross national income) is necessarily something that will lead to better outcomes for human well-being, happiness, and the environment.[13] By honestly including natural capital[14] on the balance sheets of planetary profit and loss we can change

7   David W. Pearce and R. Kerry Turner,
    *Economics of Natural Resources and the
    Environment* (Baltimore: Johns Hopkins
    University Press, 1989).

    Ellen MacArthur Foundation, "Towards
    the Circular Economy: An Economic and
    Business Rationale for an Accelerated
    Transition" (2012), PDF publication online
    at https://www.ellenmacarthurfoundation.org.

8   Kanyinke Sena, "Renewable Energy Projects
    and the Rights of Marginalised/Indigenous
    Communities in Kenya" (International Work
    Group for Indigenous Affairs, 2015), PDF
    publication online at http://www.iwgia.org/
    iwgia_files_publications_files/0725_REPORT21.pdf.

9   Maya Lin, September 17, 2009, Lecture at
    the California Academy of Sciences, San
    Francisco, CA, http://www.sfartscommission.org/
    pubartcollection/pubart-press-releases/2009/09/17/
    press-kit-maya-lin-debuts-final-memorial-at-
    california-academy-of-sciences.

10 Naomi Klein, *This Changes Everything* (New
    York: Simon & Schuster, 2014).

11 (1) LAGI Glasgow (supported by Glasgow
    City Council and igloo Regeneration,
    and in collaboration with ecoartscotland,
    Scottish Canals, and BIGG Regeneration):
    LAGI managed an invited competition
    for an urban regeneration site along the
    Scottish Canals with an emphasis on
    an ecological place-making approach to
    community-building. The winning design,
    Wind Forest, will be installed as an integrated
    component, giving back to the surrounding
    neighborhoods with a public park that
    provides clean electricity to 300 of the
    homes in the new development.
    See http://landartgenerator.org/glasgow.

the metrics by which we measure success, and shift incentive structures toward favoring regeneration rather than exploitation. The high-carbon world has much to learn about how localized agriculture, energy-efficient vernacular architecture, holistic medicine, and steady-state economies can help to pull us back from the brink of global environmental catastrophe. Until we can accept with humility that the predominant value set of the twentieth century—a view of nature as a thing to manage and of people as consumers—is counterproductive to climate solutions, we have a frustrating road ahead in the twenty-first century.

The global free market has shown that it isn't capable on its own of quickly providing the incentive structures that can make it a mechanism for achieving harmony with nature. Given the limited time that we have to get things right, we could take a lesson from the triumphs of large-scale public-sector investment and policies that led to the midcentury golden era for the middle class.

If every "high-carbon world" country implemented a new Sustainable Works Progress Administration (SWPA) we could mobilize collective action with the force of a planetary patriotic duty. Within decades we could build our new energy infrastructure, establish regenerative economic policies, and give our cities the long-term resiliency they need to prosper. The United States has made this kind of public-sector investment many times before. It's just that it is usually mobilized for destructive rather than constructive ends. This time we need a war on climate change.

Similar to the WPA in the 1930s United States,[15] an SWPA project offers the opportunity to realize the potential for infrastructure projects to provide an outlet for creative expression and contribute to our culture in meaningful ways. Imagine the majestic beauty of the massive infrastructures that will power our prosperity for the next hundred years, regeneratively designed with input from creatives, that will allow the planet to heal.

In every sense, design is the key driver of positive change and climate action: design of infrastructure, design of buildings and cities, design of regional planning systems, design of closed-loop industrial systems, design of waste management, design of cradle-to-cradle consumer goods, and the design of good public policy and regulations.

Cities that recognize the value of arts and culture have long benefited from percent for art programs. It has become expected (and in many cases required) for large-scale development projects to invest at least 1% in the arts, especially when there is public funding involved, either by bringing an artist onto the project team to produce an on-site work, or by investing in a fund that is pooled for larger projects throughout the city.

As we increase our focus on large-scale environmental and climate design solutions—resilient infrastructures, environmental remediation, regenerative water and energy projects—it is high time that a similar percent for art requirement be placed on these projects as well. This simple policy standard could bring great benefit to communities that otherwise find themselves left out of the process. Even when their net benefit to the environment is clear, if these projects have not been considered from a cultural perspective, they risk being ignored at best. And at worst they risk alienating the public and sparking pushback against similar future projects.

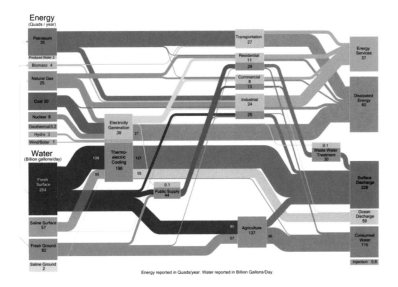

Water-Energy Nexus Sankey Diagram
United States Department of Energy

(2) Art+Energy=Camp (supported by Google Community Grants, the Heinz Endowments, Three Rivers Community Foundation, and in collaboration with Homewood Renaissance Association and Conservation Consultants Inc.): In 2015 LAGI held our first summer camp for renewable energy public art design and construction. The Camp gave 20 kids from Pittsburgh's historically underserved Homewood neighborhood a summer of activities and learning on energy science, conservation, and public art, and led them through their own design process to conceive of and help to construct a 4.2 kWp solar sculpture that helps to power a local community center.
See http://artenergycamp.org.

(3) Maasai Solar is a LAGI collaboration with Tereneh Mosely, the founder of Idia'Dega, who has been working with the Olorgesailie Maasai Women Artisans (OMWA), a group of 30 women in the South Rift Valley. The partnership is bringing aesthetically and culturally relevant renewable energy infrastructure to the Maasai community in Olorgesailie, Kenya, and expanding Idia'Dega + OMWA's sustainable economic model. Sales on the global market of solar accessories crafted by OMWA with Maasai beadwork will be reinvested by OMWA in community projects, and the prototypes will stay in Olorgesailie to provide much needed electrification. See http://maasaisolar.org.

Involving artists in the process can instead deliver a more holistic approach to sustainability that addresses social equity, environmental justice, aesthetics, local needs, and other important cultural considerations. As we have said from the founding of LAGI, "Sustainability is not only about resources, but it is also about social harmony."

One percent for the arts for energy applied to a trillion dollars' worth of infrastructure will yield a cultural legacy that will mark this important time in human history. These monuments to future generations will let them know that we understood the impact of the industrial revolution on the planet and that we at least tried to make things right. These will be places where tourists of the future will go to be inspired—like visitors to the Hoover Dam today—not only because of the infrastructural aspects, but because of the beautiful artistry and design aesthetic of the place.

Art always reflects society—whether past, present, or future—and serves a function by showing us ourselves as we are (and as who we might become). It is never purely art for art's sake. It is always art for human's sake. Today the stakes are higher than ever for art to help us become something better.

Embracing the fact that the great energy transition will have a resounding influence on the design of public space in the coming decades, the time is now to proactively address the influence of these new machines on city planning, urban design, zoning ordinances, and building codes. The entries to the 2016 Land Art Generator Initiative design competition give us a glimpse of a future in which the aesthetic influence of clean energy technologies becomes a welcome and positive contribution to well-planned cities.

It's a future in which we provide the water needs of cities in ways that do not have externalized environmental impacts, and that celebrate the sustainable technologies that make it possible through contemplative and playful installations in public space. LAGI 2016 recognizes the fact that there can be no distinction between energy and water in regions like Southern California where so much electricity is used to pump and move water. The massive Edmonston Pumping Plant that brings water to the south over the Tehachapi Mountains along with the other pumping plants in the State Water Project together use eight billion kilowatt-hours of electricity each year,[16] enough to power over one million homes.

As Christopher Sjoberg and Ryo Saito, the winning team of this year's LAGI design competition, wrote in their narrative statement:

> Many say the new sustainability ethos is "water is the new energy." California has recently experienced one of the most prolonged droughts in its modern history, almost certainly made worse by climate change, putting strain on water resources depended upon by industry and residents alike. Los Angeles, which obtains a mere 13% of its water from local ground well sources,[17] depends on a vast and energy-intensive network of water transport infrastructure to move water from distant reservoirs into the city.

(4) The Solar Tapestry (the first project is planned in partnership with Yakima Neighborhood Health Services): This participatory design project for community energy is bringing people together to tell a story through mural making. Instead of using paint, the composition uses solar panels of custom colors and dimensions to translate the image into a performative south-facing solar wall.

[12] Elizabeth A. Stanton, Frank Ackerman and Ramón Bueno, "Reason, Empathy, and Fair Play: The Climate Policy Gap" (United Nations Department of Social and Economic Affairs, Working Paper No. 113, 2012), PDF publication online at http://www.un.org/esa/desa/papers/2012/wp113_2012.pdf.

[13] These measures are evolving as a part of the 2015 implementation of the UN Sustainable Development Goals (SDGs), although there is still a focus on "growth" over steady-state, regenerative economics; see http://www.un.org/sustainabledevelopment.

Lynge Nielsen, "Classifications of Countries Based on Their Level of Development: How it is Done and How it Could be Done" (IMF Working Paper, 2011), PDF publication online at https://www.imf.org/external/pubs/ft/wp/2011/wp1131.pdf.

[14] Ellen MacArthur Foundation, "The Circular Economy, Schools of Thought." https://www.ellenmacarthurfoundation.org/circular-economy/schools-of-thought/regenerative-design, accessed on July 15, 2016.

The Sankey diagram included in a 2014 report by the United States Department of Energy highlights the entanglements between water and energy. The yellow lines represent all of the electricity produced and where it is consumed.[18] Notice the high levels of "surface discharge" and "dissipated energy" on the right-hand side. These are opportunities for designers.

Jane Jacobs writes in *The Nature of Economies* about how a complex forest makes the most efficient use of energy through cycles of recombination and recycling, driven by and reinforcing a diversity of species.[19] Our cities should aspire to function in this same way, with a complex and diverse ecosystem of energy and water infrastructures that allows nothing to go to waste. Every new building and public park can be designed as a clean energy power and water plant for the benefit of the surrounding city.

As we wrote about in *New Energies*, the LAGI 2014 publication, energy cooperatives can point the way to equitable community-oriented climate solutions when supported by a framework of laws that encourage such citizen-led efforts. We are inspired by the progress that is being made, and hopeful that artists will be more frequently invited to be a part of local and regional infrastructure projects.

When asked by Rebecca Ehemann (Founder of Green Public Art) to bring LAGI to Southern California in 2016, we knew immediately that it would be the ideal site for a competition. Renewable energy is a top priority in California, and the state is leading the conversation on the global stage. At the forefront are cities such as Santa Monica, where policy and planning are setting an example for sustainable development and social well-being.

The ongoing water crisis also presented the opportunity to expand our design brief to include drinking water harvesting technologies (in addition to renewable energy technologies) as media for public artwork proposals responding to a site adjacent to the historic Santa Monica Pier.

This coastal site offered the platform to utilize new energy technologies, including tidal power and wave energy conversion. In the pages of this book you will find interesting visual expressions of wave power buoys, from translucent jellyfish to honking swans!

The Santa Monica Pier provided a picturesque and playful backdrop. The pier already boasts a solar-powered Ferris wheel and is in the process of major water conservation planning efforts. What if a new public artwork could provide all of the pier's power and water needs, while also enhancing the delicate balance between beauty and spectacle that defines this place?

The vibrancy of the pier informed the title of this edition. "Powering Places" reminds us that our infrastructure does not exist alone in a vacuum. The distant power plant out of sight and out of mind is no longer relevant in the era of renewable energy technologies. These objects can coexist with us, and the closer they are to the places we live and work the more efficient and resilient they become. Because they require access to natural energies such as the sun and the wind, their workings can be an active part of our visual landscape. They can add to our experience, making our favorite and most cherished places more colorful, more fun, more interesting, and more enlightening.

LAGI 2016 was perhaps our most complicated design brief yet. Not only were we asking for conceptually rich public art that generates clean electricity at a utility scale, but we also added considerations for water harvesting. We provided a site boundary completely within the ecologically sensitive waters of Santa Monica Bay and adjacent to one of California's most cherished

[15] The WPA was in operation for nearly a decade. In its initial year 1935, the WPA was appropriated nearly $5 billion (1935 dollars not adjusted for inflation), or 6.7% of GDP. A 6.7% of GDP investment in 2016 would equate to over one trillion dollars. Robert D. Leighninger Jr., *Long-Range Public Investment: The Forgotten Legacy of the New Deal* (Columbia: University of South Carolina Press, 2007).

[16] "The Department of Water Resources Report on Reducing Dependency on Fossil Fuels and Changes to the Power Contracts Portfolio" (California Department of Water Resources, 2013), PDF publication online at http://www.water.ca.gov/legislation/docs/2013-FossilFuelReport.pdf.

[17] Ken Murray, "How Los Angeles Can Become Water-Independent," *Time*, October 10, 2013, http://ideas.time.com/2013/10/11/how-los-angeles-can-become-water-independent. (cited by Christopher Sjoberg and Ryo Saito, designers of *RegattaH2O* in their narrative statement for LAGI 2016).

[18] Diana Bauer, Mark Philbrick, and Bob Vallario, "The Water-Energy Nexus: Challenges and Opportunities" (US Department of Energy, 2014). Image courtesy of the U.S. Department of Energy, https://commons.wikimedia.org/w/index.php?curid=47882040.

[19] Jane Jacobs, *The Nature of Economies* (New York: Random House, 2000).

cultural landmarks. The site encompassed the old breakwater, which is already in need of some attention after more than 80 years of neglect.

The rich history of the Santa Monica Pier, brought yet another layer of consideration to the brief. As you'll read in the essay by James Harris (p. 20), the Santa Monica Pier and breakwater have been reimagined in many different iterations, beginning with the railroad wharfs of the late nineteenth century, and continuing through the grandiose plans of the 1970s to build a new island (abandoned in the face of public opposition).

LAGI 2016 offers the City of Santa Monica and its people the chance to dream yet again about the potential for their pier to be something even greater, while in keeping with the core values of the city to protect the environment and set the highest standard in sustainable design.

The creative and ecological approaches to wave energy, fog harvesting, and desalination in this publication are all inspired by the cultural context of Santa Monica, but the artful applications of the technologies can find resonance for other coastal cities as well.

The essays in this edition help to provide a framework for learning about the LAGI 2016 entries. Framed by the wonderful introductory words from Craig Watson (p. 8) and Shannon Daut (p. 10), and following on Jim Harris's history of the Santa Monica Pier, you'll discover a wider history and contemporary context for energy and water infrastructure in Southern California through the insightful writing and information graphics provided by Barry Lehrman (p. 30). Patricia Watts (p. 40) teaches us of the rich contemporary landscape of Ecological Art and the issues that it is addressing in California. Finally, Glen Lowry (p. 46) continues the conversation about social equity in the context of twenty-first-

century infrastructure with an elegant introduction to the study of spatial justice. Glen's essay makes clear that we can no longer externalize risks to other places and that, "new times require new cultural imaginaries."

The secret to innovation is strengthening a diverse creative community driven by an empathic desire to help people everywhere. Educators recognize the value of the arts to inspire young people to dig deeper into science, technology, engineering, and math (STEM subjects), and policies are being written to bring the arts into STEM, creating STEAM. LAGI artworks are the perfect way to engage young minds in energy and climate science. In 2015, building on the success of our STEAM outreach to schools and our Art+Energy Flash Cards—and while we were engaged in our first Art+Energy Summer Camp—we decided to run a parallel "Youth Prize" in addition to the biennial LAGI design competition for professionals. You can read more on page 222 and see some of the results from five of the participating schools.

Let's collaborate to solve the critical issues of the twenty-first century by taking a positive and empowered approach. Starting today we can begin to build the infrastructural foundations for regenerative energy and water systems that will sustain us in prosperity for one hundred generations. The world is ready for this kind of thinking.

Our thanks goes out to all of those who participated in LAGI 2016 Santa Monica in every capacity, many of whom are listed in the acknowledgments on page 239.

LAGI 2016
DESIGN GUIDELINES

The LAGI 2016 design guidelines were developed closely with the City of Santa Monica.

The guidelines constituted the rubric for determining qualified entries to the LAGI 2016 competition.

*For example, a proposal to generate potable water by desalinating ocean water must take into consideration the downstream effects of brine disposal and the impacts of the process on the marine ecosystem.

PROJECTS MUST:

Consist of a three-dimensional sculptural form that has the ability to stimulate and challenge the minds of visitors to the site. The work should aim to solicit contemplation from viewers on such broad ideas as ecological systems, human development and habitation, energy and water resource consumption and production, and/or other concepts at the discretion of the design team;

Convert natural energy into electricity and/or drinking water at the site. The artwork must have the ability to store and/or transform and transmit the electrical power it generates to a grid connection point to be designed by others. Consideration should be made for artfully housing the required transformer and electrical equipment (balance of system) within the project boundary and restricting access to those areas for the safety of visitors to the site. Similar considerations should be made for drinking-water production and transmission technology if incorporated;

Be pragmatic and constructable, employing technologies that can be scalable and tested. There is no limit on the type of technology that is specified. It is recommended that the design team make an effort to engage the owners of proprietary technology in preliminary dialogue as a part of their own research and development of the design entry. The more pragmatic the proposals are, the greater the likelihood will be that one of them may get built;

Not create greenhouse gas emissions and not pollute. The work must not impact the natural surroundings negatively.* Each entry must provide a brief (approximately 300 words) environmental impact assessment as a part of the written description. The statement should include a list of the effects of the project on the natural ecosystem and should propose a mitigation strategy to address them;

Be well informed by a thorough understanding of the history, geography, restrictions, and details of the design site, and the broader surrounding and regional contexts;

Be safe to people who would view it. Consideration must be made for viewing platform spaces and boundaries between public and restricted areas. Boats can access the area around the breakwater, but swimming out to, or near the existing breakwater is prohibited;

Be designed specifically to the constraints of the design site at the Santa Monica Pier as shown in the Location Plan (available for download). Designs can (but are not required to) allow visitors to walk within the project boundary;

Designs must not exceed 80 meters in height (2× the height of the Pacific Ferris Wheel).

LAGI 2016 JUDGING CRITERIA

The LAGI 2016 jury made their decisions based on the following criteria:

- Adherence to the Design Brief;

- The integration of the work into the surrounding environment and landscape;

- The sensitivity of the work to the environment and to local and regional ecosystems;

- The estimated amount of clean energy and/or drinking water that can be produced by the work;

- The way in which the work addresses the public;

- The embodied energy required to construct the work;

- The perceived return on capital investment of the work, judged by the complexity of the design in relation to the energy it produces each year;

- And the originality and social relevance of the concept.

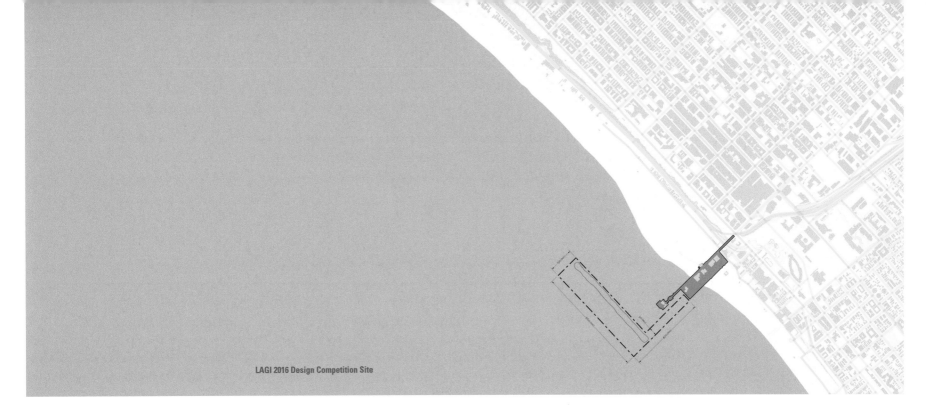

LAGI 2016 Design Competition Site

The jury and voting process took place through an online format over the month of June 2016.

OFFICIAL LAGI 2016 JURORS

Ben Allen
Senator, California State Senate (District 26); Chair, California State Legislature Joint Committee on the Arts

Kevin McKeown
Mayor, City of Santa Monica

Ned Kahn
Ned Kahn Studios

Craig Watson
Director, California Arts Council

Eric Corey Freed, RA, LFA, LEED AP
Vice President Global Outreach, International Living Future Institute

Dean Kubani
Director, Office of Sustainability and Environment, City of Santa Monica

Jack Becker
Executive Director, Forecast Public Art and Public Art Review

Jessica Cusick
Cultural Affairs Manager, City of Santa Monica

Elizabeth Corr
Manager Art Partnerships & Events at the National Resources Defense Council (NRDC)

Tom Ford
Executive Director, The Bay Foundation

Dominique Hargreaves
Executive Director, USGBC-LA Chapter

Shari Afshari
Deputy Director, County of Los Angeles Department of Public Works

Pauline Kamiyama
Interim Director of Civic Art, Los Angeles County Arts Commission

David Hertz, FAIA
Founder and President, The Studio of Environmental Architecture (S.E.A.)

Freya Bardell and Brian Howe
Principals at Greenmeme

Phillip K. Smith III
pks3.com

Trevor Lee
Principal, Suprafutures

Vicki Scuri
Vicki Scuri SiteWorks

Laura Watts
Associate Professor, Technologies in Practice (TiP) Research Group, IT University of Copenhagen

Santiago Muros Cortés
LAGI 2014 First Place Winner

One of the Santa Monica Pier's longtime supporters was a woman named Colleen Creedon. She helped rally the community to save the pier from demolition in the early 1970s and even lived in an apartment above the merry-go-round.

Colleen dreamed of making the Santa Monica Pier completely sustainable. When Herb Alpert introduced her to his architect, Harry Newman, she saw the opportunity to put her ideas on paper.

This sketch from 1978 is the result of their working session—a continuous unraveling on a roll of yellow tracing paper documenting their shared ideas about how renewable energy can be a beautiful part of the constructed world around us.

The image is reproduced courtesy of Harry Newman, and was provided by Jim Harris from the City of Santa Monica archives.

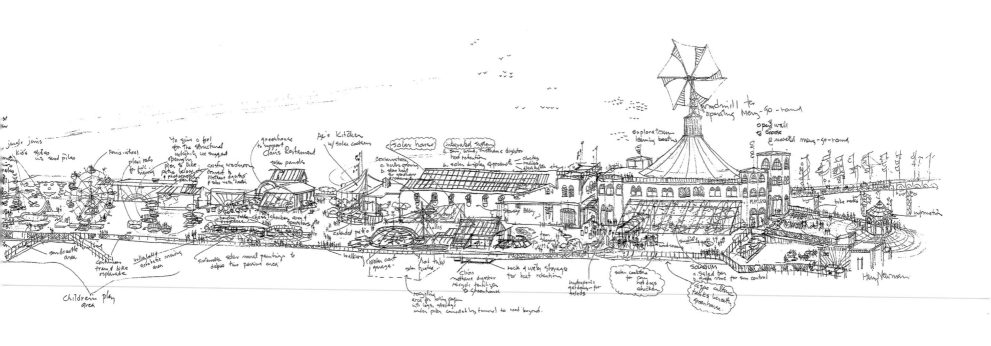

Solar Power For the Santa Monica Pier
Conceived & Developed by: Colleen Creedon
Associate Harry Newman Architect AIA

21

ESSAY

Santa Monica's Beach and Pier

James Harris

FIRST INHABITANTS: THE TONGVA AND THE CHUMASH

The first people to inhabit the area that we know today as Santa Monica Beach were of two hunting and gathering groups—the Tongva (also known as the Gabrielinos), who occupied the area southeast of Topanga Canyon, and the Chumash, who occupied the area from Topanga Canyon to Malibu Creek. It is estimated that these groups first inhabited the area sometime between 2,000 BCE and 700 CE.

"THE TEARS OF SANTA MONICA"

In 1769 Father Juan Crespí, a member of Spanish soldier/explorer Gaspar de Portolá's Alta California expedition, happened upon a pure water spring in the area and declared the spring to be "The Tears of Santa Monica," a reference to the story of the tears that the fourth-century Saint Augustine's mother shed for her son prior to his elevation to pious status.

RANCHEROS

In 1839 the Mexican government issued land grants to the area that would eventually be known as Santa Monica to three ranch families, those of Francisco Marquez, Ysidro Reyes, and Francisco Sepulveda. Marquez and Reyes partnered to raise cattle in what is known today as Santa Monica Canyon, with their land expanding throughout the neighboring beach areas.

CITY OF SANTA MONICA

With the induction of the State of California into the United States in 1850, travel into the area began and building rapidly increased. As Americans discovered the beach they frequently enjoyed it either for a day or for an extended camping excursion. In 1875 the City of Santa Monica was officially founded by Robert S. Baker and Nevada Senator John Paul Jones. Land parcels were sold and plans for a railroad from the sea to Los Angeles were soon underway.

EARLY RAILROAD WHARFS

Senator Jones used his land in Santa Monica to build a railroad from the beach to Los Angeles, ultimately connecting with a railway running from Los Angeles to his silver mine operations in Independence, California. His railway was intended as a direct threat to Collis Huntington's already well-established Southern Pacific railway which ran from San Pedro to Los Angeles. In November 1875 Jones opened his Los Angeles & Independence Wharf, which served his railway of the same name, starting what was ultimately a very short railroad war. Within two years Jones's railway system was forced into bankruptcy and in January 1879 the wharf was deemed unsafe and was dismantled.

And yet, Santa Monica captured Collis Huntington's attention. Southern California's growing popularity inspired other competing railroads coming into the Los Angeles area. Recognizing the potential of Santa Monica Bay as a seaport, Huntington sought to beat his competition's efforts westward and establish an official deep-water harbor for the City of Los Angeles, moving his own operations out of San Pedro and into Santa Monica.

In July 1892 Huntington began construction of a new railway through the town of Santa Monica, then north along the beach until a point just south of Santa Monica Canyon. At this terminus Huntington built a 4,720-foot-long wharf and dedicated it as Port Los Angeles. The project triggered a nine-year battle between San

Pilings used in the construction of the
Santa Monica Pier, August 31, 1908
Image courtesy of Santa Monica Public Library
Image Archives/Photographed by Consulting
Engineer Edwin H. Warner

Santa Monica Municipal Pier opening
day, September 9, 1909
Image courtesy of Santa Monica Public Library
Image Archives/Western Publishing and Novelty
Company (Los Angeles)

Pedro, Redondo Beach, and Santa Monica as to which location would become the official Los Angeles Harbor. Ultimately San Pedro won the designation. The wharf, which from the beginning was most often referred to as the "Long Wharf" due to its extraordinary size, remained active as railway service for shipping until 1913. It stood for several years afterward and was used as a fishing pier until it was dismantled in 1920.

BATHHOUSES AND AMUSEMENT PIERS

By the early 1900s Santa Monica's beachfront gained growing recognition for its recreational pleasures rather than any dreams of a seaport. The first, modest bathhouses were established in the late 1890s and in 1901 Santa Monica's North Beach Bathhouse extended heavy ropes from their establishment out into the ocean so that bathers, in their heavy wool bathing suits, could safely wade out into the ocean and enjoy the fresh ocean waves.

In 1897–98 the Ocean Park Pier was built by developers Abbot Kinney and Francis Ryan in the newly formed community of Ocean Park, located just south of Santa Monica. In 1905 Kinney ventured on his own to create a new dream, the "Venice of America." A nod to Venice, Italy, Kinney built this new community just south of Ocean Park using man-made canals instead of streets, complete with gondolas as the primary means of travel. He also developed his own pier, the Abbot Kinney Pier. Upon this pier Kinney built a dance hall, introducing to the region an entirely new concept—the amusement pier.

Long Wharf freight pier built by
the Southern Pacific Railroad
Company in 1893
Image courtesy of Santa Monica Public
Library Image Archives

Throughout the first half of the twentieth century these two piers in Ocean Park and Venice explored and pushed the boundaries for what amusements could be placed atop a pier, including roller coasters and thrill rides of all types.

SANTA MONICA MUNICIPAL PIER

In 1907 the City of Santa Monica faced a crisis—what to do with their accumulating sewage. City Commissioners agreed to build a 1,600-foot municipally owned pier that would support a pipeline designed to carry treated sewage out past the incoming tide and send it out to sea. Plans called for this pier to be made entirely of concrete—the first of its kind established on the West Coast of the United States—thus giving it a distinction unmatched by the amusement piers in Ocean Park and Venice. On September 9, 1909, the Santa Monica Municipal Pier officially opened to the public to great fanfare, with a parade, ocean and beach races, and fireworks, along with a U.S. Navy flotilla anchored just off of the pier's end.

LOOFF PLEASURE PIER

Citizens of Santa Monica were less than satisfied in being known for their "sewer pier." Almost immediately after the Municipal Pier's unveiling came calls for an amusement pier to rival those of the neighboring communities just south of Santa Monica's border. Enter Charles I. D. Looff, a very well known carousel carver turned amusement park entrepreneur. On June 12, 1916, he opened the doors of his first and cornerstone attraction, the Looff Hippodrome, home to a new carousel. Opening shortly thereafter were the Blue Streak Racer roller coaster, a few thrill rides, and a bowling and billiards hall.

In 1924 the Looff family sold their leasehold to a group of Santa Monica realtors. The new group replaced the Blue Streak Racer with a larger, faster coaster called the Whirlwind Dipper, then extended the amusement pier westward several hundred feet and built upon it the world's largest ballroom—the La Monica Ballroom. On its opening night the La Monica drew more than 50,000 people just to view it. The event is credited as the cause of Santa Monica's first recorded traffic jam. Unfortunately the new, improved pier and ballroom never reached the level of success that Santa Monicans hoped for. Storms damaged much of the pier in 1925 and, not long after recovery and reopening, the stock market crash of 1929 ended hopes altogether. The thrill rides were removed by 1930 and the ballroom was leased to the City of Santa Monica for use as a convention center.

THE GOLD COAST

In the 1920s and the 1930s Hollywood's elite essentially claimed the beach area north of the Santa Monica Pier. Screen legends and producers such as Douglas Fairbanks, Mary Pickford, Louis B. Mayer, and Daryl Zanuck enlisted the era's most coveted architects to design and build their homes on the beach. The most noteworthy of these architects was Julia Morgan, who was hired by publishing tycoon William Randolph Hearst to build a 100-plus room palatial estate for his mistress, Marion Davies.

SANTA MONICA YACHT HARBOR

In September 1931, in a Depression-era effort to create jobs for local workers as well as a new revenue source via yacht moorings, Santa Monica voters passed a $690,000 bond measure to fund the construction of a breakwater and, hence, Santa Monica Yacht Harbor. The breakwater was originally to be composed of concrete cribs, which would be accessible by fishermen and pedestrians via a bridge extended from the west end of the Santa Monica Pier. In March 1933, shortly after the first crib was prepared and set into place a few hundred feet from the end of the pier, a crack was discovered in its structure. The new breakwater appeared doomed.

City officials consulted with the United States Army Corps of Engineers, who advised the City to use the remaining funds to build a more affordable, more reliable rock mound breakwater. The City proceeded with this change of plans and quickly began shipping rocks in from Santa Catalina Island, working steadily for a full year on the construction. One life was lost during the project, that of a popular fisherman-turned-construction-hand named "Scotty" McPherson. A plaque was placed upon one of the breakwater rocks in his honor as construction resumed. On July 30, 1934, the breakwater was complete. Santa Monica celebrated on August 4 with the first annual Santa Monica regatta.

During construction of the breakwater an unforeseen development emerged as a result of the new structure's effect upon ocean currents: sand began to accumulate just north of the Santa Monica Pier, causing the beach in that area to expand. This was problematic in that the widening beach meant a shrinking

La Monica Ballroom and Santa
Monica Pier, 1926
Image courtesy of Santa Monica Public
Library Image Archives

Paddleboard races in Santa Monica Bay,
August 13, 1949
Image courtesy of Santa Monica Public Library
Image Archives/Del Hagen Studios

Santa Monica breakwater construction
began in 1934.
Image courtesy of Santa Monica Public Library
Image Archives

yacht harbor with less space for moorings, a key component of the harbor's revenue model. Furthermore, local private beach clubs saw their beaches disappearing due to this change in current, inducing some to sue the City of Santa Monica for the impact upon their beach environment. Ultimately, after many years of dredging efforts to fight the beach expansion, the City conceded to the new course of nature.

LIFEGUARDS, PADDLEBOARDS, AND SURFBOARDS

With the new yacht harbor began certain activities that helped to develop what would ultimately become known as the "Southern California beach lifestyle." In 1933 Santa Monica Lifeguard Service established their headquarters on the Santa Monica Pier. Employing some of the most skilled watermen in the world, the Santa Monica Lifeguard Service took advantage of the newly pacified waters of the harbor to help develop innovative new tools to aid in rescue and water safety. Among these creative minds were surfing legends Tom Blake and Preston "Pete" Peterson.

Tom Blake, who discovered surfing and honed his skills in Hawaii in the 1920s, was already a well-seasoned waterman by the time he joined the Santa Monica lifeguards. In 1929, while still in Hawaii, he crafted the first-ever hollow surfboard. He patented the concept and, in 1932, permitted the Thomas Rogers Company of Venice, California, to build hollow paddleboards using his design. These paddleboards were immediately adopted by the Santa Monica lifeguards as their primary rescue tool, and soon afterward lifeguard services all along the Pacific Coast followed suit.

Pete Peterson also used Blake's hollow design to build his own paddleboards. Considered by both his contemporaries and today's surfers and paddlers to be the greatest waterman who ever lived, he was equally skilled as a craftsman. His paddleboards, skiffs, and dories are widely coveted by modern collectors, but it is his developments advancing the rescue tube that had the greatest impact upon water safety and rescue. Two versions of the "Peterson Tube"—the inflatable tube and the foam tube—have been adopted by lifeguard services in pools, lakes, and oceans worldwide. The foam tube is still in use by most services to this day.

While the lifeguards saw the paddleboard as a vital lifesaving tool, it didn't take long for the public to recognize its potential as a recreational delight as well. Paddleboards became accessible to the public in the mid-1930s and soon Santa Monica Yacht Harbor became home to the United States mainland's first organized paddleboard races. Paddleboard clubs emerged, inspiring challenges between communities. By the mid-1940s paddleboard water polo and paddleboard water ballet shows began to entertain people not only at Southern California beaches but in water shows that toured throughout the United States, giving people in cities like Chicago, Illinois, and Phoenix, Arizona, a taste of the culture that was developing in the Santa Monica Bay.

As the twentieth century reached its midway mark, though, the public's interest in paddleboarding began to subside in favor of the sport's more exciting cousin—competitive surfing. Malibu emerged as the dominantly preferred area for the surfing community due to its point break, but the figures most integral to the development of surfing—the surfboard shapers—called Santa Monica home. Among these were Dale Velzy and Dave Sweet in the 1950s and, later, Jeff Ho and Rich Wilken in the 1970s.

Yachts in the Santa Monica Yacht
Harbor, 1935
Image courtesy of Santa Monica Public
Library Image Archives/Carolyn Bartlett
Farnham Collection

CAUSEWAY AND SANTA MONICA ISLAND

By the early 1960s the Santa Monica Pier was falling into a state of disrepair. The once proud, colossal La Monica Ballroom was condemned and demolished, the breakwater was crumbling to the point that it did little to pacify the harbor, and the pier deck and substructure grew increasingly weak. City officials often referred to the pier as an eyesore and continually expressed concerns over the financial burden it created.

In 1963 a proposal to build a causeway—a series of islands connected by bridges to form a highway over the sea from Santa Monica to Malibu—was seriously considered, using the pier as the initial bridge. The plan ultimately fell through. In the late 1960s Santa Monica's City Manager, Perry Scott, proposed the construction of a man-made island with a resort hotel and convention center, using the pier as a bridge to the island. The proposal was presented to the voters for funding, but failed.

In 1971 City Manager Scott presented an updated plan for the island to the City Council, this time with a developer attached to fund the project. The project also called for the demolition of the Santa Monica Pier in favor of a newly built bridge as its replacement. The Council approved the project in the summer of 1972, but received immediate backlash from a community that had witnessed the disappearance of the area's neighboring piers. Abbot Kinney's Venice Pier was dismantled in 1947 and Ocean Park's "Pacific Ocean Park" went bankrupt in 1967. The Santa Monica Pier was the last of the significant piers still standing.

A long, difficult battle ensued. The island was defeated by protests from environmental organizations coupled with the calculated costs associated with its upkeep. The Santa Monica Pier, however, remained doomed due to its continual maintenance costs. In a timely twist of good fortune for pier supporters, three City Council members were running for re-election in the spring of 1973. The community embarked upon a relentless campaign against the incumbent Council members until they ultimately relented, changed their minds, and saved the pier.

STORMS OF 1983

In the winter of 1983 Mother Nature effectively accomplished much of what City officials failed to achieve ten years earlier. A series of storms battered Santa Monica Bay unlike any previously recorded year and nearly destroyed the Santa Monica Pier in the process.

On January 27, 1983, a storm approached in which swells were expected to reach crests of 10 feet. The lower fishing deck of the Santa Monica Pier was perched just 8 feet above the mean high tide, leaving that area little chance of surviving the incoming storm. The pier was evacuated shortly after dawn that morning as a crowd of hundreds stood atop the palisade overlooking Santa Monica Beach to observe the fate of the pier. As expected, massive waves poured over the fishing deck and demolished it with ease.

The day after the storm, City officials assured the public that the pier's lower fishing deck would be rebuilt, and within a couple of weeks they dispatched a crane to the end of the pier to clean up the damage and prepare for the reconstruction.

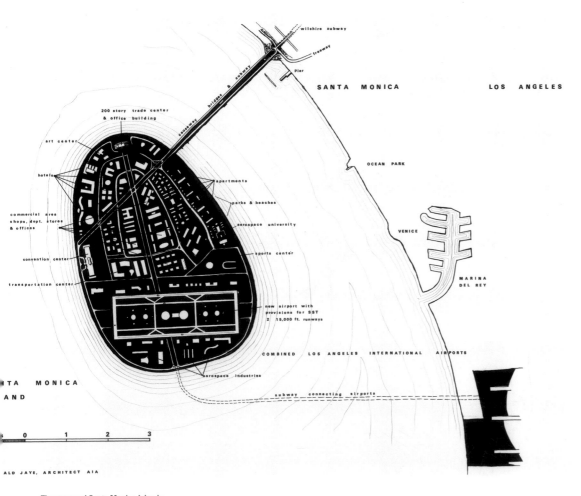

The following labels appear on the map:

wilshire subway

freeway

Pier

200 story trade center & office building

art center

hotels

commercial area shops, dept. stores & offices

convention center

transportation center

apartments

parks & beaches

aerospace university

sports center

new airport with provisions for SST 2 15,000 ft. runways

aerospace industries

subway connecting airports

SANTA MONICA   LOS ANGELES

OCEAN PARK

VENICE

MARINA DEL REY

COMBINED LOS ANGELES INTERNATIONAL AIRPORTS

NTA MONICA

AND

0   1   2   3

ALD JAYE, ARCHITECT AIA

The proposed Santa Monica Islands
Image courtesy of Herald-Examiner Collection/
Los Angeles Public Library

On March 1 an equally large storm struck the pier, rocking it so violently that the crane toppled into the ocean and effectively acted as a battering ram as it knocked loose the pier's pilings and created a sea full of destructive debris, tearing away at the aging pier until the entire west end was demolished. By the time the storm subsided, one-third of the total surface of the pier had vanished.

RESTORATION AND WORLDWIDE FAME
The destruction left by the storms of 1983 actually provided the Santa Monica Pier's fate a "silver lining." A decade earlier the Santa Monica Pier was saved from demolition, but since that time no progress was made in regard to improving the pier or making it viable. All of a sudden the City was presented, quite literally, with a clean slate to build upon. Input from community meetings showed strong support for making the pier more family-friendly. Plans to build an amusement park were conceived—an homage to the amusement piers that once defined Santa Monica Beach.

In the late 1980s reconstruction of the pier's west end took place, culminating in an official dedication on April 6, 1990. In 1992 a fine-dining restaurant was built upon the new west end, and on May 25, 1996, a new full-scale amusement park, Pacific Park, offered visitors thrill rides on the pier for the first time in 66 years.

Today Santa Monica is known worldwide for its century-old iconic amusement pier and for its broad, accommodating beaches. Millions of people visit the area every year, recognizing and celebrating its undisputed status as representative of the past, present, and future of Southern California's beach lifestyle.

Santa Monica Yacht Harbor from the
Santa Monica Pier looking toward
the shore
Image courtesy of Santa Monica Public Library
Image Archives/Randy Young Collection

View of the Santa Monica Harbor, pier,
and breakwater looking toward the City,
September 3, 1936
Image courtesy of Santa Monica Public Library
Image Archives/Spence Air Photos

ESSAY

**Los Angeles Aqueductsheds
and Energysheds**

Barry Lehrman

HISTORY OF POWER TRANSMISSION IN CALIFORNIA

Southern California was a center of innovation in the development of electrical power and long-distance transmission at the end of the nineteenth century. The gold mining industry had already cultivated expertise in high-pressure hydraulic engineering, and cities were located in relatively close proximity to viable hydropower locations.

NOTABLE FIRSTS

1886

Highgrove Hydroelectric Plant, Redlands, California (64 miles east of Los Angeles) was the first direct current electrical power plant built in Southern California.

1891

The world's first high-voltage single-phase alternating current (10 kV) line connected 14 miles between Pomona Powerhouse (on San Antonio Creek in the San Gabriel Mountains) to Pomona, California (30 miles east of Los Angeles) to run refrigeration equipment in the citrus packing houses. California Historic Marker #514 is located on an overlook above the powerhouse's location N 34° 12.735', W 117° 40.564'.

1893

Mill Creek Plant No. 1 in Riverside, California, used the world's first three-phase alternating current generators (built by General Electric) and the first three-phase power lines covering 7½ miles to Redlands Plant No. 1 and the power line were designed by A. W. Decker, the engineer of the Pomona Powerhouse and power line.

1905

Nevada Power Mining and Milling Company built a 113-mile power line from Bishop Creek (Inyo County, California) to mines in Nevada.

1912

The first 220 kV transmission lines were built to connect the hydropower Big Creek Plant (near Fresno, California) 241 miles to the Eagle Rock Substation in Los Angeles.

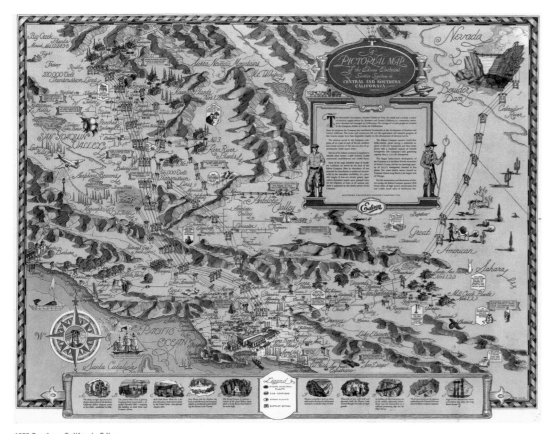

1935 Southern California Edison

Image courtesy of David Rumsey Map

Collection, www.DavidRumsey.com

1947 Southern California Edison

Image courtesy of David Rumsey Map

Collection, www.DavidRumsey.com

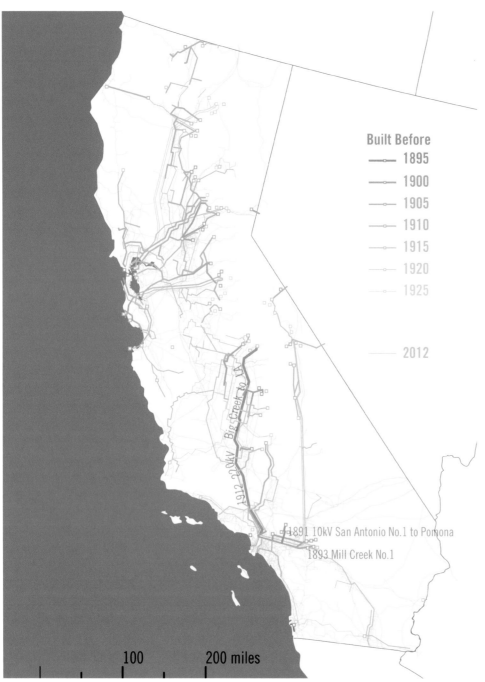

Built Before
— 1895
— 1900
— 1905
— 1910
— 1915
— 1920
— 1925

— 2012

1912 220kV Big Creek to LA

1891 10kV San Antonio No.1 to Pomona

1893 Mill Creek No.1

100   200 miles

Historical powershed of Los Angeles
Image courtesy of Barry Lehrman

POWERSHED OF LOS ANGELES

Los Angeles was connected to hydropower in the Sierra Nevada Mountains before construction on the Los Angeles Aqueduct began. Today, the electrical power supply system that is owned and operated by the Los Angeles Department of Power and Water and Southern California Edison encompasses a greater territory than the aqueductshed for metropolitan Los Angeles (even if you ignore the entire Western Area Power Administration's power grid that covers all of the contiguous states west of the Rocky Mountains).

CELILO AC-DC CONVERTER STATION

PACIFIC DC INTERTIE

INTERMOUNTAIN GENERATING STATION 1,900MW

INTERMOUNTAIN DC INTERTIE

OWENS GORGE

NAVAJO GENERATING STATION

Diablo Canyon Nuclear Power Plant
[decomissioned] 18,000 MW

Santa Susan Field Laboratories
Experimental Nuclear Reactors
[Superfund Site]

Edmonston Pumping Plant

HOOVER DAM 2,080 MW

SYLMAR AC-DC CONVERTER STATION

MOHAVE POWER STATION

ADELANTO AC-DC CONVERTER STATION

San Onofre Nuclear Power Plant
[decomissioned] 2,710 MW

Parker Dam 120 MW

PALO VERDE NUCLEAR GENERATING STATION

Energyshed Key

━━━ LADWP

──── Southern California
Edison

──── Other Electricity
Systems

○ AC-DC Converters

Substations

▢ Powerplants 1,000MW+

▫ Powerplants 100-999MW

▫ Hydro-Power Plants 100+MW

▫ Hydro-Power Plants 30-99.9 MW

◎ Pumping Plants (SWP & CoRA)

100   200   400   600   800   1,000 miles

Energysheds of Los Angeles
Image courtesy of Barry Lehrman

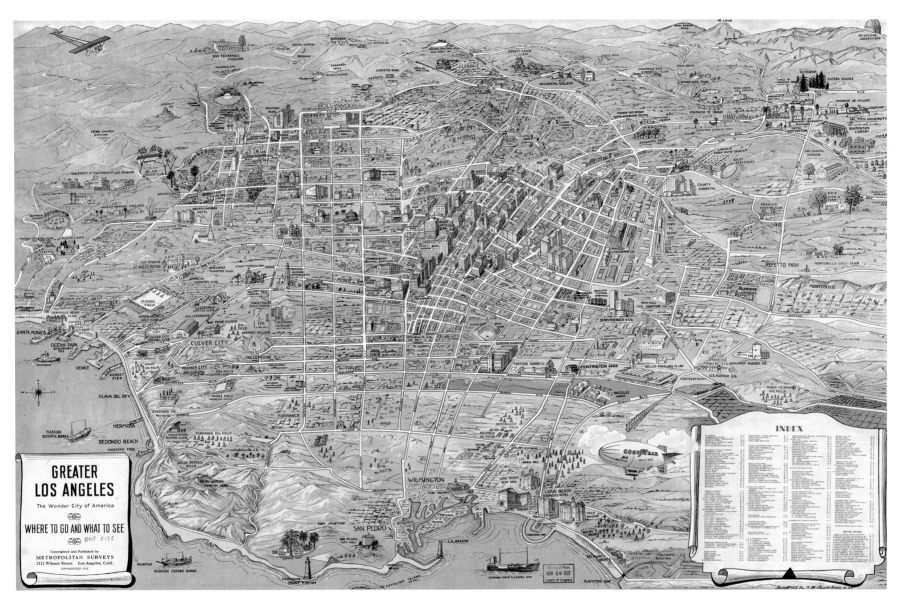

1932 K. M. Leuschner's Greater
Los Angeles: The Wonder City
of America
Image courtesy of Library of Congress

Santa Monica Sheet

1888 Hammond Irrigation Map

Image courtesy of David Rumsey Map

Collection, www.DavidRumsey.com

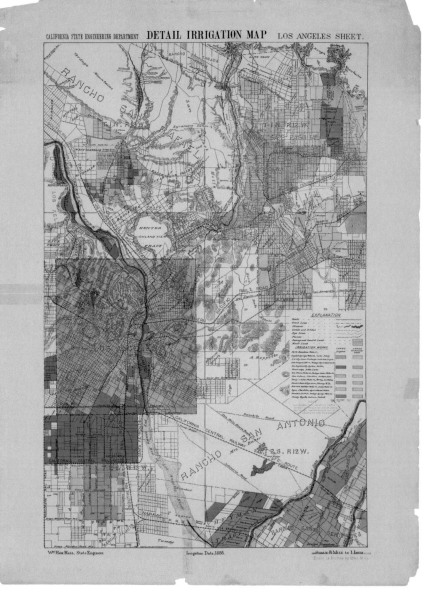

Los Angeles Sheet

1888 Hammond Irrigation Map

Image courtesy of David Rumsey Map

Collection, www.DavidRumsey.com

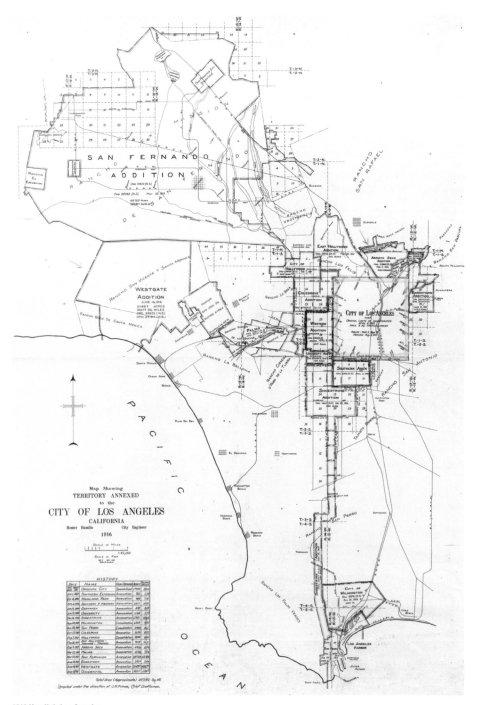

Map Showing
TERRITORY ANNEXED
to the
CITY OF LOS ANGELES
CALIFORNIA
Homer Hamlin   City Engineer
1916

1916 Hamlin's Los Angeles
Annexation

Image courtesy of Library of Congress

AQUEDUCTSHED OF LOS ANGELES MAP

As Los Angeles boomed from the extraction of oil and real estate speculation at the beginning of the twentieth century, the city's elites started prospecting for a new water source to quench the insatiable demands of development. In 1907 the city chose to build an aqueduct 200 miles north to the Owens Valley (where Mayor Fred Eaton owned more than 20,000 acres, which he then sold to the city) over nearer sources such as Malibu Creek and the Mojave River (which didn't have enough water), and the Kern River and San Gabriel River (where too many people already lived).

In 1939 the Colorado River Aqueduct (built by the newly formed Metropolitan Water District of Southern California) began providing imported water to the eastern suburbs. It was the MWD that first defined the Los Angeles Metropolis as encompassing all of Southern California from Oxnard down to San Diego. Los Angeles continued to expand the extraction of water from the Eastern Sierras with a tunnel connecting the Owens River to the Mono Basin in 1941, and a second "barrel" to the aqueduct, which was completed in 1970.

California began dreaming of building an aqueduct to export the plentiful water from northern California's Feather River into the arid San Joaquin Valley and Southern California before World War II, but it wasn't until the 1950s that the legislation and funding to create the State Water Project were passed. With help from federal funding for the Central Valley Project, construction began in the mid-1960s. The first water deliveries to Los Angeles arrived in 1974, with substantial completion of the West Branch to Santa Barbara and the East Branch down to San Diego occurring in 1997.

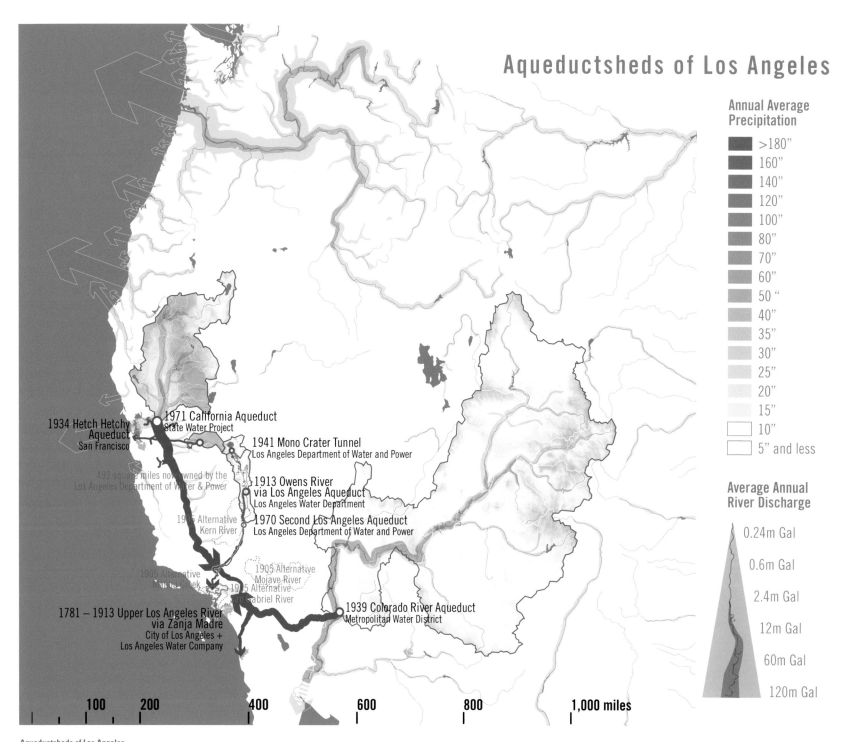

Aqueductsheds of Los Angeles

Annual Average Precipitation

>180"
160"
140"
120"
100"
80"
70"
60"
50 "
40"
35"
30"
25"
20"
15"
10"
5" and less

Average Annual River Discharge

0.24m Gal
0.6m Gal
2.4m Gal
12m Gal
60m Gal
120m Gal

1934 Hetch Hetchy Aqueduct
San Francisco

1971 California Aqueduct
State Water Project

1941 Mono Crater Tunnel
Los Angeles Department of Water and Power

492 square miles now owned by the
Los Angeles Department of Water & Power

1905 Alternative
Kern River

1913 Owens River
via Los Angeles Aqueduct
Los Angeles Water Department

1970 Second Los Angeles Aqueduct
Los Angeles Department of Water and Power

1905 Alternative
Malibu Creek

1905 Alternative
Mojave River

1905 Alternative
San Gabriel River

1939 Colorado River Aqueduct
Metropolitan Water District

1781 – 1913 Upper Los Angeles River
via Zanja Madre
City of Los Angeles +
Los Angeles Water Company

100   200   400   600   800   1,000 miles

Aqueductsheds of Los Angeles

Image courtesy of Barry Lehrman

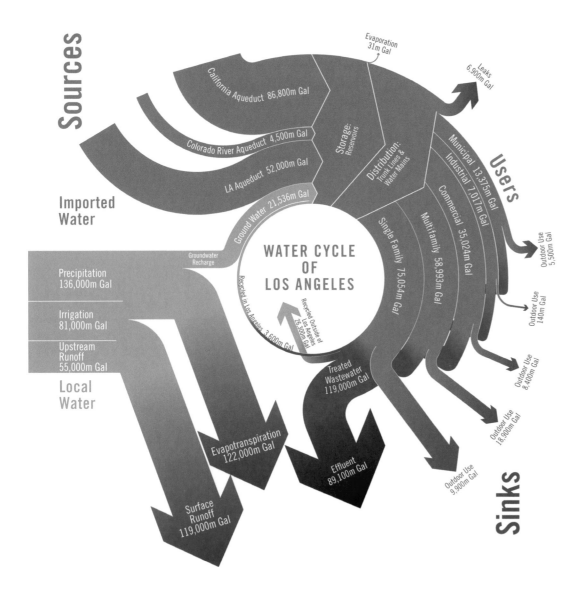

Sources

California Aqueduct 86,800m Gal

Colorado River Aqueduct 4,500m Gal

LA Aqueduct 52,000m Gal

Ground Water 21,536m Gal

Imported Water

Groundwater Recharge

Precipitation 136,000m Gal

Irrigation 81,000m Gal

Upstream Runoff 55,000m Gal

Local Water

Storage: Reservoirs

Distribution: Trunk Lines & Water Mains

WATER CYCLE OF LOS ANGELES

Recycled in Los Angeles 3,600m Gal

Recycled Outside of Los Angeles 26,300m Gal

Evaporation 31m Gal

Leaks 6,900m Gal

Users

Municipal 13,375m Gal

Industrial 7,017m Gal

Commercial 35,024m Gal

Multifamily 58,993m Gal

Single Family 75,054m Gal

Treated Wastewater 119,000m Gal

Outdoor Use 5,500m Gal

Outdoor Use 140m Gal

Outdoor Use 8,400m Gal

Outdoor Use 18,900m Gal

Outdoor Use 9,900m Gal

Evapotranspiration 122,000m Gal

Surface Runoff 119,000m Gal

Effluent 89,100m Gal

Sinks

LOS ANGELES WATER CYCLE

The water supply for the City of Los Angeles is an intertwined mix of imported and local water. This Sankey diagram reveals critical opportunities to improve the resilience of the local water supply by enhancing runoff capture and recycling water for direct reuse and indirect groundwater recharge. If every available drop of water was recycled, the region would gain 502 million gallons of water a day, enough to slake the thirst of at least 5.5 million people (and enough to retire the Los Angeles Aqueduct). Currently, there is a system of purple pipes distributing a small amount of non-potable recycled water to industrial and municipal users, but no large-scale recycling of water in Los Angeles County.

Capturing precipitation and runoff is more challenging due to the intermittent and highly variable nature of rain in Southern California—but distributed small-scale efforts (such as rain barrels and rain gardens) are starting to make a substantial difference.

Note: quantities have been converted from acre-feet into million gallons. Data utilized was a mix of water year, fiscal year, or calendar year—so quantities may not total 100%. One U.S. liquid gallon equals 3.78541 liters.

Water Cycle of Los Angeles

Image courtesy of Barry Lehrman

SOURCES: HISTORY OF POWER TRANSMISSION IN CALIFORNIA

Ronald Burgess, "Redlands Powers the World—How the San Bernardino Valley Developed Modern Electric Power First" (The Fortnightly Club of Redlands, California, 2007), http://www.redlandsfortnightly.org/papers/burgessRon07.htm.

"Santa Ana River Hydroelectric System: Written Historical and Descriptive Data" (Historic American Engineering Record, HAER No. CA-130, 1992), https://cdn.loc.gov/master/pnp/habshaer/ca/ca3700/ca3707/data/ca3707data.pdf.

"Mill Creek 2 and 3 Hydroelectric Systems: Written Historical and Descriptive Data" (Historic American Engineering Record, HAER CA-2272, 2010), https://cdn.loc.gov/master/pnp/habshaer/ca/ca3700/ca3714/data/ca3714data.pdf.

"Big Creek Hydroelectric System East & West Transmission Line: Written Historical and Descriptive Data" (Historic American Engineering Record, HAER No. CA-167, 2012), http://lcweb2.loc.gov/master/pnp/habshaer/ca/ca3900/ca3976/data/ca3976data.pdf.

Laurence Shoup, "The Hardest Working Water in the World: A History and Significance Evaluation of the Big Creek Hydroelectric System" (Southern California Edison, 1988), http://www.cpuc.ca.gov/environment/info/esa/sjxvl/SCE_DRs/DR6/DR6_attachment.pdf.

A Brief Outline of California's Great Community Electrical Enterprise (Southern California Edison, 1935), http://www.davidrumsey.com/luna/servlet/detail/RUMSEY~8~1~274153~90047929:Text--A-Brief-Outline-of-California.

Pictorial Map of the Edison Electrical Service System in Central and Southern California (Southern California Edison, 1935), http://www.davidrumsey.com/luna/servlet/detail/RUMSEY~8~1~274154~90047930:A-Pictorial-Map-ofthe-Edison-Elect.

Electrical Generation Stations and Major Transmission Systems in Central and Southern California (Southern California Edison, 1947), http://www.davidrumsey.com/luna/servlet/detail/RUMSEY~8~1~271932~90045781:Southern-California-Edison-Company-.

Thomas Taylor, "Santa Ana River No. 1: A Pioneer in Hydro Generation, Power Transmission," *Hydro Review* (August 1999), http://www.hydroworld.com/content/dam/hydroworld/siteimages/1805_HallofFame.pdf.

W. G. Vincent, Jr., "Interconnected Transmission System of California," *Journal of Electricity* 54, no. 12 (1925), https://ia800702.us.archive.org/23/items/journalofele541151925sanf/journalofele541151925sanf.pdf.

James C. Williams, *Energy and the Making of Modern California* (Akron, OH: University of Akron Press, 1997).

SOURCES: POWERSHED OF LOS ANGELES

California State Water Project (SWP) Facilities (California Department of Water Resources, n.d.), http://water.ca.gov/swp/docs/SWPmap.pdf.

California's Electric Transmission Lines (California Energy Commission, 2012), http://energy.ca.gov/maps/infrastructure/Transmission_Lines.pdf.

Solar Power Plant Licensing Projects (California Energy Commission, 2014), http://energy.ca.gov/maps/renewable/Solar_Power_Plant_Licensing_Projects.pdf.

2012–2016 California's ISO's Electricity Road Map (California Independent System Operators, 2012), https://www.caiso.com/Documents/2012-2016StrategicPlanElectricityRoadMap.pdf.

LADWP Sources of Power-By Plant & Type of Generation (City of Los Angeles Information Technology Agency, Los Angeles Department of Water and Power, 2014), https://data.lacity.org/A-Livable-and-Sustainable-City/LADWPSources-of-Power-By-Plant-Type/gyz8-bf3p.

"2015 Briefing Book, Putting Customers First" (Los Angeles Department of Water and Power, 2015), http://www.ladwpnews.com/external/content/document/1475/2606574/1/2015%20Briefing%20Book%2002-26-2015LR.pdf.

Colorado River Aqueduct Profile and Map (Unknown Author, n.d.), http://www.ecommcode.com/hoover/hooveronline/hoover_dam/before/read/010l.jpg.

SOURCES: AQUEDUCTSHEDS

Barry Lehrman, Jonathan Linkus, and Cal Poly Pomona Students, *Aqueduct Futures Project* (2013).

Aqueduct Futures Exhibition, http://www.aqueductfutures.com.

Barry Lehrman and Cal Poly Pomona Students, *After the Aqueduct Exhibition, Aqueduct Futures Project* (2015).

Michael Bostok, *US Rivers* (2013), https://github.com/mbostock/us-rivers & https://bost.ocks.org/mike/us-rivers.png.

Matthew Heberger and Peter Gleick, *American Rivers* (Pacific Institute, 2013), http://www2.pacinst.org/wp-content/uploads/2013/06/pacinst-americas-rivers-creativecommons.jpg.

"Owens Valley Land Management Plan" (Los Angeles Department of Water and Power, and Ecosystem Sciences, April 28, 2010), http://inyo-monowater.org/wp-content/uploads/2011/09/ladwp013763_OV_Land-Managment-Plan_final.pdf.

Service Area Map (Metropolitan Water District of Southern California, n.d.), http://www.mwdh2o.com/PDF_In_The_Community/3.3_service_area_map.pdf.

Groundwater Basins in Southern California (Metropolitan Water District, N.D.), http://www.wwdh20.org.

Nelson Minar, *Map of American Rivers* (2013), https://www.flickr.com/photos/nelsonminar/sets/72157633504361549.

William Mulholland, "Complete Report on Construction of the Los Angeles Aqueduct" (Los Angeles, CA: Department of Public Service of the City of Los Angeles, 1916), https://books.google.com/books?id=xLA_AQAAMAAJ.

William Mulholland and Lippencott & Parker Consulting Engineers, "Water Commissioners' Report for the Year Ending November 30, 1905" (Los Angeles, California, 1906), https://books.google.com/books?id=DIFKAQAAMAAJ.

Robert A. Sauder, "Patenting an Arid Frontier: Use and Abuse of the Public Land Laws in Owens Valley, California," *Annals of the Association of American Geographers* 79, no. 4 (1989): 544–69, http://www.jstor.org/stable/2563647.

Californian Rivers and Lakes (US Geologic Survey, 2004), http://nationalmap.gov/small_scale/printable/images/pdf/outline/rivers_lakes(u).pdf.

California Precipitation Map (US Geologic Survey, 2005), http://nationalmap.gov/small_scale/printable/images/pdf/precip/pageprecip_ca3.pdf.

Watershed Boundary Dataset (US Geologic Survey, n.d.), http://water.usgs.gov/maps.html.

SOURCES FOR LOS ANGELES WATER CYCLE

Miscellaneous data and documents regarding the California Aqueduct (California Department of Water Resources, n.d.), http://www.water.ca.gov.

Reference Evapotranspiration (California Department of Water Resources, n.d.), http://www.cimis.water.ca.gov/App_Themes/images/etozonemap.jpg.

Barry Lehrman, *Recharge City. Dry Futures Competition, Los Angeles, CA* (Archinect.com, and Arid Lands Institute, Woodbury University, 2015), http://archinect.com/news/article/136734973/ recharge-city-3rd-place-winner-in-dry-futurespragmatic-category.

Sewer Maintenance Districts of Los Angeles County (Los Angeles County Public Works, 2013), https://dpw.lacounty.gov/smd/smd/ssmp.pdf.

"Twenty-Fifth Annual Status Report on Recycled Water, Fiscal Year 2013–14" (Los Angeles County Sanitation District, 2015), http://www.lacsd.org/civicax/filebank/blobdload.aspx?blobid=10780.

"2015 Briefing Book, Putting Customers First" (Los Angeles Department of Water and Power, 2015), http://www.ladwpnews.com/external/content/document/1475/2606574/1/2015%20Briefing%20Book%2002-26-2015LR.pdf.

Water Main Break Data (Los Angeles Department of Water and Power, 2015), https://data.lacity.org/A-Livable-and-Sustainable-City/DWP-Water-Main-Breaks-Quarterly-/khdk-aiwb.

LADWP Water Supply in Acre Feet (Los Angeles Department of Water and Power, 2015), https://data.lacity.org/A-Livable-and-Sustainable-City/LADWP-Water-Supply-in-Acre-Feet/qyvz-diiw.

Urban Water Management Plan (Los Angeles Department of Water and Power, 2015), http://www.ladwp.com/uwmp.

Stormwater Capture Master Plan (Los Angeles Department of Water and Power, August 2015), https://www.ladwp.com/ladwp/faces/wcnav_externalId/a-w-stormwatercapturemp.

Sewer System Management Plan (Los Angeles Sanitation Department, February 2015), https://www.lacitysan.org/cs/groups/public/documents/document/y250/mdey/~edisp/cnt012545.pdf.

Integrated Resource Plan (Metropolitan Water District of Southern California, 2015), http://mwdh2o.com/Reports/2.4.1_Integrated_Resources_Plan.pdf.

Miscellaneous data and documents about groundwater in the San Fernando Valley (Upper Los Angeles River Watermaster, n.d.), http://ularawatermaster.com.

Miscellaneous data and documents related to groundwater in the LA Basin (Water Replenishment District of Southern California, n.d.), http://www.wrd.org.

ESSAY

Rising from the Ocean: ECOlogic LA

Patricia Watts

1 "La Brea Tar Pits," Wikipedia, https://en.wikipedia.org/wiki/La_Brea_Tar_Pits.

2 Rachel A. Surls and Judith Gerber, *From Cows to Concrete: The Rise and Fall of Farming in Los Angeles* (Santa Monica: Angel City Press, 2016), 29.

3 Helen Mayer Harrison and Newton Harrison, "Arroyo Seco Release: A Serpentine for Pasadena," in *The Time of the Force Majeure: After 45 Years Counter-force Is on the Horizon* (New York: Prestel, 2016), 176–179.

4 Lauren Bon, 2010, stated in a red neon sign on a wall of her Metabolic Studio, downtown Los Angeles.

5 Christopher Hawthorne, "How Frank Gehry's L.A. River Make-over Will Change the City and Why He Took the Job," *Los Angeles Times*, August 9, 2015, http://www.latimes.com/local/california/la-et-la-river-notebook-20150809-story.html.

6 Andy Lipkis, stated in a video on the Tree People website, https://www.treepeople.org/about.

In the current epoch, unofficially called the Anthropocene, environmental baselines in the landscape are shifting at such a rapid rate that the human mind can barely compensate for the loss of spectacular natural features that were present historically. In fact, most people think of Southern California as a desert, although that perception is the result of long-term droughts. Because of the accelerated pace of our recent human evolution, the imagination has become our most prized survival mechanism. Given this premise, let us imagine the Los Angeles Basin of 1.7 billion years ago, as it lay beneath an ancient sea. Imagine large rivers coursing from the Nevadan Mountains 65 million years ago, transporting sediments to a swampy range of marshes and lagoons hanging above the San Gabriel Mountains. Then imagine hills rising from the ocean bottom 1.8 million years ago, eventually forming mountain ranges, while at the same time the sea level was dropping. These epic transitions in the landscape are biblical in their proportions, though occurring over vast expanses of time.

If you want to get hyper-idealistic, go ahead and imagine the L.A. Basin of 10,000 to 8,000 years ago, when the climate was much cooler and more moist than it is today—more like that of California's Central Coast. Glaciers were active along the peaks of the Santa Ana Mountains, and in the Santa Monicas redwood groves flourished. It was Shangri-La! And although you could probably imagine saber-toothed tigers, giant ground sloths, dire wolves, ancient bison, bears, mammoths, and mastodons roaming the area, it would be hard to believe they had actually existed if they hadn't met their fate in the tar fields near today's Miracle Mile, leaving behind a treasure trove of fossilized bones of some 38,000 years' antiquity.[1]

The Chumash Indians, who migrated to the L.A. Basin 8,000 years ago, and the Tongva, who arrived 3,500 years ago, experienced the land in all its fecund glory. Imagine foothills whose natural springs fed into a network of streams, marshes, vernal pools, and lakes sited on lower-lying grassy plains. There was an abundance of birds, fish, sea life, and deer for the native populations to consume. However, by the late 1700s, European settlers had introduced intensive farming, and in 1804 or 1805, Franciscan missionaries planted the first significant orange grove at Mission San Gabriel.[2] Life in the basin progressed onward, yet what remains today—besides the fossils, which tell one story—are patches of fragmented landscapes that leave us with slivers of hope, future stories to be told.

Will we be able—aided by a big dose of human imagination—to piece the parts back together again? Inspired by the region's rich ecological history, could we create, in some new form, the kind of spectacular natural features that nature herself bestowed upon the Chumash and the Tongva? Is it feasible to truly recapture these images of the past through regenerative processes—remediation, restoration, and rehabilitation of nature? Probably not. However, by deploying new technologies and guided by an army of educated "-ologists," we can at the least attempt to increase sustainability by optimizing the natural resources that remain and creatively converting the waste of the nineteen million people who live in today's greater Los Angeles—ten million in Los Angeles County alone. Imagine: just two hundred years ago, a mere two thousand people resided in the area.

The single most important resource in the L.A. Basin—and one that has been severely misused over the last century—is water. The L.A. River was the sole fresh water supply for the City of Los

Angeles before the completion of the Los Angeles Aqueduct in 1913. To address flood control, 80 percent of the river was paved during the 1930s by the United States Army Corps of Engineers—in fact, it is often called the world's largest storm drain. The concrete encasement of the river signaled the beginning of the demise of wild nature in the L.A. Basin. The expanding and contracting braided river historically flowed from the San Fernando Valley toward downtown Los Angeles before heading west to the Ballona Wetlands, and after 1825, it changed course, migrating south from downtown L.A. to Long Beach. This phenomenon of nature, which traced a grand alluvial fan in the sediment, was a natural resource that, over time, was thought to threaten human development. It would later be seen as an industrial blight on the landscape.

In 1984 the Garden Club of America invited California artists Helen and Newton Harrison to Pasadena, located in the San Gabriel Watershed, inland from the L.A. River. There they saw the decimation of the Arroyo Seco riverbed, also a result of flood control efforts; another concrete channel—built by the U.S. Army Corps of Engineers and California Flood Control—fragmented the canyon. The artists were appalled by the severe destruction of an intact ecosystem and sought to decouple flood control from the destruction of rivers, using art as a tool for education and inspiration. They were invited back to Pasadena in 1987, this time by the Santa Monica Mountain Reserve, for another project. Addressing several million L.A. residents on a local radio program, the Harrisons recited text urging the restitution of waterways. This performative art piece invited listeners to "imagine every channel in the L.A. Basin covered, and land remade green, and low-flow stream beds established where the logic and the will exist."[3] Their action fueled incipient efforts by the community to restore the L.A. River.

South side of First Street Bridge overcrossing of Los Angeles River
Image courtesy of the Historic American Engineering Record (Library of Congress).
Photograph by Brian Grogan

The artists then began a dialogue with the U.S. Army Corps of Engineers to envision a long-term, hands-off approach to a sustainable future for the L.A. Basin. Concurrently, several recently formed environmental organizations were working to save or conserve the remaining natural resources. These included Tree People, founded by Andy Lipkis in 1973; Friends of Ballona Wetlands, founded by Ruth Lansford in 1978; Heal the Bay, in Santa Monica, founded by Dorothy Green in 1985; Concerned Citizens of South Central Los Angeles (CCSCLA), founded in 1985; and Friends of the Los Angeles River (FoLAR), conceived as a forty-year artwork to make the Los Angeles River swimmable, founded by Lewis MacAdams in 1986. Over the last decade, the conversation has led to more visible transformations. In 2005 artist Lauren Bon transformed 32-acres of industrial land north of Chinatown into a living sculpture— *NOTACORNFIELD*, adjacent to the L.A. River and the current site of the Los Angeles State Historic Park. She proposes that "artists need to create on the same scale that society has the capacity to destroy."[4]

The L.A. River Revitalization Corporation, a nonprofit group formed in 2009, recently invited architect Frank Gehry to create a "brand" for the river by giving it "visual coherence"—along the lines of Frederick Law Olmsted's design of Central Park. Many have expressed concerns that this approach—far from grassroots activism—could be compromised by commercial considerations. Gehry, however, says that his focus is the river's functionality and hydrology rather than the design.[5] The premises that "less is more" and that "sometimes doing nothing is doing something" are mantras frequently used by environmental activists. And although creating a greenway and bike path and restoring adjacent wildlife habitat would be welcome amenities, the reality is that most of the concrete that was laid almost one hundred years ago is not going to be removed. If anything, its impact will be mitigated mostly by adding green design features or "habitat enhancements."

Visual artists have played an important role in the cultural landscape of Los Angeles, specifically by addressing the region's natural heritage. When in 1974 the US Army Corps of Engineers invited Judith Baca to create a community mural on the walls of the Tujunga Flood Control Channel in the San Fernando Valley, she envisioned *Great Wall of Los Angeles*, a monumental environmental public artwork half a mile in length that was completed over five summers in collaboration with hundreds of youth. It depicts the long history of California, from the days of the dinosaurs up to twentieth century. In 1997 artists Susan Suntree and Jan Williamson initiated *Earth Water Air Los Angeles (EWALA)*, a performative pilgrimage with giant puppets, in which a procession of hundreds of men, women, and children walked along the path of the L.A. River to educate residents about the urgent need to save the last open spaces. The trek began at the Ahmanson Ranch, near the headwaters of the Los Angeles River, and arrived four days later at Ballona Wetland.

More recently there have been several important works by artists who have taken to heart the visibility and accessibility of urban nature in Los Angeles; they include Freyja Bardell and Brian Howe's *Riverside Roundabout*, a series of cut stone sculpture of faces that capture and filter stormwater to irrigate the surrounding landscape, completion set for 2016; Lauren Bon's *Bending the River Back into the City*, a functional sculpture with inflatable dam, waterwheel, and designed delta that connects to the L.A. River, announced in 2014; Kim Abeles's ongoing series *Signs of Life* (started in 2004), three-dimensional aerial maps whose handmade trees represent every single tree in parts of downtown Los Angeles; Sant Khalsa's ongoing project *Western Waters* (initiated in 2000), a photographic typology addressing water as a consumer product by documenting water stores throughout the Southwest; Kim Stringfellow and Amy Balkin's 2006 *Invisible-5* public audio tour, which educates about Superfund sites in the San Fernando Valley, where chemicals leeched into groundwater in the 1950s; L.A. Urban Rangers, who offered guided hikes and campfire talks beginning in 2007, as well as interpretive tools to shine a light on fragile habitats within Los Angeles's megalopolis; the collaboration Fallen Fruit, which in 2004 started mapping fruit trees whose branches extend over public property; and Fritz Haeg, who in 2006 worked with a family in the city of Lakewood, between the San Gabriel and Los Angeles Rivers, creating a front-yard food garden for his *Edible Estates* series.

It is estimated that human development has destroyed 95 percent of Southern California's wetlands—the largest loss of any region in the nation. This includes the historic Ballona Wetlands, west of downtown Los Angeles. Starting in the 1930s, as automobile usage boomed, street paving extended from downtown, eventually reaching the ocean, and Ballona Creek was also concretized. The city's population moved west at lightning speed, a process impeded by intermittent stops for oil production. When Marina del Rey Harbor was created in the 1950s–1960s, the dramatic transformation of the landscape decimated over nine hundred out of the two thousand acres of historic wetlands, including marshes, mud flats, salt pans, and sand dunes. In the late nineties, hundreds of acres of the wetlands were again under threat with the development of Playa del Rey, inland from the Marina. Today there are only 600 acres left; they make up the Ballona Wetlands Ecological Reserve.

In response to this history of environmental manipulation in the L.A. Basin, the City of Santa Monica, in the Santa Monica Bay Watershed, has become one of the most environmentally activist municipalities in the nation. It was one of the first cities to adopt a comprehensive sustainability plan, including establishing waste reduction and water conservation policies for both the public and private sectors and implementing the Community Energy Independence Initiative. In 2000, in partnership with the Santa Monica Cultural Affairs Department, the City built the Santa Monica Urban Runoff Reclamation Facility (SMURRF), which treats an average of a half million gallons per day of urban runoff by removing trash, sediment, oil, grease, and pathogens. The processed runoff is sufficiently clean to be used for landscape irrigation and for the flushing of toilets. This project, the first of its kind, was created in collaboration with a public artist, Richard Turner, who contributed to architectural design features, landscaping, and education programs.

In 2013 the Los Angeles County Museum of Art (LACMA) rebooted its Art and Technology Program, originally initiated by then senior curator Maurice Tuchman; it ran from 1967 to 1971. The program paired artists with technology companies to support groundbreaking experimentation. Early participants included ecological artists Newton Harrison and Hans Haacke, Light and Space artists Larry Bell and Robert Irwin, and Land Art artists Walter de Maria, Christo, and Robert Smithson. The program produced a wide range of partnerships between artists and scientists and was the springboard for further explorations combining diverse domains, in which artists developed more informed work addressing environmental and social problems. This legacy of interdisciplinarity led to LACMA's current Art + Technology Lab.

Similarly, the Land Art Generator Initiative (LAGI) design competitions support deep collaborations in the now-expanded fields of art, science, and architecture, on projects with humanitarian purposes. Both conceptually and technically, the opportunities adjacent to the Santa Monica Pier abound. They can be seen as "post-nature" geographies that employ emerging technologies to envision large-scale public art that utilizes energy: wave and tidal, wind and solar.

This region has historically been seen as a leader of the nation in lifestyle and business innovation, as well as a health mecca and even a Mediterranean-style paradise. In the late 1970s, architect Glen Small, seen as an innovator in green architecture, proposed his *Biomorphic Biosphere*, an ecologically based vertical city that would lift the buildings of Los Angeles off the ground like hovering space-age sustainable megastructures. Today, large, high-end buildings are being erected at record speed, including the Santa Monica City Services Building, registered for full Living Building Challenge (LBC) certification by the International Living Future Institute (ILFI), the world's most rigorous sustainable-rating program, which is challenging buildings to meet their own energy and water needs on site. LAGI also encourages whole cities to evolve into coordinated "living districts." Such districts would have sustainable infrastructure designed into the fabric of their buildings, parks, and public places, thus reducing or eliminating reliance on externalized resources and waste streams.

Through a combination of artistic and other creative practices, a visionary urban resilience approach is within reach. Traces of our water history are etched on the landscape for our inspiration. Imagine a raised Culver Boulevard running over the remaining Ballona Wetlands and a return of native plants and wildlife below. Imagine the winning design from the LAGI 2016 open call realized at the Santa Monica Pier, feeding the city with additional energy and drinking water. In the words of Andy Lipkis, "If we take a really smart approach and use the design principles of nature, and nature itself, we can restore and retrofit this city."[6] The Los Angeles Basin emerged from the ocean a million years ago, and here we are now waking up to the unlimited possibilities to reconnect with what has been lost over the last two centuries. Imagine that!

View north along the Los
Angeles River

Image courtesy of the Historic American
Engineering Record (Library of Congress).

Photograph by Brian Grogan

ESSAY

**Power Redesigned Is Power
Redistributed—Spatial Justice and
LAGI's Human-scale Energy Productions**

Glen Lowry

Cultural subjects "play themselves" for multiple
audiences: the police, state agencies, generations,
ancestors, the tribe, animals, and a personal God.
Subjectivity is plural and not simply a matter of turning
toward power, as in Althusser's famous fable (1972). It
can also involve turning away, falling silent, keeping
secrets, using more than one name, being different in
changing situations. — James Clifford[1]

RE:BUILDING—A NEW PASTORAL / GOATS ON THE ROOF

This may be apocryphal, but I'd like to share a story told to me
by an architect friend. The narrative recalls a senior colleague's
plan for persuading clients to accept new, contentious design
elements. Faced with convincing clients to sign off on a budget
overrun or other sticky issue, the architect advised the team to
put "goats on the roof"—i.e., to add a few goats to the drawings
or model. Apparently, the out-of-the-box goats had the power to
captivate the client, and in so doing, they would allow other, more
controversial elements of the proposed building to go unnoticed. I
like this example because it is an architectural nod to the pastoral
that provides more than a cynical bait and switch. Instead, the
goats help to create a context for innovative design solutions by
recalling other forms of social interaction or economic production.
Imagining the goats enables the client to think about different
forms of the built environment and to redraw, even momentarily,
the line between the building and green spaces.

Borrowing from Welsh cultural historian Raymond Williams's
study, *The Country and the City* (1973), we might say that the
architect's ability to blur the line between rural and urban points to
a deeper engagement with interconnected spheres of interest, or
what Marxists refer to as modes of production. As Williams argues,
the landscapes popularized in nineteenth-century literature and
poetry provided a functional, ideological difference that effectively
situated rural Britain outside of an emergent industrialization.
Setting the country apart from the expanding, centralized powers
of *the city*, these idealized representations of nature elided shifting
industrial relations by glossing over growing social and economic
disparities separating urban and rural development. Read against
this longer history of labor relations, industrialization, and
hegemonic representations of *the country*, the figurative goats
gesture toward recognition of the interdependence of urban and
rural spaces in a dominant mode of production. A poetic reminder
of a disappearing commons and the vital link between cities and
vast tracts of rural land, the goats provide a symbolic representation
of the dependence of industrial centers on the rural territories that
are systemically subsumed by industrial development and our
avaricious appetite for water, electricity, and fossil fuels.

I'm reminded of these goats when I look at the exquisite
renderings that now support the LAGI design briefs for Dubai,
Copenhagen, New York, and Santa Monica. The idyllic renderings
that play on beautiful sweeps of light and breeze transport viewers
to vital spaces of possibility that are both a turning toward and
away from the dominant power. In this other world, the blazing
sun of the Arabian desert, the desolate winds of a capped New
York landfill, the ambiguous haze over a decommissioned shipyard

along the Copenhagen waterfront, or crashing waves on the beaches of Santa Monica are returned to beneficence. In these images, the sun, wind, and water are transformed into friendly elements. In many ways, this imaginary drive is a crucial function of the artists, architects, and designers brought together by LAGI. Their collective strength rests with an ability to see these formative elements as positive agents in a new ordering of urban life. Returning to the basic features of the Santa Monica shoreline, these creative designs take viewers beyond futuristic visions of micropower plants. As the best public art plans do, these proposals resonate with new and different approaches to a range of immediate and contemporary social concerns.

Leafing through these proposals, we begin to desire not only the artworks but perhaps more importantly, the world they envision. This is the true power of art. Vibrant engines, the capacity of these proposed works outstrips their ability to deliver essential amenities (power and water). They engender bold changes to everyday life— to the way we live and how we want to live. Goats on the roof. A chicken in every backyard. Community-owned power plants. These are the objects and practices needed to help redefine the spaces we live in. Positive responses to global challenges, they also provide the means with which to reestablish local control over our cities and countries. They provide a visual means for rethinking power, and offer a rich databank of solutions that require us to regrid power relations, redesigning the production, consumption, and—implicitly—the distribution of electricity on a scale and in a manner that effectively replaces the massive and now floundering infrastructures of twentieth-century development.

RESCALING: CULTURAL SUBJECTS, SUBJECTS OF CULTURE

The monumental, seemingly monolithic enterprises of post-war modernity crumble and disintegrate all around us; once stirring images of industry and power fade before our eyes. The architectural wonders—the freeways and power plants, the universities and courthouses, stock exchanges and factories—that made possible twentieth-century growth and prosperity, across North America and throughout the so-called developed world, falter under the strain of twenty-first-century imperatives. Nevertheless, as the proposals gathered here in LAGI 2016 suggest, all is not lost.

New times require new cultural imaginaries—new power, new power plants, new dreams of progress, but also new technologies and new social relations. Compare these evocative proposals to the monuments of hydroelectric power. Think, for example, of the Sir Adam Beck and Robert Moses Power Stations on the banks of the Niagara River, the Hoover Dam across the Colorado, James Bay Hydroelectric, and the Robert Bourassa Power Station; think of the Kashiwazaki-Kariwa Nuclear Power Plant in Japan or the Bruce Nuclear Generating Station on Lake Huron; or think of the structures of late oil—the tar sands of the Athabasca outside Fort McMurray, oil fields of the Persian Gulf, rigs offshore in the Gulf of Mexico or the North Atlantic, massive tankers, and snaking transcontinental pipelines. The manageable scope and renovated scale of the LAGI projects collected here provide a stark contrast to the brutality of twentieth-century industrialism, which were based on massive expropriations of land, often from Indigenous peoples, and ever-present threats of ecological devastation. The narrative subjects embedded or depicted in the following pages are human figures who might be seen to perform across a variety of local sites.

Circulating beyond the exigencies of a specific design brief or single set of circumstances, Santa Monica, the plans and proposal presented in this book become part of an archive or databank that provide images of renovated civic engagements and human-scale urban developments. Continuing to echo the language of James Clifford, we might say that the subjects imagined or represented here turn toward power, or more directly toward public involvement in power generation and sustainable approaches to carbon neutrality, but they also turn away from overdetermined narratives of control and hegemonic dominance. Art, design, architecture, engineering, research, or innovation—the selected projects respond to and perform different identities as they "play themselves" across a range of social situations, political contexts, and discursive formations. These site-specific interventions invite us to make connections that extend beyond the local; they invite readers to see what is possible in Santa Monica as concrete examples of what is needed elsewhere. Bearing more than one name, they enter multiple fields of force and invite us to follow their lead across faraway places and very different geopolitical locations. They encourage us to wonder what new forms of power (and power generation) might look like in Kitimat, Vancouver, Fort McMurray, Attawapiskat, Doha—the list grows. They invite us to want to reestablish meaningful connections with other people and places with whom energy is shared. Or put in another way, the proposals gathered here encourage us to think about energy and citizenship across new networks that are capable of rebalancing and countering past inequities and disparities.

RE:GENERATING—SPATIAL PRACTICE

To outline how we might read LAGI's utopic vision/s within a more overtly political context, one that is rooted in questions of social justice and equitable access to resources, I'd like to reframe this discussion in the context of contemporary urban theory. Arguably, artworks that focus on energy generation are a priori political, and as such, can be seen to be embedded in a representational confluence that connects art, philosophy, science, government, and the economy. Public art that self-consciously represents or imagines new forms of power tends to invite thinking about political efficacy and our collective access to material resources—including fuel, energy, and social power. But how do we begin to read these works? Beyond saying that they provide politically provocative imagery, how do we begin to plug them into dynamic debates about power, the environment, and social equity? Peak oil, global warming, and other related forms of environmental crises tend to highlight concerns around government control over power (energy) as a material resource (renewable or not). However, they also suggest opportunities for new social formations, based on new thinking and new possibilities for transformative and transformational social engagement. To work through what I see as the inherently political nature of the LAGI platform, I want to suggest that the associated geographies of power that define the unique sites taken up by LAGI 2010 through LAGI 2016 are of central importance to our interpretation or assessment of proposed interventions.

Situating LAGI in relation to the "spatial turn" in cultural criticism allows us to consider the geographic elements of these proposals and the vast networks of geopolitical power in which they are situated. Instead of focusing attention on the natural or environmental aspects of each LAGI site in isolation, I want to outline a spatial approach that is based on an assumption that any successful attempt to harness or reflect energy—solar, wind, tidal—requires integration with the power grid. As such, the most provocative proposals offer a point of access to thinking about the specific power relations that define the spatial or geographic aspect of the site. It is beyond the scope of my short text to explore the geopolitical contingencies of Santa Monica or Southern California, let alone compare them to those at play in the United Arab Emirates, Denmark, or New York. Nevertheless, I want to provide a thumbnail sketch of how we might approach LAGI's strategic objective, its drive "to advance the successful implementation of sustainable design solutions by integrating art and interdisciplinary creative processes into the conception of renewable energy infrastructure"[2], through the lens of social power and justice.

Too often global warming is discussed as a temporal concern. The media presents historical causes for increasingly apparent climate changes (for example, the overconsumption of cheap/subsidized oil, overdevelopment, and globalization), or pundits offer timelines to help viewers understand the effects (past) and to underline the growing seriousness of the problem (future). The effect of these narratives is to disempower the public; the forces and impacts are too great for individuals to comprehend, let alone resist. When specific geographical locations or regions enter discussion (for example, dwindling polar ice caps, disappearing rain forests, and growing deserts), they tend to be elsewhere—places with little direct connection with everyday life in the powerful metropolitan centers. More to the point these distant sites come to be subsumed in larger historical narratives. These remote spaces and the ecological devastations they are asked to represent are put forward as objective proof that older generations have made terrible mistakes that younger generations will need to respond to or live with. There is a clear and persuasive logic to these arguments and the growing intergenerational chasm they foment. However, when the rain forests, deserts, and polar ice caps are located within dominant linear histories, their immediate relevance is denied; they are spaced out or distanced from local political concerns. Dominant narratives downplay our connections with ecological turmoil by systemically banishing the geography of environmental devastation from thinking about the here and now—an increasingly urban here and now.

In response, instead of separating these sites from urban centers, contemporary cultural theorists have sought to reassert the primacy of spatial thinking, arguing for a reintegration of space, alongside time, in social analysis. Proponents of this "spatial turn" draw on the works of Henri Lefebvre, Michel Foucault, and Edward Said, each of whom sought in different ways and across distinct disciplinary configurations to reestablish the subject of geography in social critique. We might also cite influential social geographers David Harvey and Edward Soja, among others, who build on the work of Lefebvre (and to a lesser extent Foucault and Said) to explore North American urban contexts. In this critical context, the urban focus of the LAGI projects represented in this publication becomes important and provides a means of articulating the project within a larger discussion of social justice as a regional or territorial concern. Borrowing from this work, I seek to position LAGI 2016 as a means of thinking through connections between environmentally engaged art and what Soja (2010) terms *spatial justice*. Highlighting LAGI as spatial practice allows us to consider some of the more radical possibilities that come to light in its growing archive of images and ideals.

At the core of this line of reasoning is the work of Lefebvre, whose 1974 publication *The Production of Space* proffers a radical break from the historicism of postwar social thought, Marxist in particular.[3] This break hinges on the contention that space should be understood as social process. Lefebvre argues that space is neither a stage nor an empty container for historical events to take place. Space, he contends, is better thought of as a social dynamic, the means for producing and reproducing social relation. Controlling space, crucial to the growth of industrial capitalism, can therefore be seen a locus of control and of emancipation.

Highlighting the critical importance of lived experience, Lefebvre's theory of social space moves beyond a conventional binary that pits materialist perceptions of space or descriptive analyses against idealist conceptions of space—images and ideal representation. It offers instead an understanding of spatial consciousness that rests on a three-part social production that brings together scientific description, philosophical speculation, and embodied engagement or everyday life. Countering the dehumanizing drive of scientific rationalism and the Enlightenment,

Lefebvre sought to describe a multiscalar geography power. Against the objectifying drive of European expansion, which sought to assert economic, political, and philosophical control over massive expanses of the planet—through imperial expansion and the emergent power of modern industrial nations—Lefebvre provides a blueprint for redefining the inter- or cross-disciplinary connections among philosophers, mathematicians, astronomers, geographers, artists, and designers.

Lefebvre's work offers an excellent means for understanding the political efficacy of public art and engagement. The micro-power plants planned and designed for LAGI 2016 might thus be understood as more than fanciful visions. They are more than simply creative responses to what might happen at a particular site along the Santa Monica waterfront. Representing the Santa Monica shoreline as a social space or site for public arts, they embed its natural splendors in complex geopolitical processes and suggest ways of redefining and reorganizing social relations. The public that is depicted, or in some cases implied, by the works collected here are already involved in reliving power relations and our immediate access to public energy. They experience electricity and water as renewable resources and basic human rights. As responses to an emergent shift in larger modes of production (postindustrial, global, carbon-neutral), these proposals have already begun to reimagine and remake sustainable energy and social relations.

RE:DISTRIBUTION—TOWARD SPATIAL JUSTICE

Taking up the work of Lefebvre, linking the concept of social space directly to questions of social justice, cultural geographer Edward Soja's *Seeking Spatial Justice* develops the idea of spatial justice.[4] Soja argues that discussions of universal justice, social justice, and distributive justice tend to hinge on a dialectic focused around the historical struggles of a social group (class) and time-based injustice. With *spatial justice*, he seeks to introduce "space," or more particularly the concerns around space as social process, into the equation. Revisiting John Rawls's idea of distributive justice, Soja explores examples in which spatial issues impact, or even lead to injustice. Access to justice (as well as the geographic basis of injustice) needs to be understood in relation to theory-praxis dialectic, or so he contends. Drawing on examples from Los Angeles, including the bus riders strike and the Rodney King protests, Soja suggests that justice is shared or meted out through space and time, and that communities are empowered or they are marginalized by their geographic location:

> Human spatiality in all its forms and expressions is socially produced. We make our geographies, for good or bad, just or unjust, in much the same way it can be said that we make our histories, under conditions not of our own choosing but in real-world context already shaped by sociospatial process in the past and the enveloping historically and socially constituted geographies of the present. This profoundly displaces the idea of space merely as external environment or container, a naturalized or neutral stage for life's seemingly time-driven social drama. (p. 103)

His work invites us to think about what types of space-driven drama we might want or need to radically change the course of history and the apparent impacts of global warming.

For Soja, spatial justice involves a radical shift in thinking about cities. Discussing the work of the Marxist geographer Harvey's work around urban struggle, as well as the writings of Lefebvre, Soja rearticulates "the right to the city" as basic citizenship rights. He argues that human rights and civic rights, which are linked conceptually with notions of the citizen as city-dweller, need to be expanded to comprise larger interconnected geographies of power. The creation and administration of things in space and time, or better the distribution of goods and services, are spatially determined and need to be reasserted in our discussion of justice, including social and environmental justice. This is at the heart of Soja's argument. It is also, I suggest, crucial to how we make sense of both LAGI 2016 and the larger network of projects LAGI has initiated. The place-based nature of the proposals challenge us to think about how access to the power grid—flows of electricity and water, like ideas and political power—are spatial. The focus of these projects is geographic, about how this place at this time might be reimagined and reused. Providing a rationale by which a community, or even a few houses, might move off the larger power grid and onto different networks—networks charged and running through contemporary art and culture, I might add—the proposed projects remind us of the often-taken-for-granted systems of power, the megaprojects and vast resources developments that are required to maintain so-called modern conveniences. The disparity in scale between LAGI projects and the megaindustries of a state or national economy give us pause to think about how our power consumption might be distributed and better redistributed.

"CHANGING SITUATIONS"

Collapsing expressways, underfunded public school systems, and abandoned social services—bold dreams of universal public health and well-being—too often give way to overmediated stories of despair and reckless abandon. The genius of the too "long neoliberal moment" (Derksen)[5] has been to use bleak images of inevitable futures to justify growing private interests and entrenched divisions between those who have too much and those who have too little. However, amid crumbling urban infrastructures, above the din of populist hysteria, there are alternatives, or so the artists, architects, engineers, and designers involved in this publication contend. Their work provides bold views of how the grid might be meticulously dismantled and repurposed. While bureaucratic systems fail to meet local needs and national economies obsess with the fleeting, capricious interests of increasingly mobile, detached elites, there is growing frustration not only among the working poor and disenfranchised, but also among the socially conscious, critically engaged artists and theorists. Older divisions of culture and labor, separations of utility from function, differences linking here and elsewhere flicker and disappear; the brittle old stock rips and burns before falling to the floor of a derelict projection room.

Tentative, pixelated to begin with, the new, shared imagery that LAGI taps into vies for attention on our streets, across abandoned lots, and along the harbor. Gradually, almost imperceptibly, new images take shape. This is how I read the meticulous drawings rendered here. With each iteration (or page turn), the display refreshes, resolution and definition filling in. Dynamic range, dimensionality and image depth become more realistic. As I think about what is needed and possible in Santa Monica, I think of LAGI's impressive and growing network of interconnected projects. My mind travels to other cities, following Robert and Elizabeth home to work with youth in the inner city of Pittsburgh or Maasai women in Kenya. Tracking closer to home, I think about how similar projects might function among Aboriginal communities. I see these relatively small-scale public gestures intertwining themselves with the longer lines of power—the power lines of a massive North American grid, and in so doing, they demonstrate new approaches—energy and support—for others who are willing to think through and combat structural inequalities. Distinct alongside stories about the rising tide of ecological devastation and social unrest, the generous and generative potentials that open out of this 2016 version of LAGI provide much-needed counterpoints to the increasingly bleak but also probable futures of peak oil and global warming. Placed alongside the reports on forced migrations, police brutality, and genocide, these urban interventions propose creative, critical re-evaluations of everyday life and its significance in positive political change.

Taken as both platform and process, LAGI 2016 offers a vital lexicon or rich visual repository with which to imagine alternatives to what sometimes feels like the overwhelming lethargy of public debate. The innovative contributions featured here represent a

LAGI Art+Energy Camp, 2015,
Pittsburgh, PA
Image courtesy of the Land Art
Generator Initiative

1 James Clifford, *Returns: Becoming Indigenous in the Twenty-First Century* (Cambridge: Harvard University Press, 2013), 47.

2 See http://landartgenerator.org

3 Henri Lefebvre, *The Production of Space*, trans. Donald Nicholson-Smith, (Oxford: Basil Blackwell, 1991). Originally published 1974.

4 Edward Soja, *Seeking Spatial Justice* (Minneapolis, MN: University of Minnesota Press, 2010).

5 Jeff Derksen, "Poetry and the Long Neoliberal Moment," *West Coast LINE* 51 40.3 (2006), 4–11.

powerful grounding of the (super)structural changes that define the first decades of the twenty-first century as a crucial moment of global change and development. When I look at the new and creative approaches to power generation collected here, I am struck by growing counternarratives, which contest outmoded civic (dis)engagements; the conceptual genius of these proposals, which provoke and evoke positive urban development, is their ability to challenge dominant discourses of scarcity and neglect.

The scale and public focus of these proposed artworks provide a necessary frame or foil with which to view the crumbling monuments of state-funded energy, the built environment, and policies and practices involved in the mass production and consumption of energy. To the extent that they invite us to imagine micropower plants coming online alongside older power plants, these urban designs provide vital counterpoints to the megawatt stations of Niagara, James Bay, or the Bruce, and to the built environment of twentieth-century power and the social, political, and ecological developments these massive power stations made possible. Taken together, these proposals for public artworks provide a rich portfolio of ideas that rearticulate links across contemporary art, urban architecture, and sustainable development. These works foreground important questions about the relationship between social justice and creative practice. And they do this at a human scale and in a manner that resituates everyday life within a renovated notion of the public sphere and reflects the changing situations of place.

Elizabeth Monoian and Robert Ferry of LAGI working with Olorgesailie Maasai Women Artisans of Kenya and Idia'Dega, 2016

Photograph by Tereneh Mosley

WINNING ENTRIES

First Place Winner
Regatta H2O: Familiar Form,
Chameleon Infrastructure

Second Place Winner
Cetacea

Third Place Winner
Paper Boats

"The place-based nature of the proposals challenges us to think about how access to the power grid— flows of electricity and water, like ideas and political power—is spatial."

—Glen Lowry

Regatta H₂O
Familiar Form, Chameleon Infrastructure

What makes a human-made form beautiful? What makes a natural landscape beautiful?

Beauty is of course in the eye of the beholder, but both powerful forms and landscapes elicit strong emotional attachments, and the experience of them can inspire people into action. While each may be evaluated on their own merits and qualities, rarely do they come together without controversy.

Yet there are some man-made forms so universally associated with their landscapes, and so steadfastly imprinted in the collective imagination—the red dairy barns of pastoral America, the terraced rice paddies of Southern China, the whitewashed villas of hilltop Greece—that they become an inseparable element of the natural landscape's identity. The sea is no different, and since civilizations first began navigating the oceans by harnessing the wind, the billowing forms of sail and mast have occupied an omnipresent place in the mental image of the seaside.

Regatta H₂O repurposes this familiar maritime form as infrastructure, which harvests fog to create fresh water, and harnesses the wind in order to power its operations.

The sails of *Regatta H₂O* are fog-harvesting meshes. Collection troughs are designed as veins within the sail surface, transporting harvested moisture to the mast where it can be piped to storage vessels at the Santa Monica Pier. When the moisture content of the air falls below a certain threshold, the sails are retracted to reveal the horizon line of the Pacific Ocean.

While water is harvested passively, some electrical power is needed to operate the pumping and steering mechanisms and deployment of the sails. This energy is extracted from the wind via a device known as a Windbelt™, which relies on an oscillating belt suspended between two electromagnets. Each of the *Regatta H₂O* masts contains eight such generating units along its length.

At night, light rings beneath each wind band pulsate with the intensity of power being generated. This also serves as a navigational safety device, alerting boats of their presence in the dark.

Through an artistic and technological reimagining of millennia-old science, *Regatta H₂O* shows that the union of the natural environment with the climatic benefits of sustainable energy and water infrastructure can have powerful and positive impacts on how we perceive cherished landscapes.

TEAM
Christopher Sjoberg, Ryo Saito

TEAM LOCATION
Tokyo, Japan

ENERGY TECHNOLOGIES
aerostatic flutter wind harvesting (Windbelt™)

WATER TECHNOLOGIES
fog harvesting

ANNUAL CAPACITY
70 MWh (used on site)
112 million liters of drinking water

Southwest elevation: sails stowed
for sunset viewing

Southwest elevation: sails deployed
for fog harvesting

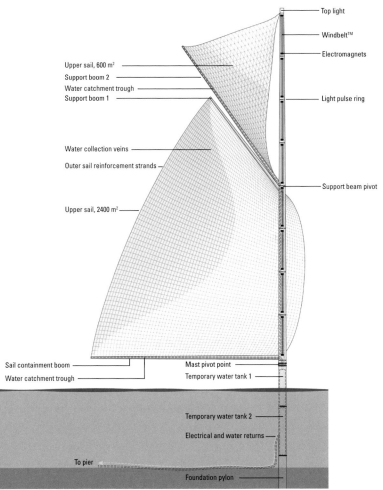

Top light

Windbelt™

Electromagnets

Upper sail, 600 m²

Support boom 2

Water catchment trough

Support boom 1

Light pulse ring

Water collection veins

Outer sail reinforcement strands

Support beam pivot

Upper sail, 2400 m²

Sail containment boom

Mast pivot point

Water catchment trough

Temporary water tank 1

Temporary water tank 2

Electrical and water returns

To pier

Foundation pylon

Typical sail detail diagram

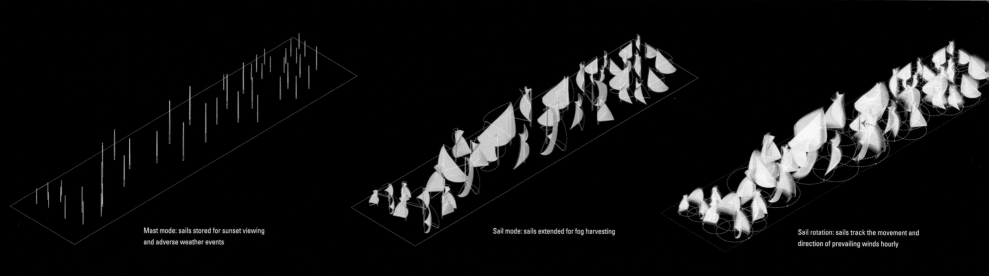

Mast mode: sails stored for sunset viewing
and adverse weather events

Sail mode: sails extended for fog harvesting

Sail rotation: sails track the movement and
direction of prevailing winds hourly

Sail phase diagram

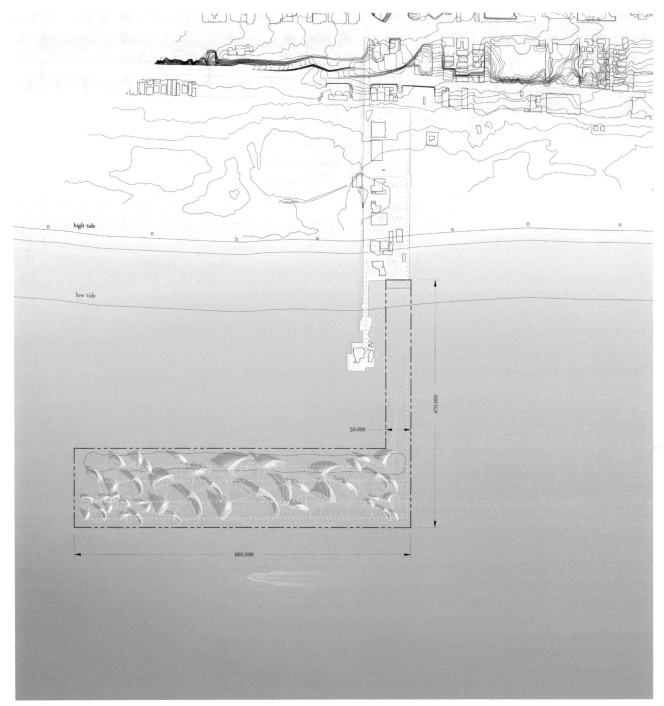

high tide

low tide

470.000

50.000

660.000

Site plan

Cetacea

Cetacea is an elegant integration of energy and art, glistening white in the Santa Monica sun, rising gracefully from the surface of the water.

Cetacea generates power by harvesting the renewable resources of Santa Monica Bay—wind, wave, and sun. Driven by the principle of "clean power for clean water," *Cetacea* reconciles water scarcity with pressing social and ecological concerns by supporting the existing water filtration facilities near the pier while providing carbon-neutral power to city residents. By connecting to the Santa Monica Urban Runoff Recycling Facility (SMURRF) and providing enough electricity to run a High-Efficiency Reverse Osmosis (HERO) system, *Cetacea* contributes to Santa Monica's 2020 sustainability goals of water and energy independence.

The blue whale is a pelagic powerhouse. Consuming upwards of four tons of krill per day, the world's largest creatures are fueled by gargantuan quantities of its smallest. *Cetacea* reimagines the blue whale's strategy of capturing microsources of energy on an even larger scale.

In place of the sprawling and unappealing profile of common renewable energy farms, a vertical configuration of wave-, wind-, and solar-powered generators within graceful, multifaceted arches maximizes energy production within a minimal footprint. Modular arch components mean that *Cetacea* can easily be expanded in the future through the construction of additional forms, meeting the needs of a changing city while continuing to generate energy beautifully and unobtrusively. Repetition and subtle variation of the arches create ethereal forms in constant interaction with the play of sea, light, and cloud across the horizon.

Wave buoys 300 mm in diameter are situated within the framework of the arches, floating at sea level to capture wave energy around the clock. The vertical movement of each passing wave induces the flow of electricity by moving a magnet through an electromagnetic coil.

Windbelts™ are stacked within the sides of each arch at one-meter intervals. Following Bernoulli's principle, the form of the arches increases wind speed as it passes through the belts. The resulting aerostatic flutter of the belts creates energy by oscillating magnets through an electromagnetic field. Photovoltaic panels positioned at the top of each arch provide maximum solar output.

Cetacea is the order of marine mammalia containing the whales and their congeners.

TEAM
Keegan Oneal, Sean Link, Caitlin Vanhauer, Colin Poranski

TEAM LOCATION
Eugene (OR), USA

ENERGY TECHNOLOGIES
wave energy converter with linear alternator, Windbelt™, photovoltaic panels

WATER TECHNOLOGIES
high-efficiency reverse osmosis (HERO™ by Aquatech) for stormwater runoff treatment

ANNUAL CAPACITY
4,300 MWh (80% used to offset the energy demand of existing SMURRF facility and power the HERO™ system) 650 million liters of drinking water

The reestablishment of kelp forests in the Santa Monica Bay calls for control of purple sea urchin populations.

Grottoes and overhangs in the sculpture foundations provide habitat for sheepshead fish and lobsters—two major predators of the sea urchin.

Pylons with rough, rocky surfaces support filter feeders and molluscs.

Power transformer

Artful power generation embodies
Santa Monica's vibrant culture and
vision for a sustainable future.

Cetacea

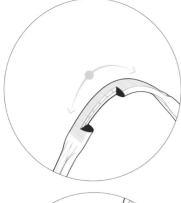

Solar Array
Solar modules capture energy from sunlight and convert it into electricity.

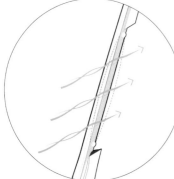

Windbelt™
Aerostatic flutter caused by the wind vibrates a belt that oscillates between magnets to generate electricity.

Wave Buoy
Vertical wave movement drives the buoy-piston linear alternator system.

Cetacea consists of five sculptures of three different sizes. Each parabolic arch ranges in height from 13 meters to 30 meters tall. A pile system uses recycled concrete and allows room for habitat reconstruction around the minimal physical footprint of the structures.

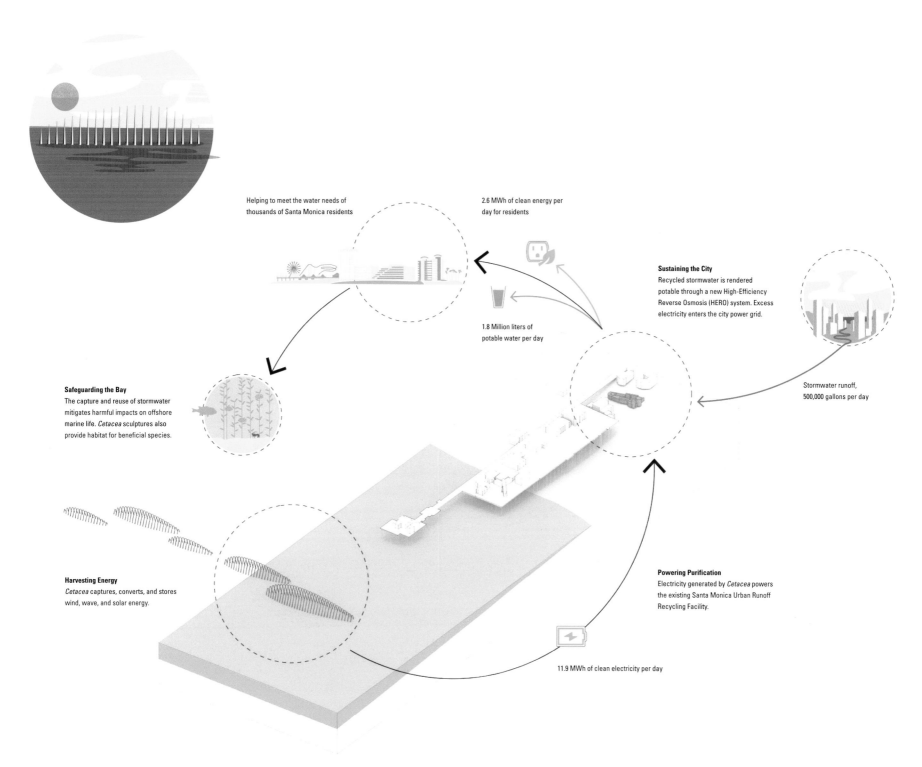

Helping to meet the water needs of
thousands of Santa Monica residents

2.6 MWh of clean energy per
day for residents

Sustaining the City
Recycled stormwater is rendered
potable through a new High-Efficiency
Reverse Osmosis (HERO) system. Excess
electricity enters the city power grid.

1.8 Million liters of
potable water per day

Safeguarding the Bay
The capture and reuse of stormwater
mitigates harmful impacts on offshore
marine life. *Cetacea* sculptures also
provide habitat for beneficial species.

Stormwater runoff,
500,000 gallons per day

Harvesting Energy
Cetacea captures, converts, and stores
wind, wave, and solar energy.

Powering Purification
Electricity generated by *Cetacea* powers
the existing Santa Monica Urban Runoff
Recycling Facility.

11.9 MWh of clean electricity per day

Paper Boats

A shimmering, iridescent mirage of swirling whites, pinks, and greens floats playfully in a sinuous line resembling a school of fish. *Paper Boats* recalls the 1930s desire to transform the Santa Monica Pier into a thriving boating and yachting destination. The breakwater constructed at that time created a protected harbor, but has eroded over the years. Today it is almost completely submerged under the ocean surface.

While recalling this history, *Paper Boats* revitalizes the ecology of the area. Throughout the years, overhunting and overfishing of some key species have allowed purple urchin to graze on the kelp without competition. This has led to "urchin barrens," which offer little in the way of genetic diversity, food, or nesting habitats. *Paper Boats* has reversed this trend by establishing pockets of coral and kelp (once commonplace here) within underwater "shipwreck" frames that anchor each boat to the historic breakwater. The rebar "shipwrecks" mirror the sculptures above and encourage coral growth with a phenomenon called accretion. First observed by Wolf Hilbertz, accretion is a process where a trickle of direct current electricity (provided by the solar collector above) is run through the rebar to accelerate coral growth up to five times faster than normal.

Paper Boats uses a combination of special Fresnel lenses, reflectors, and holographic photovoltaic cells. Each boat's four sails work as concentrated photovoltaic collectors. The outer shell of the "sail" utilizes Fresnel lenses to channel incoming light.

Beneath the sails are a series of holographic photovoltaic cells that pair laser-etched glazing with bi-facial silicon panels to trap sunlight from both directions with incredible efficiency. The intricately cut patterns also refract light, giving them the shiny, iridescent quality that glows beautifully—especially at sunset.

The solar panels are attached to a ceramic-clad aluminum framework. The structure conceals the CPV conduits and acts as a passive heat sink. A trickle of energy is diverted to the "shipwrecks" before entering the main conduit. This small charge provides a catalyst for coral growth, strengthening the local marine ecosystem.

TEAM
Christopher Makrinos, Stephen Makrinos, Alexander Bishop

TEAM LOCATION
Pittsburgh (PA), USA

ENERGY TECHNOLOGIES
concentrated photovoltaic (CPV), reflectors, Holographic Planar Concentrator™ (HPC) technology developed by Prism Solar Technologies

ANNUAL CAPACITY
2,383 MWh

The location of the installation makes it the perfect centerpiece for large-scale, national events.

An iconic form, the paper boat is nostalgic, simple, and instantly recognizable. It acts as a surreal memorial to the history of the Santa Monica Pier and its underlying ecologies.

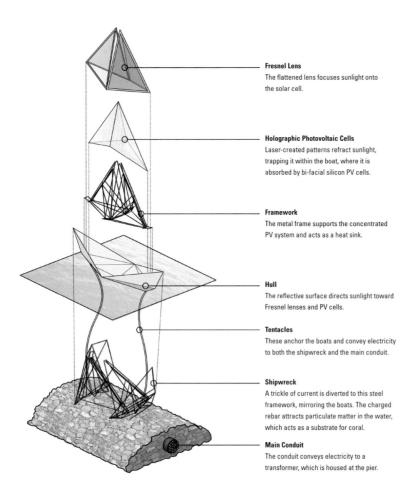

Fresnel Lens
The flattened lens focuses sunlight onto
the solar cell.

Holographic Photovoltaic Cells
Laser-created patterns refract sunlight,
trapping it within the boat, where it is
absorbed by bi-facial silicon PV cells.

Framework
The metal frame supports the concentrated
PV system and acts as a heat sink.

Hull
The reflective surface directs sunlight toward
Fresnel lenses and PV cells.

Tentacles
These anchor the boats and convey electricity
to both the shipwreck and the main conduit.

Shipwreck
A trickle of current is diverted to this steel
framework, mirroring the boats. The charged
rebar attracts particulate matter in the water,
which acts as a substrate for coral.

Main Conduit
The conduit conveys electricity to a
transformer, which is housed at the pier.

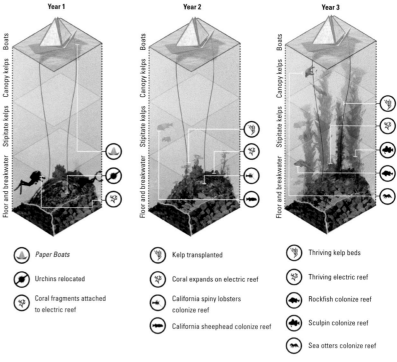

**Restoring a reef with electricity
and kelp forests**

A section through Santa Monica
Bay shows the relationship of *Paper
Boats* to the breakwater, both above
and below the surface of the water.

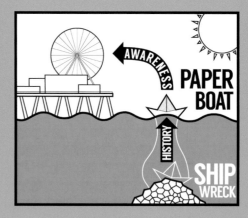

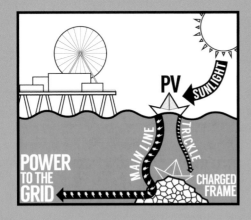

Recognizing a disconnect between the surface and subsurface landscapes of the pier, *Paper Boats* work to raise awareness and reestablish a connection between ecological and human activities. On the surface, *Paper Boats* calls attention to the history of the breakwater as a historic yacht harbor, and the "shipwrecks" below raise awareness of the negative impact of past human activity on marine ecosystems. In order to reflect the positive impacts of the installation, the "shipwrecks" manifest themselves into successional marine ecosystems—the surface energy directly resurrecting subsurface ecologies and providing tangible benefits to the local flora and fauna.

12,000
LBS OF CARBON OFFSET PER DAY

ABLE TO POWER
28
FERRIS WHEELS FOR A YEAR
(2,383,000 KWH/YR)

$650,000
ECOSYSTEM SERVICES
RENDERED PER YEAR

The electric reef would not only revitalize the local marine ecosystems, it would establish a thriving tourist industry centered on scuba diving, snorkeling, and other noninvasive water activities.

SHORTLISTED ENTRIES

ESTHER

Breakwater Make Water

Flowerpops

Santa Monica Ocean's Breath

Aurora

The Flying Steelhead of Santa Monica

Follies and Fog

Horizon Lines: The Transparency of Energy

Subsurface

The Pipe

sky + music + fountain + water

The Clear Orb

Sun Towers

2000 Lighthouses Over the Sea

Big Beach Balloon

Wake Up

Noctilucales

Ring Garden

Catching the Wave

Cnidaria Halitus

Weightless Balloons

"The enormity of the problem cannot be overstated, and we will need all hands on deck to stem the tide of climate change. Artists and the arts can play a significant role in helping us meet this challenge head-on by humanizing global issues, deepening community engagement, and stimulating creative solutions to seemingly intractable problems."

—Shannon Daut
City of Santa Monica Cultural Affairs Manager

ESTHER

ESTHER captures the ephemerality of motion through water and air, harnessing these elements to generate purified water and clean energy. The design is conceived as two parts, an underwater point absorber buoy that harvests wave energy, and a piezoelectric torque generator "mast" that collects wind energy as it sways above water.

This two-part design takes inspiration from synchronized swimming, as epitomized by the classic aqua-musicals of Esther Williams from the golden years of Hollywood in the 1940s and 1950s. Like the swimmers in an aquatic ballet, *ESTHER* elegantly moves in unison above and below water, creating a spectacle of the periodic movements of the tides and the forces of the wind. This dynamic movement is accentuated by the reflective fiberglass material, which creates a play of shadows across the surface of the water. At the same time, the water is mirrored on the masts, reflecting

a fragment of the sea into the horizon. The form of the masts is derived from the abstraction of a synchronized swimmer's leg and aerodynamic sailing spars.

The eccentric spacing created by the elliptical formation allows viewers from the Santa Monica Pier to understand the installation as an object rather than a nondirectional field, much as the bodies of synchronized swimmers collectively form an elaborate pattern. The top of the masts light up at night allowing observers to enjoy the installation at all times of the day and in all weather conditions. The light is amplified by a Fresnel lens, which sits on top of the masts and powers a small solar updraft tower during the day.

A point absorber power buoy is just below the surface of each mast generating 100 kWh of electricity every day by harnessing the ever-present wave energy within the ocean.

TEAM
Peter Coombe, Jennifer Sage, Eunkyoung Kim, Charlene Chai, Kaitlin Faherty (Sage and Coombe Architects)

TEAM LOCATION
New York (NY), USA

ENERGY TECHNOLOGIES
point absorber wave energy converter (CETO™ system developed by Carnegie Wave Energy), piezoelectric stacked actuators, Fresnel-assisted convection turbine

ANNUAL CAPACITY
2,800 MWh

Visitors to the Santa Monica Pier on an overcast and rainy day will take pleasure in the performance of the glowing lights of *ESTHER*.

The masts employ technology developed for the Windulum, a piezoelectric wind turbine that transforms wind into electricity without generators while eliminating any potential hazards to birds posed by traditional wind turbines.

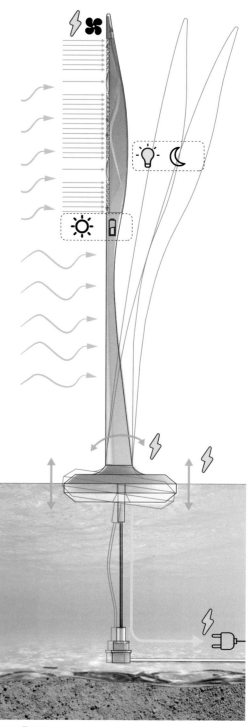

Energy diagram

Movement of *ESTHER* and
synchronized swimming

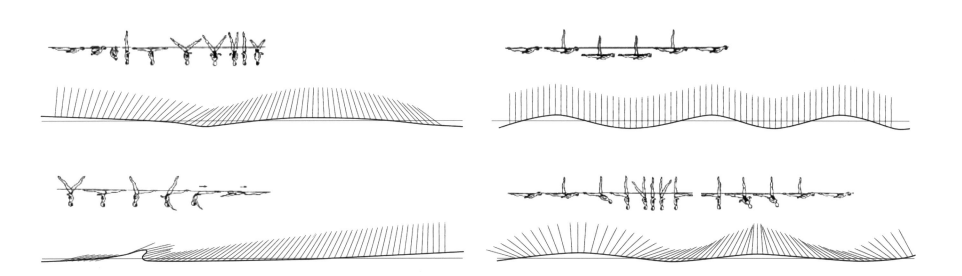

Breakwater
Make Water

Not often is there an opportunity to generate ideas for an offshore location and to create a feature that directly responds to its maritime setting. The scale of the site creates visibility from around the whole of Santa Monica Bay. *Breakwater Make Water* is therefore an installation that is both eye-catching and visually sensitive to its setting.

Contributing to Santa Monica's strong identity is the fog that comes rolling in off the Pacific Ocean almost every morning. Using a technology similar to that already successfully used in projects in South America, fog-harvest netting is shaped into sails to recall the harbor that once occupied the site.

Energy generation is accomplished with a buoy-type wave energy converter that powers an underwater turbine by moving vertically with the waves and tides. The hull of the boat acts as the float of the buoy and the boat's mast continues below the water to form the absorber. The turbine unit is anchored to the sea floor with a fixed deadweight, which also houses the pipe and cable infrastructure as it joins into each adjacent unit.

Sixty boats are spaced out within the site area on the far side of the breakwater. Each boat measures 24.5 meters from the base of the hull to the top of the mast and is 15 meters long. The base of the hull sits about one meter below the water level, rising and falling with a range of four meters between high and low tide. There is a minimum spacing of 10 meters between each boat to allow for efficient harvesting of fog and to provide an intermittent view of the horizon from the beach and pier.

Wind carries fog particles through the material, trapping droplets of water. Gravity then causes these droplets to fall to the base of the sails before flowing into the pipe infrastructure. Resources produced would first supply the pier and waterfront businesses.

TEAM
Elizabeth Anne Case

TEAM LOCATION
Wallingford, UK

ENERGY TECHNOLOGIES
point absorber wave energy converter (similar to Ocean Power Technologies™)

WATER TECHNOLOGIES
fog harvesting (similar to FogQuest™)

ANNUAL CAPACITY
400 MWh
13 million liters of drinking water

As the sun goes down over the Santa Monica Bay, the fleet of sailboats comes to life with solar-powered lights that have been charging throughout the day. The programmable LED lights can either be a static glow or cycle through color combinations, allowing for infinite creative possibilities that could tie in with the promotion of special events and holidays.

The boats take advantage of the prevailing wind direction to harvest the seasonal fog into their sails and supply Santa Monica with drinking water.

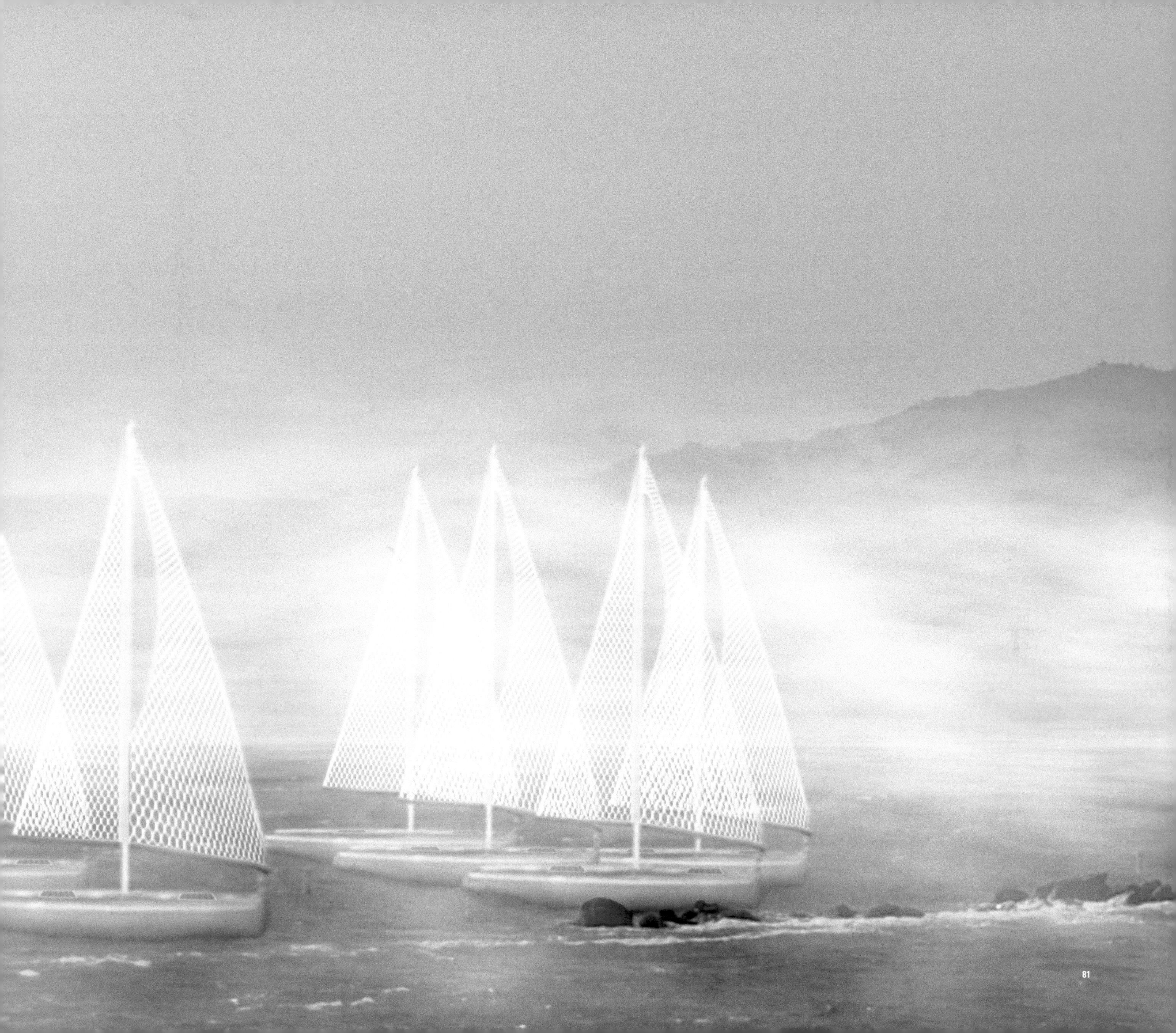

The fleet of 60 boats is sensitive to
the marine setting and acts as an
iconic centerpiece for Santa Monica
residents and tourists.

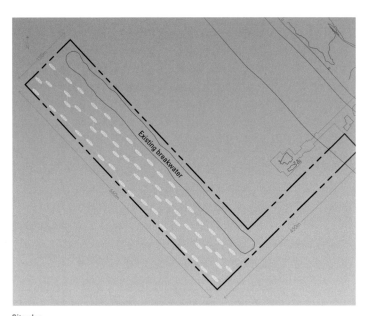

Site plan

Existing breakwater

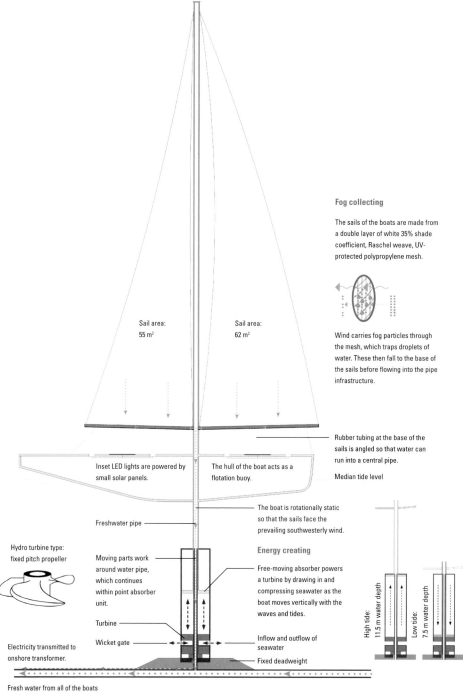

Fog collecting

The sails of the boats are made from a double layer of white 35% shade coefficient, Raschel weave, UV-protected polypropylene mesh.

Wind carries fog particles through the mesh, which traps droplets of water. These then fall to the base of the sails before flowing into the pipe infrastructure.

Sail area: 55 m²

Sail area: 62 m²

Rubber tubing at the base of the sails is angled so that water can run into a central pipe.

Median tide level

Inset LED lights are powered by small solar panels.

The hull of the boat acts as a flotation buoy.

The boat is rotationally static so that the sails face the prevailing southwesterly wind.

Freshwater pipe

Energy creating

Free-moving absorber powers a turbine by drawing in and compressing seawater as the boat moves vertically with the waves and tides.

Hydro turbine type: fixed pitch propeller

Moving parts work around water pipe, which continues within point absorber unit.

Turbine

Wicket gate

Inflow and outflow of seawater

Fixed deadweight

Electricity transmitted to onshore transformer.

High tide: 11.5 m water depth

Low tide: 7.5 m water depth

Fresh water from all of the boats is conveyed to shore through a pipe infrastructure by gravity.

83

Flowerpops

Just off the Santa Monica Pier there is an artificial giant garden, vibrant and full of life, with everything moving and the sound of the wind whistling between the stems. Here and there, one part of the system catches the eye for a moment. As Lewis Carroll suggests, perhaps it is necessary to invert the size relationships between humans and nature to uncover the laws that regulate the balance between the parties.

Flowerpops integrates a new technology park with the spectacular character of its ocean setting. The famous funfair skyline on Santa Monica Bay is extended toward the horizon line near the breakwater. Five different technologies for energy production are brought together there. The devices are designed in five natural shapes in order to compose an artificial ecosystem.

"Wind flowers" come in four different sizes and use Vortex Bladeless™ technology. "Flying pollen" are realized in colored PET-G plastic, weighing no more than 750 grams and driven by a mechanical system that is set in motion by the energy produced by some "wind flowers." "Floating water lilies" exploit wave power and are configured as a carpet of undulating buoys that dot the sea horizon. The "tulip binders" are pools of rainwater harvesters that rise and fall depending on the difference of pressure generated by the water collection. "Sun flowers" use photovoltaic film to convert sunlight into electricity.

TEAM
Augusto Audissoni, Silvia Cama (lab[zerozoone]), Elisabetta Lo Grasso, Elisa Tozzi, Nicolò Mossink

TEAM LOCATION
Genoa, Italy

ENERGY TECHNOLOGIES
Vortex Bladeless™ wind turbine, thin-film photovoltaic (similar to AltaDevices™), point absorber wave energy converter

ANNUAL CAPACITY
13,000 MWh

The system—learning from nature—is formed by a great variety of independent elements that interact, producing physical transformations and energy.

Flowerpops

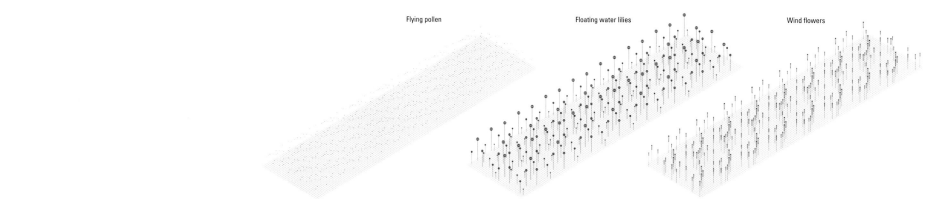

Flying pollen

Floating water lilies

Wind flowers

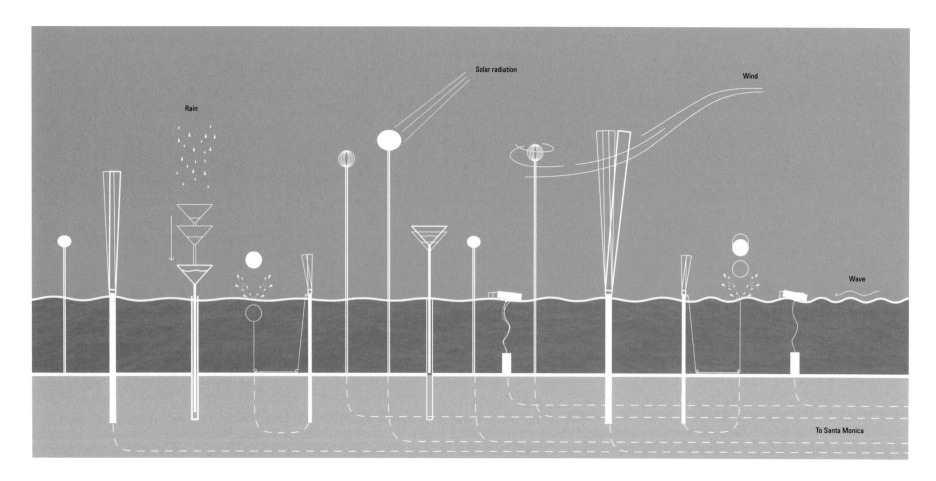

Solar radiation

Wind

Rain

Wave

To Santa Monica

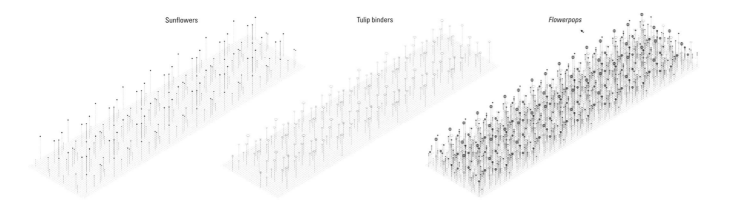

Sunflowers

Tulip binders

Flowerpops

During the passing of the day the surrounding playground changes according to weather and time. At night the stored energy powers over 2,000 LED lights, reflecting the starry sky onto the ocean.

Santa Monica
Ocean's Breath

The Santa Monica Pier is a continuation of the city into the ocean represented through play and entertainment. *Santa Monica Ocean's Breath* continues to enrich the link between the ocean and the city in a fun and visible way.

The energy potential of wave movement is enormous and the conversion to electricity is relatively simple.

The 78 floating buoys, situated 100 meters from the breakwater rocks, produce clean energy that is used to supply Santa Monica Pier activities.

By night, a small part of the produced energy is used to light up the buoys and their connection to the pier. Each buoy has a vertical illumination bar that is activated in proportion to the energy produced by the ocean—a synchronized dance of light with waves.

Santa Monica Ocean's Breath delivers enough clean energy to make the pier net-zero while creating a unique atmosphere that can attract tourists and set an example for other coastal cities.

TEAM
Fabio Azzato

TEAM LOCATION
Florence, Italy

ENERGY TECHNOLOGIES
point absorber wave energy converter

ANNUAL CAPACITY
1,000 MWh

View from the beach

Aerial view of the power buoy farm

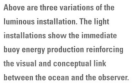

Above are three variations of the luminous installation. The light installations show the immediate buoy energy production reinforcing the visual and conceptual link between the ocean and the observer.

During the night the buoys display the generous energy potential that exists within the ocean, turning a small amount of this power into a spectacular play of light and data.

The lights react instantaneously to the waves energetic production, creating a different show for each visitor and moment.

Night view from the beach

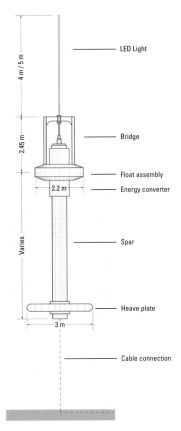

LED Light

Bridge

Float assembly

Energy converter

Spar

Heave plate

Cable connection

4 m / 5 m

2.45 m

2.2 m

Varies

3 m

Power buoy

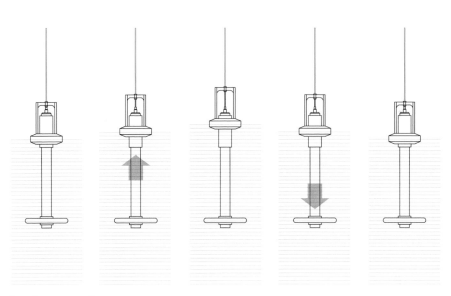

Power buoy wave reaction

Energy farm cross section

Aurora

Aurora gifts visitors a dreamlike and immersive experience of walking surrounded in a cloud with just the noise of the waves and the wind. The artwork makes palpable the ineffable, reachable the limitless, and measurable the invisible. It is a rich public space where multiple social and cultural activities can take place.

The wooden floor—an extension of the existing pier—represents stability. The cloud—coated with thermochromic paint—represents lightness and transparency. It is set up in elevation so as not to obscure the view from the beach to the horizon. Above the horizon line is a cloud that changes its shape, size, and appearance with the direction of the wind and temperature, causing boundaries to completely blur. The synesthetic impact of the artwork cannot be adequately captured with photography or film. It can only be experienced directly on location. It is formless, massless, dimensionless, and weightless. It speaks to the color of the sky, the reflection of the ocean, and the emotions of the visitors.

Aurora provides clean electricity with a tidal turbine, and drinkable water with solar distillation within the cloud. It is a hybrid system prefabricated in boxes that are set into the existing breakwater. Every element works together in a closed loop. The free-flow underwater turbine system harnesses the ocean as a predictable and sustainable power source. The system transfers kinetic energy to electricity while minimizing visual impact. An intake pipe is included at the point of highest pressure to draw water up to the solar distillation process.

Following the distillation, drinking water is channeled for collection, while the brine goes to power lamps that use salt to generate electricity. The prefabricated boxes include the pillars that support the cloud along with the distillation tray and other integrated systems. The cloud works as a container of heat and water. The greenhouse effect creates a microclimate in which water evaporates and then condenses on the inside surface of the cloud skin. The Venturi effect drives the process by which water is conveyed to and from the distillation chamber.

The circle is complete, from the ocean to the sky, from the heaviness of the rock to the lightness of the air. The system is integrated as a modular, simple, and self-sufficient structure in which aesthetics, concept, energy production, and social aspects come together.

TEAM
Daniel Martín de los Ríos, Francisco Vilar Navarro (Pistach Office)

TEAM LOCATION
Rotterdam, The Netherlands

ENERGY TECHNOLOGIES
tidal turbine (similar to Open-Centre Turbine by OpenHydro™), SALt™ (Sustainable Alternative Lighting)

WATER TECHNOLOGIES
solar distillation (brine waste powers site lighting)

ANNUAL CAPACITY
30,000 MWh
100 million liters of drinking water

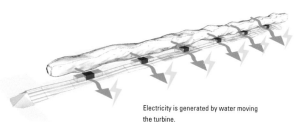

Electricity is generated by water moving the turbine.

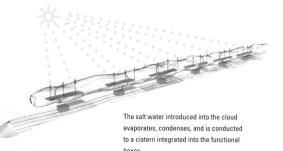

The salt water introduced into the cloud evaporates, condenses, and is conducted to a cistern integrated into the functional boxes.

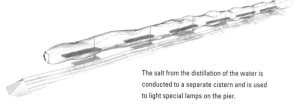

The salt from the distillation of the water is conducted to a separate cistern and is used to light special lamps on the pier.

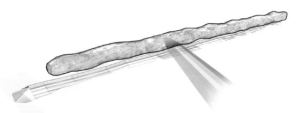

Thermochromic paint filters the white light and creates a colorful palette underneath, making the experience unforgettable.

The intervention is powerful yet respectful, dramatic yet silent, strong yet necessary. The transparency and lightness of *Aurora* makes it appear to float over the bay, a minimal and sensitive design that does not obscure the ocean view.

Synesthesia is the neurological phenomenon in which stimulation of one sensory cognitive pathway leads to automatic, involuntary experience in a second sensory or cognitive pathway.

Colors express emotions and emotions have color. The lights are controlled by the users, depending on their emotions. *Aurora* is a mirror of the population, the environment, and the city.

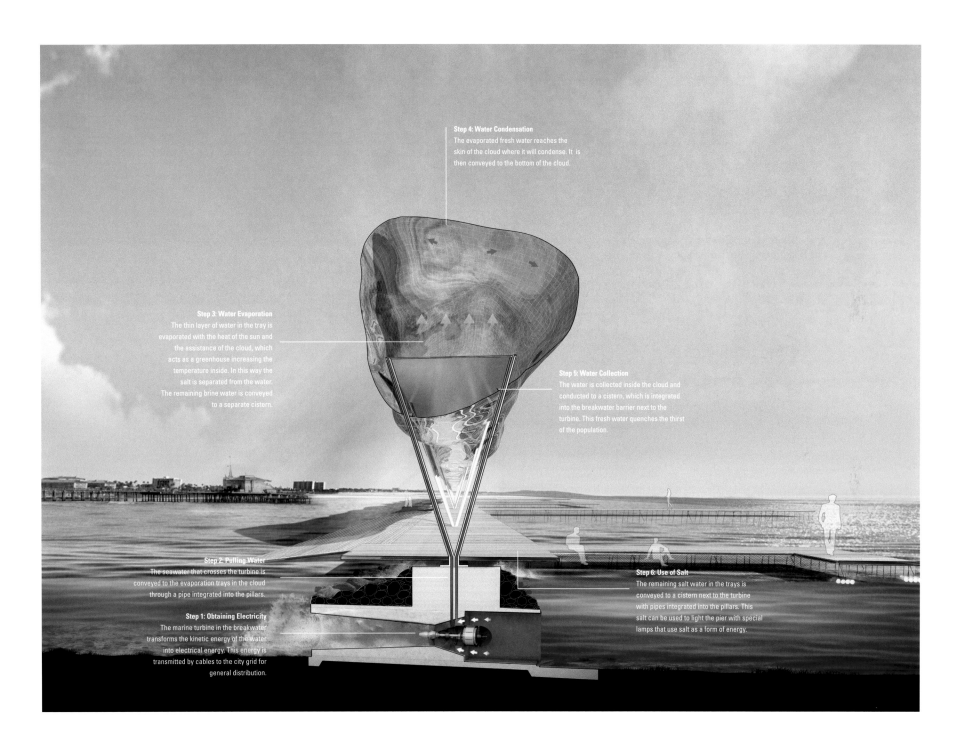

Step 4: Water Condensation
The evaporated fresh water reaches the skin of the cloud where it will condense. It is then conveyed to the bottom of the cloud.

Step 3: Water Evaporation
The thin layer of water in the tray is evaporated with the heat of the sun and the assistance of the cloud, which acts as a greenhouse increasing the temperature inside. In this way the salt is separated from the water. The remaining brine water is conveyed to a separate cistern.

Step 5: Water Collection
The water is collected inside the cloud and conducted to a cistern, which is integrated into the breakwater barrier next to the turbine. This fresh water quenches the thirst of the population.

Step 2: Pulling Water
The seawater that crosses the turbine is conveyed to the evaporation trays in the cloud through a pipe integrated into the pillars.

Step 1: Obtaining Electricity
The marine turbine in the breakwater transforms the kinetic energy of the water into electrical energy. This energy is transmitted by cables to the city grid for general distribution.

Step 6: Use of Salt
The remaining salt water in the trays is conveyed to a cistern next to the turbine with pipes integrated into the pillars. This salt can be used to light the pier with special lamps that use salt as a form of energy.

The Flying Steelhead of Santa Monica

A school of enormous steelhead swimming through the sky power our world by dancing with the wind.

Dozens of gleaming fish the size of school buses swim low in the sky, just above and beyond the pier. Their swim is slow but steady, even in a soft breeze. At sunset they dance in unison, reflecting the sky and sea. At night, out on the pier, they are surreal ghostly giants swaying to the sound of the surf. In their mood and in their color, the fish reflect the weather, the time of day, and the time of year. They follow the wind in direction and in speed. As the wind picks up, the bodies of the fish start to straighten and the tails move faster. On cloudy days the fish look flat and steely as they swim faster into an oncoming storm.

On their journeys, steelhead sew the land to the sea, reminding us how this is one fabric, one ecosystem, that we are all a part of. The heroic journey that the steelhead take upstream is assisted by their refined shape, an evolutionary reflection of the rivers themselves. The Los Angeles River had steelhead spawning pools until 1938 when it was turned into the concrete channel that it is today. The southern steelhead that swim the waters around Santa Monica are now endangered.

Each 20-meter fish is equipped with twin 400 kW generators driven by the movement of the fish. Most wind generators require strong winds and lots of space for the wind to regroup after getting churned up. These fish thrive on turbulence and their energy performance is optimized when grouped close together. As the fish swim, one side gets longer while the other side gets shorter. A chain is attached to both sides of the tail, running up the insides of the fish to a gear near the front. As the gear spins one way, then the other, the power is transferred to two flywheels that spin in opposite directions.

TEAM
Winfield Scott Balcom,
Adom Balcom

TEAM LOCATION
Ashland (OR), USA

ENERGY TECHNOLOGIES
custom wind-driven generators
(using recycled bicycle and
car parts)

ANNUAL CAPACITY
50 MWh per fish
(36 fish = 1,800 MWh)

View of a single *Flying Steelhead* as seen from the pier.

97

A school of enormous steelhead
swimming through the sky, powering
our world by dancing with the wind.

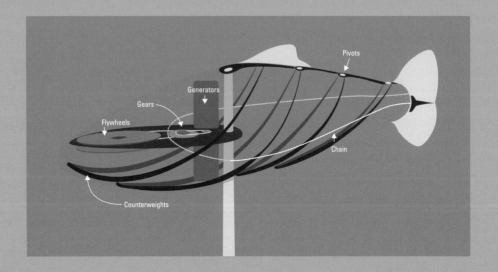

A monument to the biodiversity of
the marine ecosystem set against the
Santa Monica mountain range.

Follies and Fog

Renewable energy of the future does not need to be a blight on the landscape, or an affliction on local ecosystems, but can instead float harmlessly and almost invisibly just below the ocean's surface. *Follies and Fog* celebrates the notion that today's renewable energy sources do not require exterior cladding or to be fashioned into interesting forms, but instead can remain hidden and out of sight, while providing sustainable energy for the city.

The artwork makes visible the hidden wave energy production units below the surface of the ocean, but also uses a small amount of wave energy to conceal itself in a fog mist. As the amount of renewable energy produced nears the target of powering 1,280 homes, the amount of artificial fog is so great that it completely engulfs the artwork in a cloud of mist, obscuring it from view. It

is only when the renewable energy source begins to wane as the waves become less powerful that the viewer is able to perceive the work of art within the cloud of artificial fog.

The 128 floating follies of *Follies and Fog* each symbolize the archetypal Santa Monica dwelling and its need for energy. Each of the bright red follies is an abstraction of a house type found in a district of Santa Monica. The follies are connected to a floating grid of buoy-type wave energy converters. Each folly is directly responsible for powering 10 homes within the City of Santa Monica.

A walkway invites visitors to follow the line of the original Santa Monica Pier—a train line that extended out into the sea. There they can walk along this floating path surrounded by the abstract floating houses, as if walking along Santa Monica Boulevard.

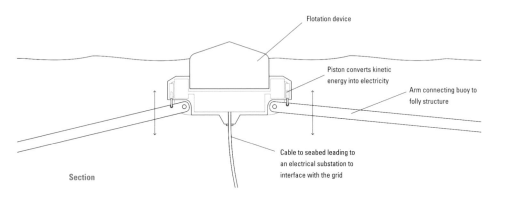

Flotation device

Piston converts kinetic energy into electricity

Arm connecting buoy to folly structure

Cable to seabed leading to an electrical substation to interface with the grid

Section

TEAM
Nik Klahre, Brooke Campbell-Johnston

TEAM LOCATION
London, UK; Copenhagen, Denmark

ENERGY TECHNOLOGIES
wave energy converter

ANNUAL CAPACITY
13,000 MWh (less the energy required to power fog generation)

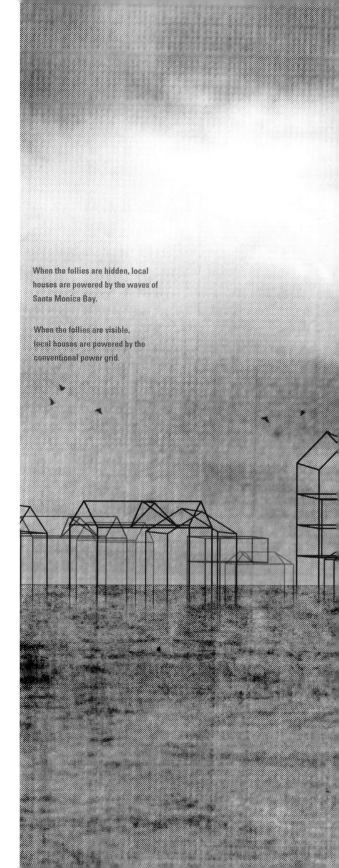

When the follies are hidden, local houses are powered by the waves of Santa Monica Bay.

When the follies are visible, local houses are powered by the conventional power grid.

Follies

The design incorporates 128 floating follies, each symbolizing the archetypal Santa Monica dwelling and its need for energy. Each of the bright red, steel follies is an abstraction of a house type found in a district of Santa Monica. Each folly is directly responsible for powering 10 homes in the city.

Walkway

Viewers make their way from a distant perspective and into complete submersion within the artwork, surrounded by the abstract floating houses, as if walking along Santa Monica Boulevard.

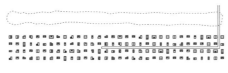

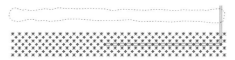

Pump Module Buoys

221 pump modules with 512 secondary buoys

Interconnected Rigid Linking Arms

The pumping modules are connected to the secondary buoys, forming a lattice grid that stabilizes the floating structure.

Section

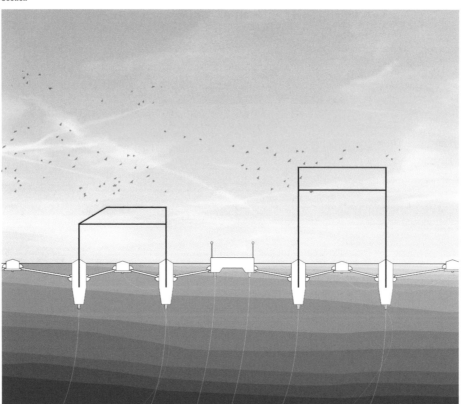

Follies and Fog reflects a typical
cross section of the city.

Horizon Lines
The Transparency of Energy

In its original form in 1909, the Santa Monica Pier was built over a sewage pipe that emptied into the ocean, working to hide the effects of humanity on the environment. *Horizon Lines* takes this one piece of Santa Monica's rich and diverse history and turns it upside down. It presents a contemporary counterpoint by creating a transparent energy source on the horizon for all to see, inspired by the form of the pier's pylons and the shape of a wave.

The project is composed of BIPV (building integrated photovoltaic) glass panels, the spacing of which is based on the crest and trough of a wave. The panels are spaced more tightly near the end of the pier to create the intensity in the crest of the wave, reflecting and refracting water and sky. The middle portion represents the trough of the wave, where the ocean becomes calm and glass-like. This pattern culminates at the far end with a tightening of the panels to signify the next peak of the wave as it heads toward shore. Walking along the beach or the pier, a visitor experiences different perceptions of the sculpture, like the glint of a wave in morning sun or a crystal-clear view through the panels to the true horizon behind.

Each panel is illuminated with an LED light strip connected to the panel's individual meter. Through the levels of illumination, visitors will be able to visualize how much energy has been produced.

TEAM
Rebecca Borowiecki

TEAM LOCATION
Boulder (CO), USA

ENERGY TECHNOLOGIES
transparent solar cell
by Onyx Solar®

ANNUAL CAPACITY
625 MWh

View from the end of the pier

View from Palisades Park

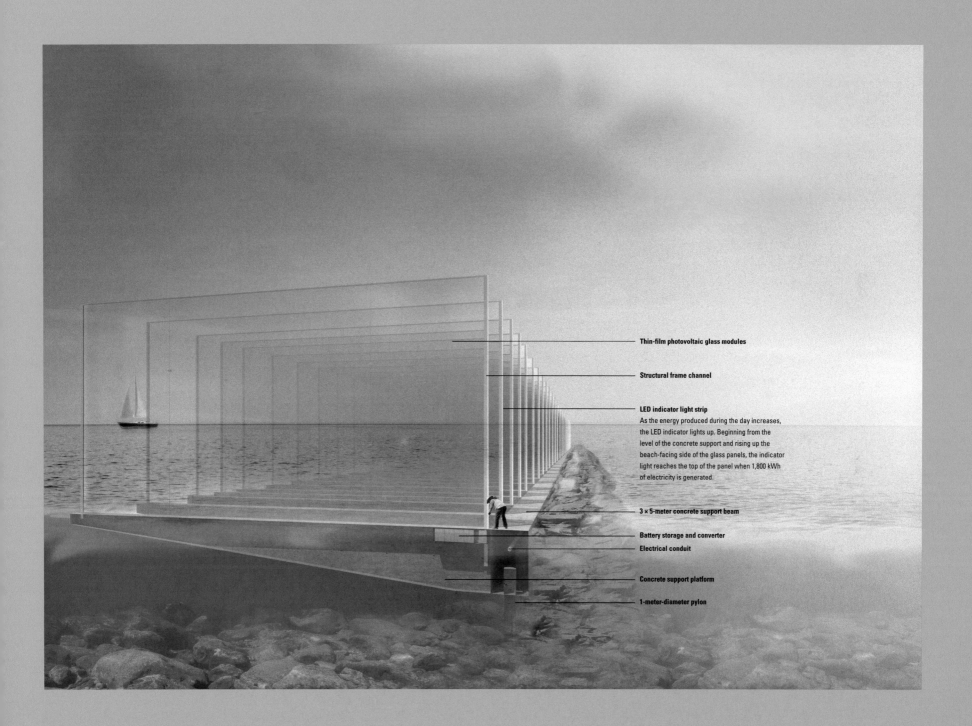

Thin-film photovoltaic glass modules

Structural frame channel

LED indicator light strip
As the energy produced during the day increases,
the LED indicator lights up. Beginning from the
level of the concrete support and rising up the
beach-facing side of the glass panels, the indicator
light reaches the top of the panel when 1,800 kWh
of electricity is generated.

3 × 5-meter concrete support beam

Battery storage and converter

Electrical conduit

Concrete support platform

1-meter-diameter pylon

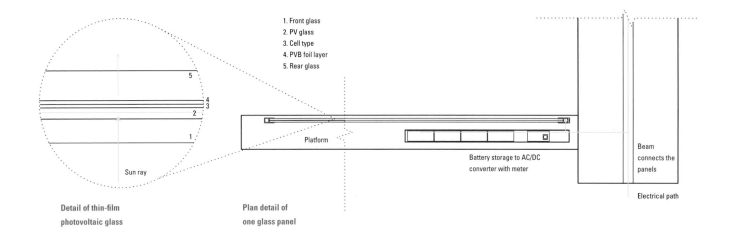

1. Front glass
2. PV glass
3. Cell type
4. PVB foil layer
5. Rear glass

Sun ray

Platform

Battery storage to AC/DC
converter with meter

Beam
connects the
panels

Electrical path

Detail of thin-film
photovoltaic glass

Plan detail of
one glass panel

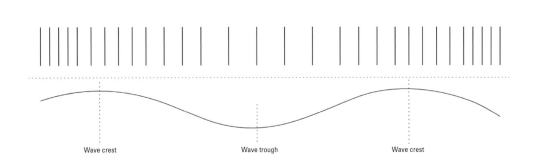

Wave crest

Wave trough

Wave crest

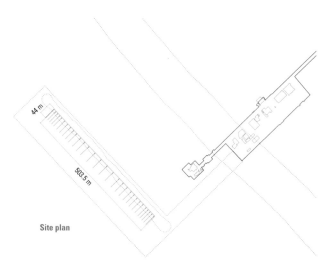

44 m

503.5 m

Site plan

View from the beach

Subsurface

Buoy-type wave energy converters capture the movement of waves in both the horizontal and vertical directions. *Subsurface* uses this kinetic energy to power hydraulic pumps and generate clean electricity.

The shape of the buoys is inspired by the problem of kelp deforestation in the Santa Monica Bay. Overfishing and stormwater runoff have led to a steady decline in kelp population as of recent years. Overfishing leads to a loss of biodiversity within the marine ecosystem, making it difficult for kelp to thrive. Stormwater runoff not only pollutes, but it also prevents oxygen from being absorbed into the water.

Subsurface encourages biodiversity and new kelp growth, generating energy from waves without disrupting the marine ecosystem. The buoys employ existing point absorber wave conversion technologies and are inspired by the buoyant pods and other natural characteristics of kelp. The resulting forms protrude gently out of the water to remind the public of the importance of renewable energy generation and the protection of the marine ecosystem below the surface.

Each buoy is designed to slowly take in water through a check valve (similar to a syringe) as the tide comes in. It then forces water back through a secondary valve as the tide goes out, adding to the energy output of the turbines. A small amount of electricity is used to power the lighting component of the artwork, while the rest is transferred to the grid.

During the day, visitors can interact with the installation by walking on the floating dock. There they can see the buoys up close and understand the workings of the remote hydraulic turbines. At night, the buoys' light can be seen from a distance, speaking to the public and celebrating sustainability.

TEAM
Ethan Stanley, Veronica Magner, Emmanuel Eshun

TEAM LOCATION
Philadelphia (PA), USA

ENERGY TECHNOLOGIES
point absorber wave energy converter

ANNUAL CAPACITY
15,000 MWh
(less energy used for lights)

The nighttime spectacle of the beacons of light emanate from the buoys below the surface.

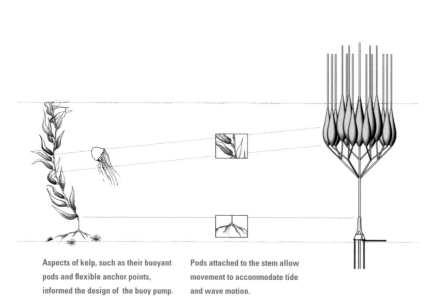

Aspects of kelp, such as their buoyant pods and flexible anchor points, informed the design of the buoy pump.

Pods attached to the stem allow movement to accommodate tide and wave motion.

Subsurface reveals the dynamics of energy in the ocean and the life beneath its surface.

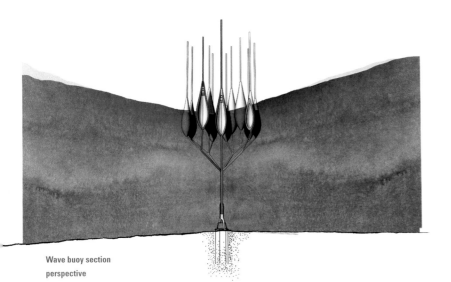

Wave buoy section
perspective

The wave buoy houses
a light within its hollow
portion that emits a
concentrated beam into
the sky at night.

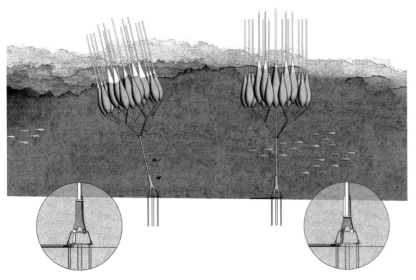

Buoy base tilted:
water intake through
check valve A

Buoy base upright:
water released into pipe
through check valve B

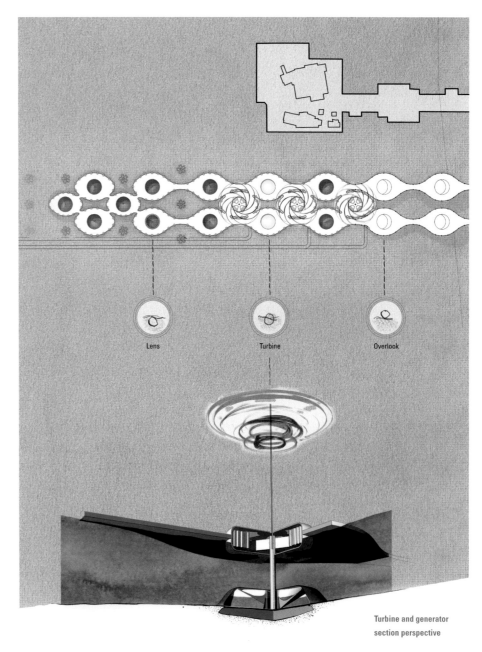

Lens

Turbine

Overlook

Turbine and generator
section perspective

The Pipe

From the beach, a gleaming pipe floats on the horizon. It's a testament to our time and reminds us about our dependence on water and about our need to appreciate and value this vital gift. It also teaches us that water is plenty and nature provides. We just need to learn to work with it, keep it clean, and appreciate it.

Multiple pools of hot and cold, crystal-clear salt water invite visitors to experience a ritual that takes them away from the stress of daily life. Relaxing on the pool deck, listening to the sound of the waves, and looking out to the ocean, visitors can be blissfully unaware of the seamless technology at work all around them.

Above, solar panels provide power to pump seawater through an electromagnetic filtration process below the pool deck, quietly providing the salt bath with its healing water and the city with clean drinking water. *The Pipe* represents a change in the future of water.

Water never leaves our planet. Rather it is simply displaced. Fresh water finds impurities and becomes temporarily unfit for consumption. These impurities can be visible or invisible. The visible particles can be filtered with basic procedures. It is the invisible impurities (dissolved solids) that make filtration complicated and costly.

Conventional desalination technology such as reverse osmosis uses excessive electricity, generates unwanted industrial waste and polluted water, and requires very expensive machinery.

Ninety-seven percent of seawater is pure water and only three percent is dissolved solids. All dissolved solids in water become ionized and can therefore be controlled through electromagnetic energy. Electromagnetic filtration uses an isolated electromagnetic field on pipes circulating seawater, separating the salts and impurities. The process is rapid and energy-efficient.

What results are two products: pure drinkable water that is directed into the city's primary water piping grid, and clear water with twelve percent salinity. The drinking water is piped to shore, while the salt water supplies the thermal baths before it is redirected back to the ocean through a smart release system, mitigating most of the usual problems associated with returning brine water to the sea.

TEAM
Abdolaziz Khalili-Araghi, Puya Kalili-Araghi, Laleh Javaheri, Iman Khalili-Araghi, Katy Kiany (Khalili Engineers)

TEAM LOCATION
Vancouver, Canada

ENERGY TECHNOLOGIES
photovoltaic panels

WATER TECHNOLOGIES
electromagnetic desalination

ANNUAL CAPACITY
10,000 MWh to generate 4.5 billion liters of drinking water

A shimmering landmark on the Santa Monica breakwater

The Pipe uses the power of nature
to purify water.

The Pipe

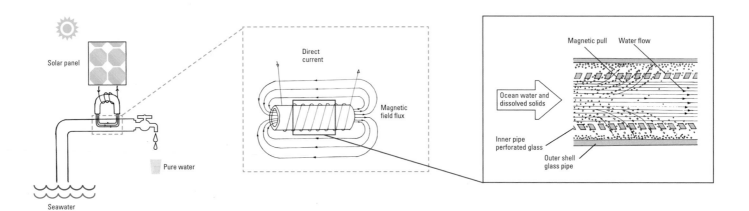

Solar panel

Seawater

Pure water

Direct current

Magnetic field flux

Magnetic pull   Water flow

Ocean water and dissolved solids

Inner pipe perforated glass

Outer shell glass pipe

The Pipe at sunset

In the center is a blissful public pool.

Warm up in the thermal bath.
Freshen up in the ocean pool.
Relax on the deck.
Repeat.

sky + music + fountain + water

The sound of a choir of dolphins and whales makes its way across the surface of the water from pipes erected in the middle of the sea. It echoes across the sea to the beach. Beautiful sprays of water accompany the chorus, their direction always changing.

A power buoy wave energy system operates under the water's surface, safe from large storms and practically invisible from the shore. The fully submerged buoys drive pumps and generators contained within the buoy itself, with electricity delivered back to shore through subsea cables for export to the grid.

The *sky + music + fountain + water* buoy design uses a translucent acrylic hull illuminated to mimic jellyfish.

Some of the energy is diverted to a pump that expels water and air. The seawater creates a constantly changing fountain while air is discharged through organ pipes. Visitors can take turns conducting this choir of sound and water from an organ-like keyboard on the Santa Monica Pier.

TEAM
Oliver Ong

TEAM LOCATION
Brisbane, Australia

ENERGY TECHNOLOGIES
point absorber wave energy converter (similar to CETO™)

ANNUAL CAPACITY
6,000 MWh (less energy used for water spray effects and sea organ)

Visible, invisible,
A fluctuating charm,
An amber-colored amethyst
Inhabits it; your arm
Approaches, and
It opens and
It closes;
You have meant
To catch it,
And it shrivels;
You abandon
Your intent—
It opens, and it
Closes and you
Reach for it—
The blue
Surrounding it
Grows cloudy, and
It floats away
From you.

A Jelly-Fish
Marianne Moore
1887–1972

The thin edge of the surface separates the ethereal underwater world and its energy generating jellyfish from the crisp Santa Monica sunset above.

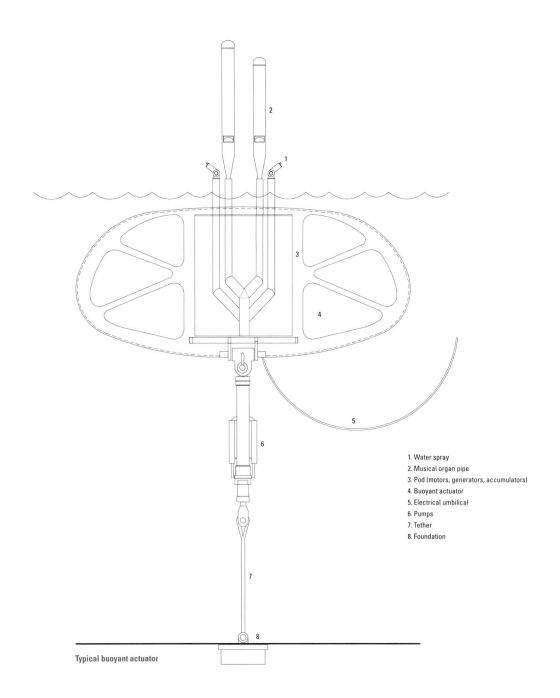

1. Water spray
2. Musical organ pipe
3. Pod (motors, generators, accumulators)
4. Buoyant actuator
5. Electrical umbilical
6. Pumps
7. Tether
8. Foundation

Typical buoyant actuator

At night the organ pipes glow like
candles floating across the sea.

The Clear Orb

Walking on the Santa Monica beach, *The Clear Orb* appears to float upon the surface of the ocean water. The colors of the sky are refracted through the translucent glass upper section, while the lower hemisphere's reflective, mirror-like surface glitters with the sunlight playing on the ocean waves.

The installation is accessible from the Santa Monica Pier by the beach boardwalk. Walking toward it, visitors gradually recognize that the pathway slopes gently below the surface of the water. The walk is an escape from our ordinary routine and the crowed city. The outside walls of this "contemplation walk" are themselves a wave-power generator installed along the existing breakwater. The inside walls along the pathway are filled with the list of extinct animals, offering an opportunity to contemplate how humans might better coexist with nature.

At the end of the pathway, visitors reach an open square just in front of *The Orb*. The square located below the ocean surface creates the feeling of visual pleasure and sharp contrast of light.

The Clear Orb is a glass sphere approximately 40 meters in diameter. The surface is made up of transparent luminescent solar concentrators. These solar cells supply the power to circulate water into *The Orb*.

The inner space of *The Orb* is a solar still that produces fresh water from seawater through evaporation and condensation. Desalinated water produced within *The Orb* pours down through the step fountain supporting it from beneath—an artful interpretation of the power of light and water to give life.

An oscillating water column wave power plant runs along the 300-meter sea-facing edge of the "contemplation walk," and provides additional energy to the solar distillation pumps and the electrical grid of the city.

TEAM
Jaesik Lim, Ahyoung Lee, Jaeyeol Kim, Taegu Lim

TEAM LOCATION
Seoul, South Korea

ENERGY TECHNOLOGIES
transparent luminescent solar concentrators, oscillating water column (OWC) wave energy

WATER TECHNOLOGIES
solar distillation

ANNUAL CAPACITY
3,820 MWh
2.2 million liters of drinking water

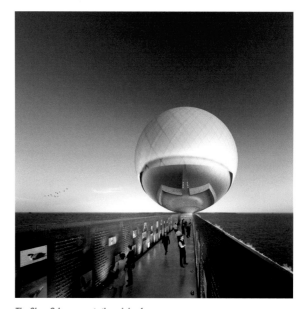

The Clear Orb represents the origin of life and energy on Earth. It produces pure water and electricity.

Communion square

The "contemplation walk" is an inviting space for visitors to enjoy a new path along their beach walk. The walls on either side generate electricity from the waves using oscillating water column chambers.

121

The Clear Orb

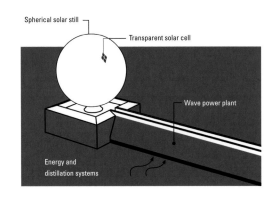

Spherical solar still
Transparent solar cell
Wave power plant
Energy and distillation systems

Distillation and solar cell orb

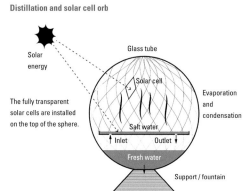

Solar energy

The fully transparent solar cells are installed on the top of the sphere.

Glass tube
Solar cell
Evaporation and condensation
Salt water
Inlet
Outlet
Fresh water
Support / fountain

Wave power plant

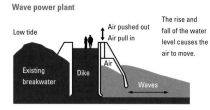

Low tide
Air pushed out
Air pull in
The rise and fall of the water level causes the air to move.
Existing breakwater
Dike
Air
Waves

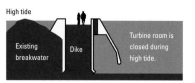

High tide
Existing breakwater
Dike
Turbine room is closed during high tide.

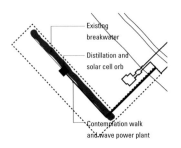

Existing breakwater
Distillation and solar cell orb
Contemplation walk and wave power plant

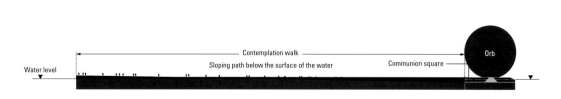

Water level
Contemplation walk
Sloping path below the surface of the water
Communion square
Orb

View from the beach

Night view

Sun Towers

The year 2016 marks a special occasion for Santa Monica. It is the 100-year birthday of the Looff Hippodrome, the gloriously eclectic carousel building that is one of the few features of Charles Looff's Pleasure Pier that remains to delight visitors today. It seems appropriate to propose a new landmark to celebrate this centennial interval in Santa Monica's history.

Sun Towers is a new type of desalination plant where low-tech solar distillation is prioritized and supplemented by renewably driven reverse osmosis. Power plant and people assimilate in an uplifting visual experience, where vertical, active, and intelligent systems constantly assess and recalibrate the local dynamic environment.

The design responds directly to the eccentricity of the site and the city. By day, opaque, elegant solar antennae float on a current of energy, strategically positioned to directly respond to the local microclimatic conditions. By night a tantalizing glimpse of striking form and color is revealed!

An extension of the promenade optimizes views to an extended sea space facing southwest, then navigates the visitor back along the loop to exciting views of the mountains and the City of Santa Monica. The panoramic terrace, located at the heart of the plant, will support a dynamic public learning center, inspired by the interpretive elements at the Santa Monica Urban Runoff Recycling Facility (SMURRF). Visitors can stroll along a unique panorama, up close to the elegant *Sun Towers*, where the drama, suspense, and beauty of solar desalination are performed.

Each solar tower is a steel-and-glass structure that contains a vertical stack of water vessels. Solar energy heats and evaporates the seawater from the vessels, which then condensates and falls to the base of the tower.

Photovoltaic panels are grouped upon vertical masts as a screen, which rotates to follow the sun path. Energy surplus generated by the PV system is used to power a micro desalination plant, situated at the bottom of the tower.

At the base of each tower is a buoy on the water's surface that rises and falls with the waves. The action drives a pump system that compresses the seawater until it reaches the solar water vessels. Tidal turbines are invisible below the water's surface to provide supplemental electricity.

This multidimensional installation celebrates the power of light and the energy of the ocean in all their myriad variations.

TEAM
John Perry, Matteo Melioli, Ramone Dixon, Terie Harrison, Kristina Butkute (BLDA Architects), Tom Kordel, Sherleen Pang, Kostas Mastronikolaou (XCO2), Steven Scott Studio

TEAM LOCATION
London, UK

ENERGY TECHNOLOGIES
photovoltaic panels, point absorber wave energy converter, tidal turbine

WATER TECHNOLOGIES
solar distillation, reverse osmosis desalination

ANNUAL CAPACITY
4,000 MWh
110 million liters of drinking water

One of the *Sun Towers*

Sun Towers complement the Santa
Monica mountain range beyond.

Sun Towers

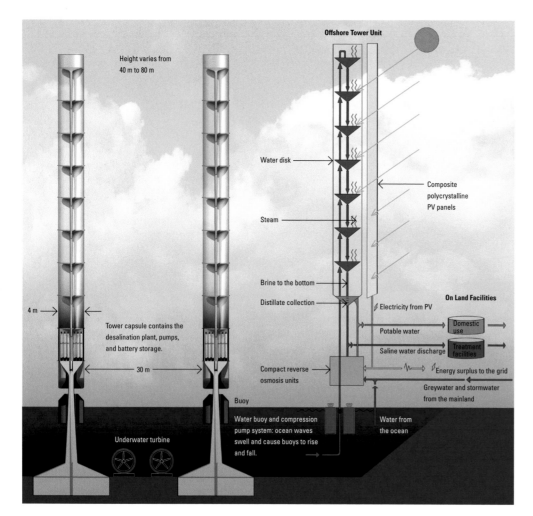

Height varies from 40 m to 80 m

Water disk

Steam

Brine to the bottom

Distillate collection

4 m

Tower capsule contains the desalination plant, pumps, and battery storage.

30 m

Buoy

Water buoy and compression pump system: ocean waves swell and cause buoys to rise and fall.

Underwater turbine

Offshore Tower Unit

Composite polycrystalline PV panels

On Land Facilities

Electricity from PV

Potable water

Saline water discharge

Compact reverse osmosis units

Domestic use

Treatment facilities

Energy surplus to the grid

Greywater and stormwater from the mainland

Water from the ocean

Sun Towers set against the cloudy sky

Sun Towers under the stars

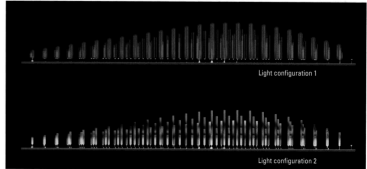

Light configuration 1

Light configuration 2

Multiple light configurations are programmable.

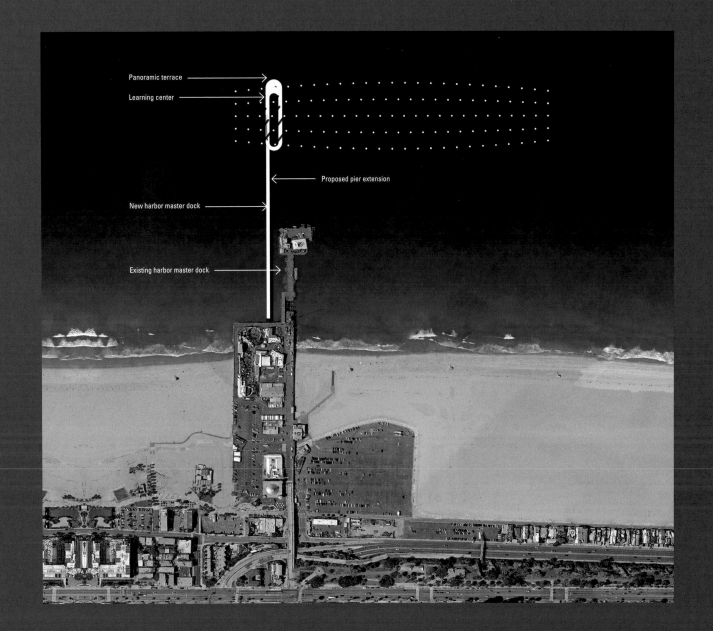

Panoramic terrace

Learning center

Proposed pier extension

New harbor master dock

Existing harbor master dock

2000 Lighthouses Over the Sea

Continuing the playful atmosphere of the Santa Monica Pier, and inspired by the 2,000 wooden piles below, *2000 Lighthouses Over the Sea* proposes 2,000 new columns that illuminate the horizon to the rhythm of the intensity of the waves and provide renewable energy to the pier and the city.

During the day, the masts could be interpreted as simple ship masts, drawing a line that catches the spectator's attention without disturbing the landscape.

The artwork invites the public to walk out on a new pier extension. As the viewer moves and descends along the new path, she can find herself in the middle of a forest of light. The movement of the masts reflects the rhythm of the waves. From the central walkway, small side piers offer different views of the work and the surrounding landscape.

The light from the tip of the masts changes in intensity according to the power of the waves. In the presence of a storm or dangerous waves, the lights will flash a red warning.

Each of the masts signifies a buoy-type wave energy converter on the water's surface. Groups of 150 masts share a synchronized collection point, from where the collected energy is transmitted to a power substation on shore.

2000 Lighthouses Over the Sea shows how it is possible to harness renewable energy resources by working in harmony with our planet, respecting marine life, and protecting the environment.

TEAM
Louis Joanne, Anaelle Toquet Etesse, Elba Adriana Bravo, Maria Rojas Alcazar, Ronan Audebert

TEAM LOCATION
Guadalajara, Mexico

ENERGY TECHNOLOGIES
point absorber wave energy converter

ANNUAL CAPACITY
4,000 MWh

Visitors enjoy the magical forest of masts, while below the power of the waves is converted cleanly into electricity.

LED light

Mast

Floater

Connecting rod

Crankshaft

Column

Concrete base

Cable to the pier's extension

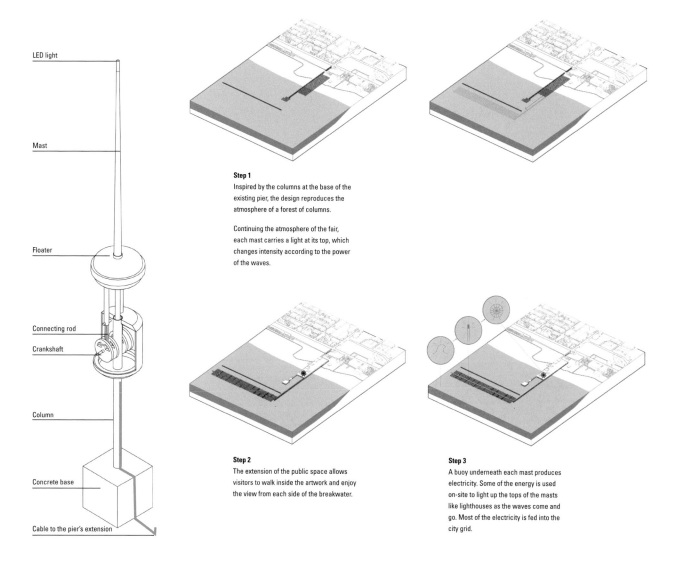

Step 1
Inspired by the columns at the base of the existing pier, the design reproduces the atmosphere of a forest of columns.

Continuing the atmosphere of the fair, each mast carries a light at its top, which changes intensity according to the power of the waves.

Step 2
The extension of the public space allows visitors to walk inside the artwork and enjoy the view from each side of the breakwater.

Step 3
A buoy underneath each mast produces electricity. Some of the energy is used on-site to light up the tops of the masts like lighthouses as the waves come and go. Most of the electricity is fed into the city grid.

2000 Lighthouses Over the Sea
extends the festive brilliance of
the carnival lights on the Santa
Monica Pier.

View from the beach at night

Big Beach Balloon

High above the bustling historic pier, *Big Beach Balloon* gently carries excited passengers skyward to experience Santa Monica from dramatic new heights. By connecting the pier's amusement park character below with spectacular panoramic aerial views above, the design celebrates Santa Monica's glorious location, while seamlessly harnessing one of its most abundant resources, the sun.

Cutting-edge, thin-film solar technology is paired with the timeless romance of motorless flight. The tethered helium balloon, 23 meters in diameter, offers 20–30 passengers a memorable 10-minute ride up to 150 meters above the pier (or as high as the Santa Monica airport flight paths will allow).

Combining solar-power generation with a new attraction at the pier is the perfect way for Santa Monica to highlight its ambitious solar initiatives in a playful way that engages people for years to come.

The spherical array of solar film allows the balloon to dynamically track the sun throughout the day. Collected energy passes through a junction box at the balloon's suspension net, and then travels down the tether cable to the landing platform for easy connection to the central grid.

One of the most precious resources of the site is the ocean vista. *Big Beach Balloon* has a small footprint, leaving the majority of the proposed site and the clear horizon view from the edge of the existing pier untouched.

The design is noiseless, allowing passengers to leave the bustle of the crowds below and listen to the music of nature.

TEAM
Matt Kuser

TEAM LOCATION
Carmel (CA), USA

ENERGY TECHNOLOGIES
thin-film photovoltaic

ANNUAL CAPACITY
300 MWh

The gondola offers breathtaking coastal views.

Imagine experiencing Santa Monica
from dramatic new heights.

133

Section

Balloon surface
detail

Buildup of layers

1. Balloon

2. Gondola

3. Tether cable

4. Suspension net

5. Landing and observation platforms

6. Thin-film photovoltaic

Site boundary

The observation platform offers an
ideal view of the balloon and beyond.

The observation platform

Forging new downtown connections

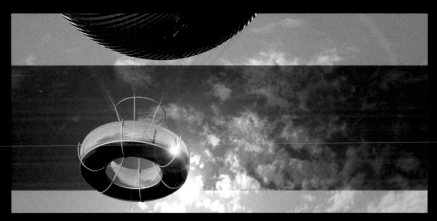

Rise above the ocean waves to
collect light waves.

Wake Up

Wake Up uses retired swan boats, giving them new life as wave energy converters.

The Santa Monica Pier—once a means of transporting waste out to the sea and now a place for social enjoyment—has a history of turning trash into treasure. *Wake Up* brings this tradition into the era of sustainability by transforming retired swan boats into contemporary energy-generating pieces of water art.

The technology behind *Wake Up* utilizes the most abundant and local force at the pier, the wake of the ocean. Wave energy converters are devices that use the natural motion of wave movements to generate usable power. One such system was developed in the 1970s by Professor Stephen Salter at the University of Edinburgh and dubbed "Salter's Duck." The "ducks" consist of a series of wedge-shaped devices located at the ocean's surface with a central axis throughout, housing the mechanics to generate power. As a wave encounters the underside of the wedges, the force pushes the wedges upward, causing rotation at the central axis. This rotation creates electrical power through hydraulic generators.

Wake Up reuses retired swan boats to function as Salter's Ducks, generating offshore energy and helping to power the pier's amusement park. The swan boat's body is modified, creating the necessary wedge shape, and a central axis links multiple boats together in staggered rows.

The system is dubbed the "Salt Swan" in reference to Mr. Salter and the atypical presence of swans in salt water. The "Salt Swans" are deployed just beyond the existing breakwater line to capture the most wave energy. When waves hit the swans, they emit a celebratory honking sound as a spectacle for the public to enjoy, and as a reminder of how the system works.

The "Salt Swans" are linked to the shore by a series of lit buoys that display the level of charge, much like a gas gauge in a car. As the onshore battery fills up, the buoys begin to light up in a suspenseful sequence. At full capacity, a dedicated, swan-inspired high striker on the pier rings its bell. Moments later, a light show ripples through the amusement park in celebration.

TEAM
Henry Moll, Mary Carroll-Coelho

TEAM LOCATION
Philadelphia (PA), USA

ENERGY TECHNOLOGIES
wave energy converter (similar to "Salter's Duck" invented in the 1970s by Steven Salter)

ANNUAL CAPACITY
1,400 MWh

HONK

Swans harvest wave energy, greeting
visitors with a celebratory "honk."

Energy is transported to the pier with
buoys displaying the progress.

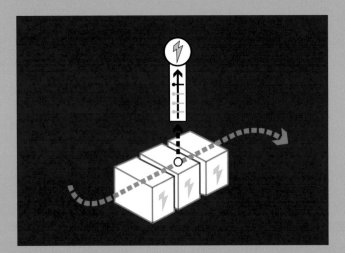

Wave energy that has been collected
and stored is shown on the markers.

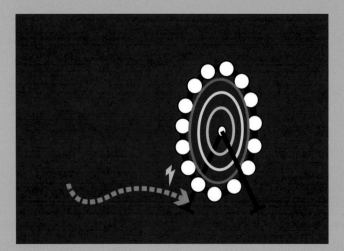

When the goal is reached, energy is
discharged to the grid.

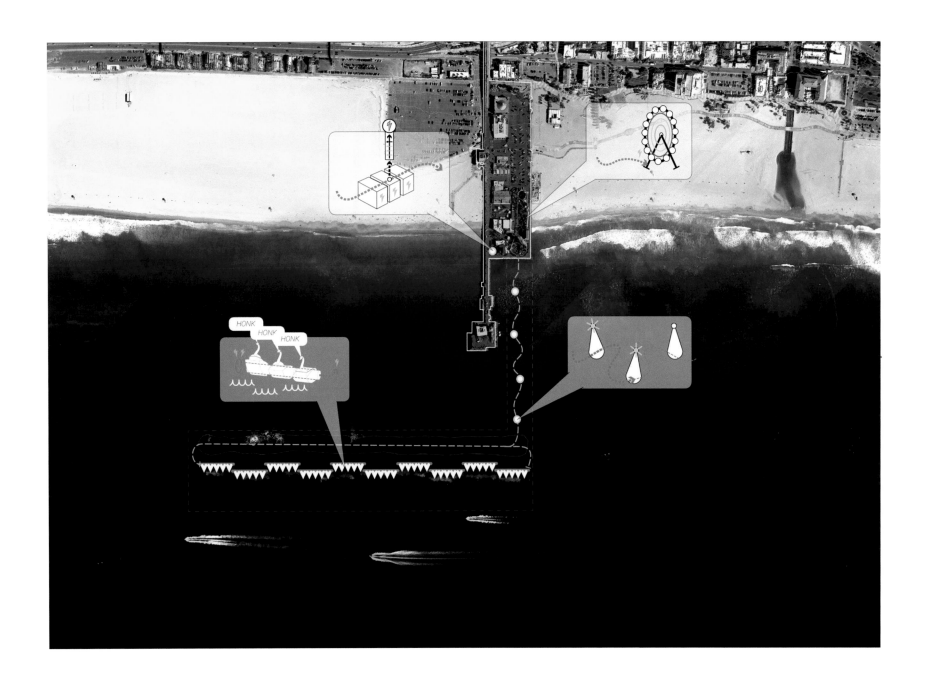

Noctilucales

Underwater view from behind the breakwater

Open spaces are essential for an urban environment to reach balance. They are a form of escape—a place to get away from the chaos of the city.

Noctilucales preserves the horizon line of the ocean—the clean and uninterrupted view, where the sea stretches out before you until it meets the sky. To compromise the horizon is to destroy the landscape.

WavePiston™ has developed one of the less visually obtrusive wave energy technologies consisting of a network of moving plates installed along cables. The movement of the plates creates hydraulic pressure, which is converted into electricity. All of the components are submerged in the ocean, making the system invisible from shore. Only the small anchored buoys on either side of each WavePiston™ string can be seen on the horizon.

Noctilucales has two main elements—the submerged wave power farm with 200 energy collectors, and an extension of the Santa Monica Pier, increasing the surface of public space and providing a secure area for the turbine/generator and desalination plant.

Underwater LED lights on top of each moving plate will cast a subtle glow at night. The energy collectors will be seen as a field of lights, producing a bioluminescent effect similar to the one created by natural noctilucales in some parts of the world.

The hydraulic pipe runs along the breakwater to a turbine station on the new pier extension. The generator is made visible, with a glass wall built on one side to show the jets as they hit the turbine. In this way, people will follow the conversion process inside one of six green cylindrical structures. The system will supply electricity for the pier and the bioluminescent installation. The surplus electricity feeds into the city grid.

Some of the wave energy is used to produce fresh water with reverse osmosis desalination. With the kinetic energy of the waves, the cost of desalination can be greatly reduced. Instead of using pumps and motors, the ocean waves are able to naturally create the necessary pressures with the movement of the plates.

The desalination plant is transparent to demonstrate the process to visitors, and drinking water fountains along the new pier provide a first taste of the fresh water produced.

TEAM
Ricardo Avella, Andrés Tabora, Michael Henriksen, Carla Betancourt, Silvia Mercader, Laura Vera, Oriana De Lucia, Martin Von Bülow, Laura Vivas, Miguel Rosas (representing: Tabora + Tabora Landscape Architecture, ATA avella taller de arquitectura, WavePiston™)

TEAM LOCATION
Caracas, Venezuela

ENERGY TECHNOLOGIES
wave energy converter (by WavePiston™)

WATER TECHNOLOGIES
reverse osmosis desalination

ANNUAL CAPACITY
4,200 MWh (less the energy used for desalination)
14 million liters per year

View from the Santa Monica
Pier extension

Night view from the Santa
Monica Pier

The system will supply electricity for the pier and the bioluminescent installation. It is also integrated with the city grid to supply its surplus.

The pressurized seawater generated by the moving plates can be used solely for electricity production, for fresh water production, or for both.

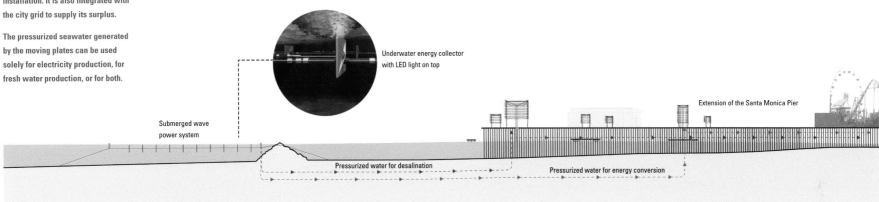

Underwater energy collector with LED light on top

Submerged wave power system

Extension of the Santa Monica Pier

Pressurized water for desalination

Pressurized water for energy conversion

Fresh Water Production
Some of the water that is pressurized by the waves is used to produce fresh water with reverse osmosis desalination.

Bioluminescent Noctilucales Effect
The system supplies electricity for the pier and the bioluminescent installation. Submersible LED lights attached to the pistons make the ocean surface glow.

Wave Power System
Energy is harvested when the waves roll along the steel wire, causing the energy collectors to move back and forth and forcing the pressurized water to an on-shore turbine for energy conversion.

Ring Garden

Agriculture is the largest user of fresh water in California. *Ring Garden* demonstrates a solution by creating a highly efficient ecosystem including a desalination plant, a rotating aeroponics farm, and an algae bioreactor. It harvests seawater, CO_2, and the sun's energy to create food, biomass, and fresh water.

Seawater enters the desalination plant through special screens that protect fish and local wildlife. Solar panels power a high-pressure pump to pressurize seawater above the osmotic pressure and through a semipermeable membrane.

The plants in the rotating farm use 60% of the water produced. The remaining 30% is sent to the city grid. The brine water is fed through the bioreactor to produce cultures of spirulina that, once mature, are sent to an offsite plant to produce biomass.

The aeroponics system uses 98% less water than conventional farming and yields on average 30% more crops without the need for pesticides or fertilizers. *Ring Garden* demonstrates that the main elements a plant needs in order to grow—water, sun, nutrients, and CO_2— are on-site and don't need to be transported.

Assisted by the power of the sun, the desalination plant provides fresh water and nutrients filtered from the seawater. On a footprint of about 1,000 m² the farm can produce vegetables that would otherwise take 26,000 m² of land and 340 million gallons of fresh water per year. *Ring Garden* consumes only nine million gallons of water per year. It saves 331 million gallons that would simply evaporate, which is water that can be redirected to 2,300 households.

The farm rotation reflects the movement of the Pacific Ferris wheel on the pier, and ensures that each "spoke" of planted area receives the appropriate amount of sunlight. The plant supports have a swivel mechanism that uses gravity to keep the plants always facing upward.

TEAM
Alexandru Predonu

TEAM LOCATION
Bucharest, Romania

ENERGY TECHNOLOGIES
photovoltaic panels, algae bioreactor

WATER TECHNOLOGIES
solar-powered osmotic desalination (with waste brine used to culture algae for livestock feed)

ANNUAL CAPACITY
440 MWh (100% goes to power desalination processes and rotation of the *Ring Garden*)
60 million liters of drinking water (40 million liters goes to agricultural production)
18,000 kg of aeroponic crop yield (conserves 331 million gallons of water) 5,000 kg of spirulina biomass for livestock feed

The structure is oriented south for the best sun exposure. *Ring Garden* is tilted approximately 8.5 degrees so that on Earth Day (April 22) the sun seen from the Santa Monica Pier will set through the middle of the wheel.

Ring Garden can be accessed by boat and offers a public space with an outdoor aeroponics garden where people can pick fresh vegetables and help plant new ones. Next to the garden is an eco awareness center.

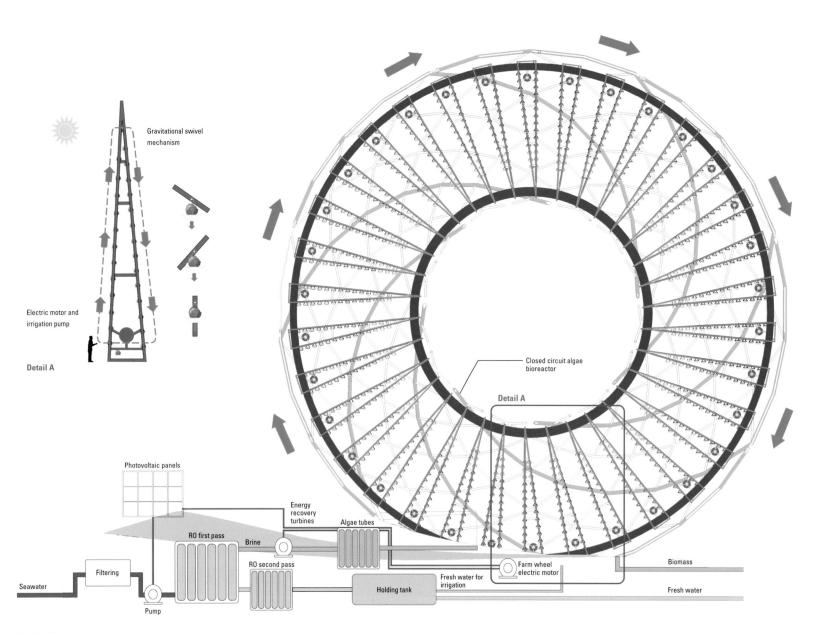

Gravitational swivel
mechanism

Electric motor and
irrigation pump

Detail A

Closed circuit algae
bioreactor

Detail A

Photovoltaic panels

Energy
recovery
turbines

Algae tubes

RO first pass

Brine

RO second pass

Biomass

Farm wheel
electric motor

Fresh water for
irrigation

Seawater

Filtering

Holding tank

Fresh water

Pump

Section diagram

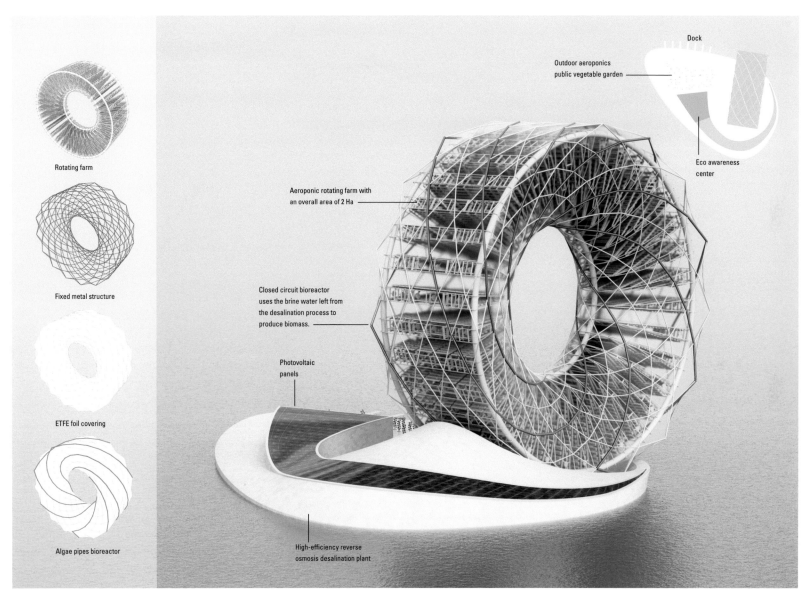

Rotating farm

Fixed metal structure

ETFE foil covering

Algae pipes bioreactor

Outdoor aeroponics
public vegetable garden

Dock

Eco awareness
center

Aeroponic rotating farm with
an overall area of 2 Ha

Closed circuit bioreactor
uses the brine water left from
the desalination process to
produce biomass.

Photovoltaic
panels

High-efficiency reverse
osmosis desalination plant

Ring Garden regenerative
systems diagram

Catching
the Wave

Catching the Wave is an artistic impression of the historical context of the Santa Monica Pier and its breakwater. The area behind the breakwater was once home to a yacht harbor filled with hundreds of sailboats and moorings. *Catching the Wave* utilizes the relationship of a sail ship and its mooring, and exaggerates the scale of both silhouettes. The fleet is moved to the west side of the breakwater to capitalize on the raw energy of the ocean's waves.

The installation is made up of 60 buoys that capture wave energy. Each "energy buoy" is eight meters in diameter. The large size increases the capacity of the buoys to capture the potential energy in each wave. Each buoy is connected to a piston mounted on the ocean floor by a flexible tether. With the upward swell of each wave, the buoy and the piston rise, allowing room for seawater to flood a large chamber. When the wave falls, the buoy and piston fall with it, pressurizing the water into pipes laid out on the ocean floor.

Back above the surface, the fleet of 15 sail ships is clustered among the sea of buoys. Each sail is 40 meters tall and is connected with two to seven buoys, which all send their pressurized seawater to the mechanical housing below the sail platform. The pressurized seawater turns a turbine within the housing to create sustainable energy for the Santa Monica grid.

As the waves increase in intensity, the sails above become brighter, illuminated by responsive LEDs. Visitors can relate in real time to the clean energy production and speculate on how bright the sails could become.

The bobbing of the blue and white striped buoys, the fluttering of the bright coral sails, and the people lounging in the summer sun on the wooden decks of the isolated platforms, all come together to create an elegant calm.

Visitors can take kayaks and paddle in and around the artwork. Passing the last sail, they will have reached the western extent of American settlement. But the frontier of environmentally conscious design is only just opening. Wave energy infrastructure is now embarking on a journey to a brave new future.

TEAM
Christina Vannelli, Liz Davidson,
Matthew Madigan

TEAM LOCATION
Hamilton (ON), Canada

ENERGY TECHNOLOGIES
point absorber wave energy
converter (similar to CETO™
by Carnegie Wave Energy)

ANNUAL CAPACITY
16,000 MWh

Catching the Wave

Fireworks celebrate infrastructure
that works in harmony with nature.

Children play safely in the surf
while the artwork generates
electricity behind them.

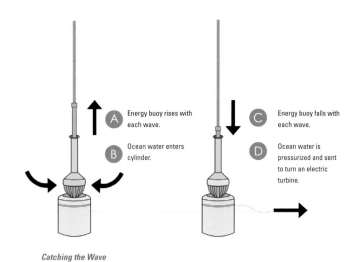

A Energy buoy rises with each wave.

B Ocean water enters cylinder.

C Energy buoy falls with each wave.

D Ocean water is pressurized and sent to turn an electric turbine.

Catching the Wave

A small amount of the electricity generated is used to light the mast and sail, communicating to the public how much energy the art installation is producing.

1. Energy buoy rises and falls with the ocean waves.
2. Tether activates piston to pressurize ocean water.
3. Pressurized water is directed toward the turbine through a network of pipes on the ocean floor.
4. High-pressure ocean water turns an electric turbine that is hidden beneath the sail platform.
5. Mast and sail lights communicate energy production to the public.
6. Energy produced is directed to an off-site grid connection.

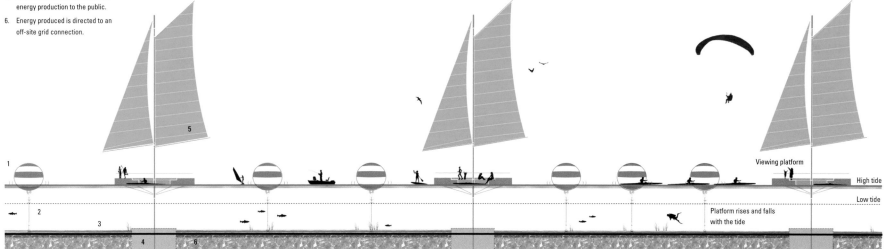

Viewing platform

High tide

Low tide

Platform rises and falls with the tide

Section

Cnidaria Halitus

Expressing the mystery and beauty of ocean life, *Cnidaria Halitus* harnesses the natural forces of the sun and the tides to produce 600,000 liters of potable water each day for the City of Santa Monica. California's buildings are on their way to becoming net zero energy, yet there is much to be done to achieve the same level of water conservation and generation that we have achieved with energy.

Cnidaria Halitus begins its water-generation process by collecting and filtering water from the ocean through a centralized system of pipes that take it to the interior of each of the boilers located at the focal point of a Fresnel lens. To maximize heat collection, the axis of the Fresnel lenses and the collectors consistently track the sun in its daily and monthly trajectory across the sky.

The sun's heat is concentrated onto the boilers, which evaporate the seawater.

The vapor condenses inside the external membrane, an ultra-lightweight transparent fabric that expands with the water vapor, further increasing the surface collection area and allowing maximum solar radiation on the boiler. The expansion and contraction of the external membrane will give the artwork a lifelike expression.

The breakwater is used to channel the currents and to concentrate them in slits, where the turbines are located, harnessing the flowing kinetic energy of the tides to generate electricity. This electricity is used to pump the water up to the boilers and to continue the evaporation process during the night.

Cnidaria Halitus provides a visible solution to the problem of water scarcity, creating awareness while providing carbon-free potable water from the ocean to the city.

TEAM
John Eric Chung, Pablo La Roche, Danxi Zou, Jingyan Zhang, Tianyi Deng (CallisonRTKL)

TEAM LOCATION
Los Angeles (CA), USA

ENERGY TECHNOLOGIES
tidal turbines (100% of energy used to pump water for distillation)

WATER TECHNOLOGIES
solar distillation with Fresnel lens

ANNUAL CAPACITY
220 million liters of drinking water

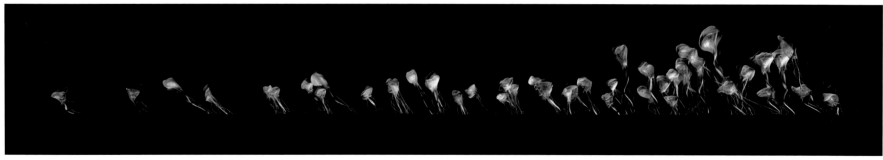

The buoyancy from the steam creates an ethereal bloom of jellyfish pulsating, hovering, and swaying above the water.

As the interior chamber heats up, the outer shell expands and subtly contracts in rhythm, breathing life into these otherworldly creatures that are designed to turn sunlight into drinking water.

Cnidaria Halitus

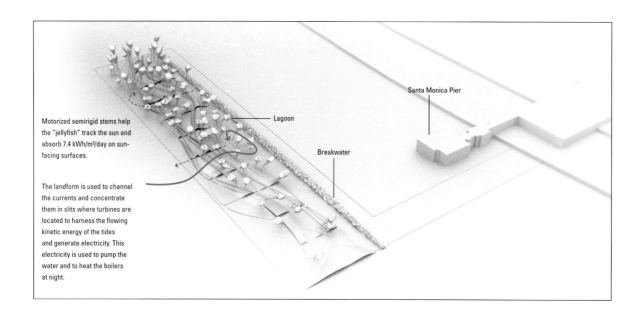

Motorized semirigid stems help the "jellyfish" track the sun and absorb 7.4 kWh/m²/day on sun-facing surfaces.

The landform is used to channel the currents and concentrate them in slits where turbines are located to harness the flowing kinetic energy of the tides and generate electricity. This electricity is used to pump the water and to heat the boilers at night.

Lagoon

Breakwater

Santa Monica Pier

View from the beach

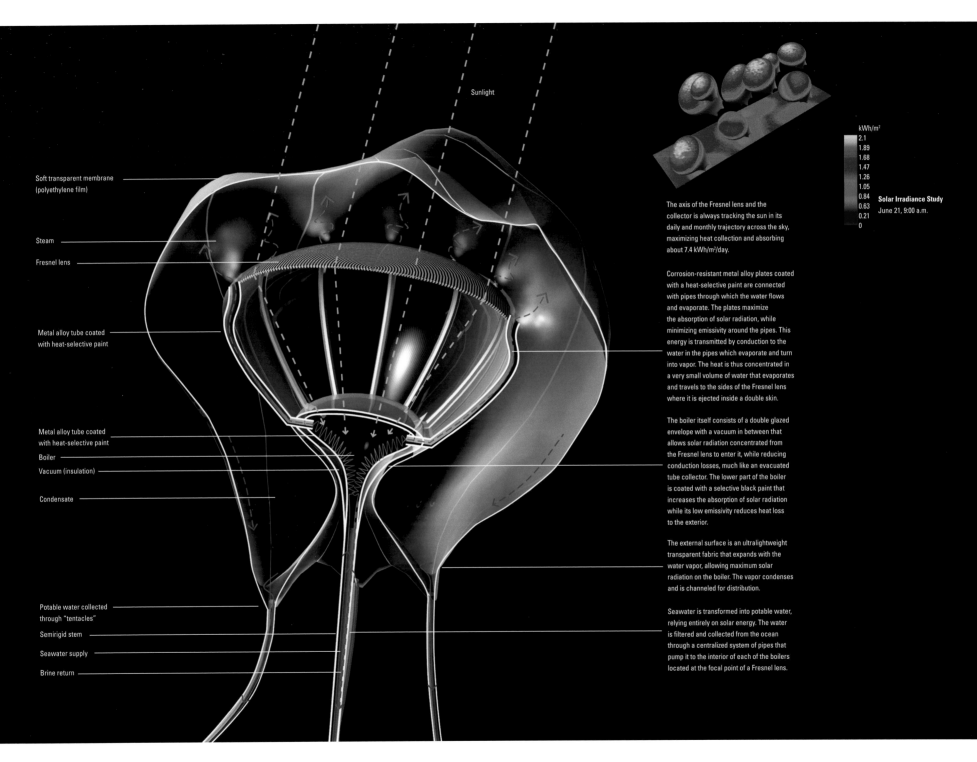

Sunlight

Soft transparent membrane (polyethylene film)

Steam

Fresnel lens

Metal alloy tube coated with heat-selective paint

Metal alloy tube coated with heat-selective paint

Boiler

Vacuum (insulation)

Condensate

Potable water collected through "tentacles"

Semirigid stem

Seawater supply

Brine return

kWh/m²
2.1
1.89
1.68
1.47
1.26
1.05
0.84
0.63
0.21
0

Solar Irradiance Study
June 21, 9:00 a.m.

The axis of the Fresnel lens and the collector is always tracking the sun in its daily and monthly trajectory across the sky, maximizing heat collection and absorbing about 7.4 kWh/m²/day.

Corrosion-resistant metal alloy plates coated with a heat-selective paint are connected with pipes through which the water flows and evaporate. The plates maximize the absorption of solar radiation, while minimizing emissivity around the pipes. This energy is transmitted by conduction to the water in the pipes which evaporate and turn into vapor. The heat is thus concentrated in a very small volume of water that evaporates and travels to the sides of the Fresnel lens where it is ejected inside a double skin.

The boiler itself consists of a double glazed envelope with a vacuum in between that allows solar radiation concentrated from the Fresnel lens to enter it, while reducing conduction losses, much like an evacuated tube collector. The lower part of the boiler is coated with a selective black paint that increases the absorption of solar radiation while its low emissivity reduces heat loss to the exterior.

The external surface is an ultralightweight transparent fabric that expands with the water vapor, allowing maximum solar radiation on the boiler. The vapor condenses and is channeled for distribution.

Seawater is transformed into potable water, relying entirely on solar energy. The water is filtered and collected from the ocean through a centralized system of pipes that pump it to the interior of each of the boilers located at the focal point of a Fresnel lens.

Weightless
Balloons

There is a profound power between the sea and sky—two endless parallel planes seeming to merge in the distance and obscured by the curvature of the earth. The pier with its thousand legs is walking inside the ocean, attempting to reach that imaginary and impossible contact point between air and water. The amusement park colonizes the platform and, in the middle of the attractions, the balloon seller offers us the fantasy of weightless deliverance—the dream of floating above our everyday struggle.

Weightless Balloons is a set of ethereal bubbles emerging from the sea, floating on the surface, moving to the rhythm of the waves. These gas spheres are protected by a metallic skeleton, like water molecules aspiring to abandon their liquid state to evaporate and blend with the air. This hope of freedom is fulfilled by the wind, which releases the balloons and makes them fly at its will. The free energy channelled into electricity derives from the fight of the bubbles against the tidal forces and the dance with the wind.

The artwork can function in two different modes for energy production. After analyzing the weather conditions, a computer determines if more power can be generated from the waves or from the wind, switching from one mode to the other as conditions warrant. Low tide sees the bubbles disappear completely behind the breakwater as they operate in "buoy" mode.

The balloons are filled with an inert gas, lighter than air, which keeps the structures floating on or over the water surface. Their skin is fabricated with double ETFE plastic layers, transparent but very durable.

The bubble's structure is attached to a coiling gear, which automatically adjusts the length of the cable to the tidal conditions, and allows the system to alternate between the "buoy" and the "aero" generator modes. The coilers work with a mechanism very similar to sailboat coilers, capable of operating in constant contact with the water, and of bearing heavy loads.

When the computer detects good wind conditions, the coils loosen to allow the structures to rise into the air and spin around their axes to produce electricity.

TEAM
Aitor Almaraz, Sonia Vázquez-Díaz

TEAM LOCATION
A Coruna, Spain

ENERGY TECHNOLOGIES
wind harvesting (similar to MARS™, Magenn Air Rotor System), point absorber wave energy converter

ANNUAL CAPACITY
2,000 MWh

The permanent transformation of the structures' arrangement conveys the impermanence of life. The perception of constant change that characterizes the universe and our lives is reinforced by the shimmering effect of the sunlight reflected onto the balloons.

Site section

Energy production diagram

Spool and Coiler

The coilers automatically adjust the length of the cable to the tidal conditions and permit the balloons to alternate between the buoy and the air generator modes. The coilers work with a mechanism very similar to a sailboat coiler. They are able to operate in constant contact with the water and bear strong loads.

Cables

The cables keep the balloon anchored to the seabed. They also have an internal conductor that transmits the electricity generated to the grid. The cable spool coils to adjust its length, adapting it to the wave or aerial condition of the generator.

Balloon

The balloon is filled with an inert gas, which is lighter than air. It keeps the structure floating on the water surface, moving with the waves. It also helps the structure to rise in the air. Balloons are fabricated with an inflatable, double EFTE plastic layer that is transparent but very resistant.

Structure

In addition to providing structural stability, the profiles are blade-shaped and oriented to obtain the best performance from the winds. The fiberglass structure is both lightweight and durable enough to withstand the harsh sea conditions.

Dynamo

The dynamo generates electricity through the axial rotation of the balloon with up to 40% conversion efficiency.

Dampers

These devices firmly link the structures to the seabed. They can convert 80% of the waves' kinetic energy into electricity.

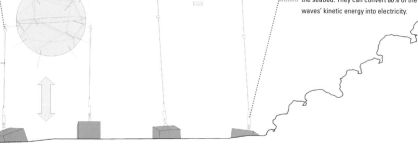

While analyzing the weather conditions, a computer determines if the power from wave energy will be greater than the power from the wind turbine.

If wind conditions are more favorable, the structures will rise in the air and spin to produce electricity as an airborne wind turbine.

The balloon seller offers us
the fantasy of weightless
deliverance—the dream of floating
above our everyday struggle.

SELECTED ENTRIES

"The Land Art Generator Initiative is devoted to bringing deep imagination and hard science to bear on a complex problem tailored to a specific location."

—Craig Watson

Director, California Arts Council

Coastal Reservoir

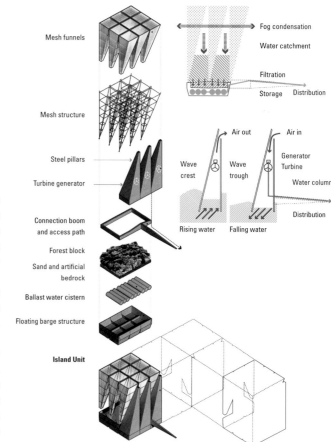

1 unit configuration

5 unit configuration

Reservoir loan

15 unit configuration

Implementation strategy

Mesh funnels

Mesh structure

Steel pillars

Turbine generator

Connection boom and access path

Forest block

Sand and artificial bedrock

Ballast water cistern

Floating barge structure

Island Unit

Fog condensation

Water catchment

Filtration

Storage → Distribution

Air out · Air in

Generator Turbine

Wave crest · Wave trough

Water column

Rising water · Falling water

Distribution

Coastal Reservoir stands as a new paradigm for creating power and water at the coast. The atmosphere of Southern California is bound together with its landscapes in a resource-harvesting cycle—an integrated energy ecology.

Though driven by wind and waves, this is not a kinetic sculpture. Though modular and floating, the assembled structure is stable and durable. *Coastal Reservoir* leverages the subtle but continuous shifts in the environment, from the undulating water levels to the shifting daily and seasonal weather patterns, and the invisible migrations of seeds.

The total dynamism of an environment is reflected in its atmosphere—its temperature, its pressure, its humidity, and its chemistry. *Coastal Reservoir* reveals these properties. With geometric slices, air is cleaved into the volume of a solid (contained in the red A-shaped pillars) and a void (framed and filled by the V-shaped mesh funnels).

Coastal Reservoir sits beyond the breakwater, its appearance constantly changing. Heavy steel, ghostly mesh, and framed void are in continuous play. On summer mornings, it appears as a slender radiant band and in winter months the morning sun breaks the form

into three distinct volumes. At midday, the mesh enclosures glow green from the interior vegetation. As the sun sets, the backlit pillars emerge and the meshes dissolve in shadow. When fog rolls in, the entire structure is obscured, its fuzzy corners merging with the atmosphere. At night, lacy shadows of the up-lighted interior vegetation play across and through the mesh scrims.

Three plate-steel "pillars," nine steel-mesh "funnels," and one "forest" form a single island unit. Each island measures 40 meters square in plan, and stands 55 meters above the water's surface. Fifteen island units make up this installation.

Coastal Reservoir generates power, water, and plant life by working with the natural properties of the surrounding atmosphere. Quite literally, it gathers its resources out of thin air. Using the principals of an oscillating water column, the "pillars" trap a volume of air that is displaced by the surrounding wave action to drive a bidirectional fan turbine. The vapor in the air creates condensate that is filtered through the mesh funnels and onto the platform below. The "forest" block at the center of each island will be established but unmanaged, and as any new island is open to colonization by seeds carried on wind and wing.

TEAM
Ivan Valin, Natalia Echeverri, Jan Henao (VALECHE Studio)

TEAM LOCATION
Hong Kong, China

ENERGY TECHNOLOGIES
floating oscillating water column wave energy converter (similar to "Mighty Whale" tested in Gokashoa Bay, Japan in 1998)

WATER TECHNOLOGIES
fog harvesting

ANNUAL CAPACITY
2,500 MWh
20 million liters of drinking water

Fog is an important dimension in coastal California's native ecosystems. *Coastal Reservoir* is not intended to provide a native habitat, but it is expected to provide optimal habitat. The vegetation and animals thriving within this machine begin from the concept of the Third Landscape, a genetic reservoir, but evolve into a New Nature, an environmental sublime.

Santa Cruz reforestation

Loss of coastal habitat due to urbanization

Species stock for fog- and salt-tolerant vegetation

California Cloud Forests
Fog supports the once-grand Redwood stands and their ferny understories in Northern and Central California. In the much drier climate of Southern California, fog is the cornerstone in stabilizing unique coastal oak and pine woodland ecosystems. With overgrazing and urbanization, many of these habitats have disappeared. Without a tree canopy, water cannot be collected from the fog. Without water, trees cannot grow. Scientists are now experimenting with artificial methods to capture fog and establish oak and pine forests on the nearby Channel Islands.

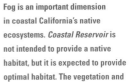

The ocean around Santa Monica is full of machines of energy extraction such as the man-made THUMS Islands near Long Beach and the oil platforms off the Santa Barbara and Los Angeles coasts. This area is also home to the Channel Islands, which harbor unique and rare ecologies.

Misty(Cal)
Fog Catchers

The low-tech water collection process and the modularity of the structure makes the design concept easily scalable and adaptable.

Misty(Cal) Fog Catchers is inspired by the way a spider web catches dewdrops from the air. In Chile's Atacama Desert, where the average rainfall is less than 0.1 mm per year, communities have successfully installed fog-catching arrays that capture the minuscule drops of water that make up fog to supply homes and irrigation systems.

Misty(Cal) is both a functional structure and a public space. The fog catchers placed in the inner part of the structure produce water for a drip irrigation system connected to gardens on the lower platform, creating a self-sustaining ecosystem. The nets that are stretched on the outer part of the structure collect water that feeds back to the city through a piping system that connects to the Santa Monica Urban Runoff Recycling Facility (SMURRF).

Coastal fog is a prevalent phenomenon throughout the year in Santa Monica peaking in May and June, also known as "May Gray" and "June Gloom." In certain years, the fog extends to July and August, occasionally referred to as "No Sky July" and "Fogust." This coastal fog is scientifically called the marine layer. The *Misty(Cal)* structure is oriented to take advantage of the prevailing southwest wind direction, as wind is a fundamental component to the fog collection process.

Most of the fog collection happens in the morning, as condensation primarily takes place at sunrise. The irrigation system linked to the gardens and orchards inside the structure reaches its full capacity during the month of June. Visitors learn about and enjoy the benefits of fog collection. As the orchards bear fruits and colorful flowers blossom through the irrigation system, "June Gloom" becomes "June Bloom"!

TEAM
Rafael Fernandez,
Marie-Adelaide Mol
(Maria Design Studio)

TEAM LOCATION
Panama City, Panama

WATER TECHNOLOGIES
fog harvesting

ANNUAL CAPACITY
36.5 million liters of
drinking water
(8 million liters used for crop
irrigation)
15,000 kg of crops

A portion of the water collected by the fog catchers is used to irrigate the public gardens and orchards, while the rest of the water supply is redirected to the Santa Monica Urban Runoff Recycling Facility (SMURRF), which treats up to 500,000 gallons of runoff water per day (approximately 4% of the Santa Monica's daily water usage).

Self-sustained orchards and gardens

Public flow and interaction

Connection to SMURRF

Collected water to SMURRF

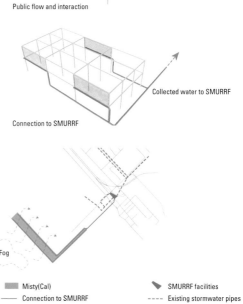

Fog

▨ Misty(Cal)
— Connection to SMURRF

◥ SMURRF facilities
- - - - Existing stormwater pipes

Misty(Cal) and the local community

Coralline

Visitors interact with the artwork.

Coralline gives visitors to the Santa Monica Pier a new and exciting visual experience on the scale of the Pacific Wheel. It is a dynamic public space in the daylight and a beautifully lit attraction in the evening.

Coralline is a portmanteau minted from the words "coral" and "line" meaning an energy line that takes a coral shape.

Coralline uses modified buoy-type wave energy converters to generate electricity. This technology typically employs three main parts: the float assembly located at the wave action, the heave plate at the seabed, and the spar that connects the two and where the kinetic energy conversion is captured.

In *Coralline* the system is turned upside down. Whereas a normal power buoy places its generator and spar under the water, *Coralline* brings the generator and spar above, leaving only the float assembly on the water's surface. Above the ocean, 305 buoys are tied together in a sculptural form over enhanced marine habitat and adjacent to a rebuilt breakwater to protect the Santa Monica Harbor.

TEAM
Faris Rajak Kotahatuhaha, Rizki Tridamayanti Siregar, Denny Lesmana Budi

TEAM LOCATION
Jakarta, Indonesia

ENERGY TECHNOLOGIES
point absorber wave energy converter (inverted)

ANNUAL CAPACITY
1,000 MWh

Aerial view

Coralline against the horizon

Coralline rises out of the
Pacific Ocean.

Flow Horizon

Flow Horizon gives the appearance of light and strength. Its transparency minimizes its visual impact on the horizon, while it serves to produce drinking water and electricity for Santa Monica.

The moment of impact of a surfboard on the waves provides the inspiration for the installation. Surfboards are designed to minimize the forces of friction on the water, but it is precisely these forces that *Flow Horizon* seeks to harness to create energy.

The installation consists of flexible connectors, which extend in different directions to support sloping planes of electroactive polymer (EAP) material. One-third of the structure is concealed beneath the surface of the water.

The EAP membranes are stretched between the steel flexible connectors. The force of the wind and the water acting on these membranes is transferred to the central column, which houses water desalination systems and the balance of electrical systems. At the top of the column is a set of concentrating lenses that channel solar radiation to assist with the desalination process.

Towering waves hit the stretched plane and create a series of vibrations that are converted into electricity by the EAP membranes. Above the surface of the water the wind works as the source of power generation.

TEAM
Kacper Kubiak, Sandra Wojtasik, Sandra Wuczynska, Kamila Politanska, Klaudia Ksiezarczyk, Marcin Burzynski

TEAM LOCATION
Kraków, Poland

ENERGY TECHNOLOGIES
kinetic wind and wave harvesting through vibration using electroactive polymers (EAP) similar to those used in HEAD's Intellifiber™ ski technology

WATER TECHNOLOGIES
solar distillation

ANNUAL CAPACITY
80 MWh
200 million liters of drinking water

Process of electricity production

Waves striking planes

Electric fibers convert vibration into electricity

Transmission of electricity to the pole

Energy flow into the condenser

Transmission of electricity to the city

Process of water desalination

Water pumping

Water lift

Lens heating up

Water evaporation

Salt and clean water

Architectural concept

Area

Steel pole

Plane with electric fibers

Twist plane fixed to pole

Multiplication

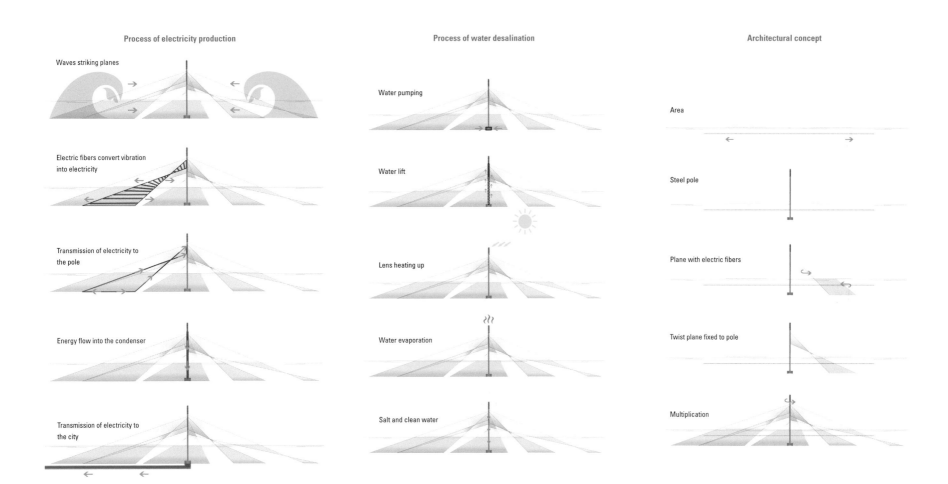

Big Balls

Big Balls creates a beautiful out-of-this-world experience connecting us with the ocean waves and tides. It is also a desalination and power plant to create drinking water and electricity for the city.

The base is composed of long floating rectangular platforms that silently and slowly move with the waves. This new landscape in the water sways in synchrony with the ocean and invites people who arrive by boat to become one with the ocean while enjoying the artwork, sunbathing, or simply walking around.

A composition of giant transparent balls, positioned and scaled to mimic the order of water molecules, show only a very thin spiral of channels running along their inner surface. The transparent material creates reflections and distortions of the background with different spheres superimposed in perspective. The vapor clouds generated inside further enrich the experience. At night, discrete lighting inside the spheres changes the horizon, creating reflection-like ghosts of the Pacific Wheel.

The movement of the platforms, powered by the waves and tides, activates a series of pistons that attach to the ocean floor and the breakwater. This movement generates pressure that activates a turbine, generating electricity 24 hours a day.

The giant spheres have a central plate onto which additional wave energy is used to pump salt water. The sun creates a greenhouse effect within the sphere, which vaporizes the water. The evaporated water then condenses on the cool outer skin and slides down the wall to collect on the spiral channels. It is stored at the bottom of the sphere before being distributed to the city. The flow of water through the spiral channels of the heat plate is constant (day and night) so that the plates will be rinsed between sunset and the next morning's sunrise, restoring the surrounding water's natural salinity.

TEAM
Jose Carlos de Silva, Leonardo de Silva, Rodrigo Marquez, Mateu-Puchades

TEAM LOCATION
Malmö, Sweden

ENERGY TECHNOLOGIES
point absorber wave energy converter

WATER TECHNOLOGIES
solar distillation

ANNUAL CAPACITY
15,000 MWh
14 million liters of drinking water

Visitors can get close and interact with the artwork.

The floating platforms are made from concrete using aggregates from demolition and recycled steel reinforcements. The floating material is recovered plastic debris from the ocean that is encased within the concrete to allow the platforms to float.

View from the beach

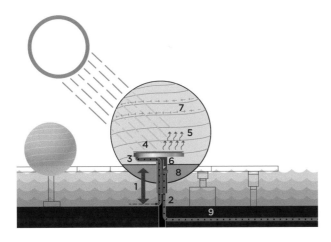

1. Waves and tides move spheres
2. Piston pumps water in and out
3. Salt water in
4. Sun heats plate
5. Water evaporates
6. Leftover salt water flows out
7. Condensed water runs on channels
8. Clean water storage
9. Clean water to the city

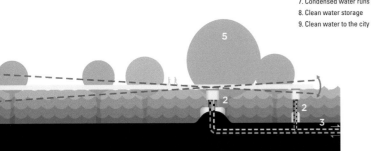

1. Waves and tides move platforms
2. Piston creates pressure
3. Pressure water to the electricity
   generator turbine
4. New public space
5. Desalination balls

Sunset from the pier

Catch a Wave

One of the strongest connections humans can make with the power of the ocean is through surfing. The force of the waves propels the surfer forward at high speed, with only the thin surfboard as the point of connection.

Inspired by the way that surfboards smoothly integrate with the water, the boards of *Catch a Wave* harness the energy of the water with wave energy converters. Instead of surfers above, thin stalks sit above to capture the power of the wind. Visitors can watch as the ocean moves the boards, forming different paths between the stalks.

There are 320 boards with 2,670 stalks. Each stalk contains piezoelectric discs that are positioned in between rigid backup plates. These piezoelectric structures compress and stretch when moved in any direction. Each motion is converted to electricity.

The artwork pays homage to the power of nature, human engineering, and the beauty of the California coast.

TEAM
Irvin Ahatovic, Ana Jugovic

TEAM LOCATION
Vienna, Austria

ENERGY TECHNOLOGIES
wave energy converter and
piezoelectric stacked actuators

ANNUAL CAPACITY
2,000 MWh

Visitors can walk between
the stalks.

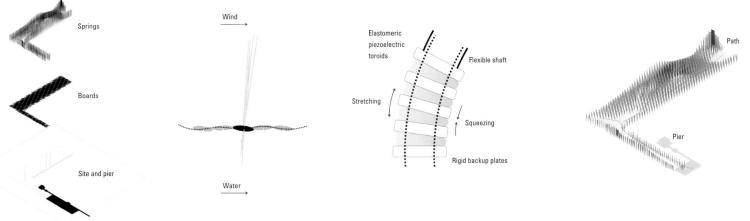

Springs

Boards

Site and pier

Wind

Water

Elastomeric
piezoelectric
toroids

Flexible shaft

Stretching

Squeezing

Rigid backup plates

Path

Pier

The Loop

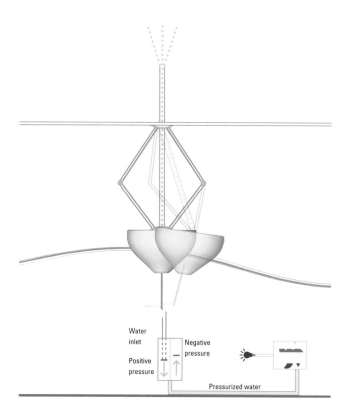

The Loop is an energy-harvesting landscape—a symbolic expression of the endless and consistent embodied energy that Santa Monica waters provide. It also serves as an extension to the already active and vibrant athletic and entertainment culture in Santa Monica, bringing visitors to the site by providing amenities such as interactive spaces, running and bicycle tracks, and additional vantage points.

The Loop demonstrates to visitors the potential of wave energy-harvesting technology, providing the opportunity for them to witness the power through a spectacular display.

The Loop extends the pier into the energy-harvesting center. As visitors walk along the new energy pier, the buoys around them work continuously to not only generate electricity but also bring beautiful fountains of water up and onto the deck, the volume of which will change depending on the intensity of the waves—a constant real-time visual representation of how much energy is being produced by the waves below.

The landscape design invites locals and visitors to experience Santa Monica from a new perspective. The power buoys can be viewed at various locations of the site and can be studied from the new pier. Their gentle movement creates an experience of contemplation.

The lateral structure that ties the platforms together consists of PTFE-woven textile, enabling human interaction with the membrane and further enhancing connections to the wave energy below. The column structure mimics the formal language of the existing Santa Monica Pier.

TEAM
Suvir Hira, Feras Alsaggaf, Dylan Catino

TEAM LOCATION
Philadelphia (PA), USA

ENERGY TECHNOLOGIES
point absorber wave energy converter (CETO™)

ANNUAL CAPACITY
11,400 MWh

View of pedestrian path looking southeast

Water Feature
Water travels vertically to the interactive space using the pressure provided by the buoy.

Translucent Shell
Fixed to the deck, this shell allows the viewers to see the linear motion within the shell. It becomes a light diffuser at night.

Pressure Piston
Arm that moves vertically to compress and release water, while visually displaying the wave conditions underneath.

Lateral Bracing
Flexible joints provide resiliency during storm events.

Fiberglass Buoy
The form of the buoy increases the linear motion for maximum movement and energy harvesting.

Water Conduit
Embedded tubing transports water from the ocean to the deck.

Water Outlet
A portion of the water is sent back up to the deck to power the interactive feature.

Seabed Piston
A fixed pressure chamber compresses the water continuously to spin turbines and produce energy.

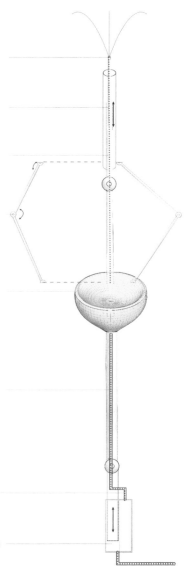

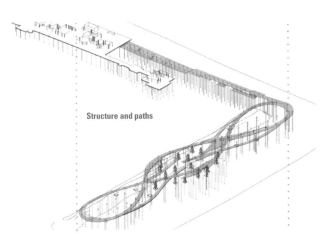

Structure and paths

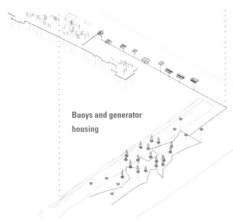

Buoys and generator housing

View of interactive deck looking northwest

Panta Rhei
Everything Flows

"Behind every image, something has disappeared. And that is the source of its fascination." Jean Baudrillard

For those who live along the coast, the passing of ships is a sight that never loses its attraction.

The idea of adding another man-made and permanent object adjacent to the Santa Monica Pier may be difficult to accept for some people. A ship however implies the idea of a journey, impermanence, and the possibility of change. Recycling one of those enormous vessels that once transported fossil fuels and has since become a kind of fossil itself is a symbolic and practical act. The oil tanker becomes a platform and location for a new philosophy. Rather than transporting oil, it is now producing energy by capturing wind, solar, and wave power to make water and electricity for the city.

The three primary wind turbines are evocative of the sails of tall ships but at the same time look like high-tech wing sails of a futuristic Americas Cup. The deck is covered with a seawater greenhouse and PV solar cells. Many of the enormous tanks become water storage. The deckhouse and bridge accommodate a research

and education center, along with residential accommodations for researchers and artists. The design provides an educational and recreational space on the sea that demonstrates different highly effective renewable energy technologies and communicates their application and impact. The income generated by the energy and water production is used to support a research and art program.

A Swell Actuated Reverse Osmosis System (SAROS™) is installed in connection with the seaward breakwater. It uses high-pressure pumps powered by the motion of waves to remove salt from ocean water. Water is collected in the ship's tanks and made available for the city.

Very little freeboard of a loaded tanker is visible. Once the vertical axis wind generators start to rotate, the ship seems to have almost disappeared. *Panta Rhei*, "everything flows," is the philosophy behind the design. As the Greek philosopher Heraclitus described the ever-present change of the world in 500 BCE, so does the power of wind and water exist in an ever-changing flow whose energy must be used in the moment before it is gone.

TEAM
Ralf Sander, Dr. Halina Sander, Professor Herbert Sander

TEAM LOCATION
Belfast, UK

ENERGY TECHNOLOGIES
photovoltaic panels, vertical axis wind turbines (similar to SeaTwirl™), wave energy converters (power on-site desalination)

WATER TECHNOLOGIES
Swell Actuated Reverse Osmosis System (SAROS™), solar distillation

ANNUAL CAPACITY
12,000 MWh (from PV and VAWT)
60 million liters of drinking water

The large vertical axis wind turbines move independently to generate electricity.

One of the challenges of large-scale desalination is what to do with all of the salt. Dumping it in shallow areas has been shown to negatively affect local marine ecosystems. A salinity plume deterrent system is designed to mix brine with ambient seawater, reducing the salinity content and temperature to benign levels.

Seventy percent of old tankers are simply run ashore in developing countries for disassembly. The low human health and environmental standards are making this practice highly profitable, but at what cost? Every day, more than 30,000 workers are risking their lives for little more than two dollars a day on Chittagong's Beach.

The sails seem to disappear through high speed rotation.

In good weather, *Panta Rhei* becomes just one of many sails that dot the skyline of the bay.

Wind Coaster

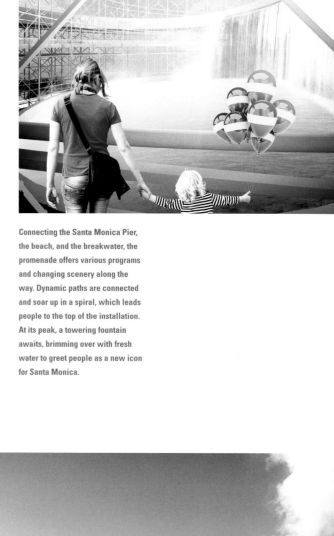

Wind Coaster brings forth memories of Santa Monica's vibrant history, while pointing to the future of renewable energy and sustainable water generation.

Many remember the massive wooden roller coaster of the old Santa Monica Pier with its bustling crowds and a vibrant atmosphere. *Wind Coaster* transfers the form of this old wooden roller coaster into a powerful and fantastic emblem of the importance of Santa Monica's environment and its memories.

The tensile brace installation stretches up to 60 meters above the sea level, offering an experience of Santa Monica on both a human and an urban scale.

Visitors to the artwork are greeted by turbines of various sizes spinning around them as they walk on the pedestrian pathways. The energy generated by these turbines is more than enough to power a seawater desalination facility that uses capacitive deionization (CDI). Electricity pumps seawater into the *Wind Coaster* rails that wind along the top of the installation. Each rail module contains two high-porous carbon electrodes inside, which separate salt and other ionized dissolved solutes from the water through electrochemical demineralization.

Visitors learn about the process of desalination through the water space experience within the installation. Along the way there, visitors are provided with a complete view of all of the equipment and the processes of the desalination and wind power systems. The water rails are arranged in sequential order so that visitors can follow the process and visually see and recognize the importance of the system.

TEAM
Kyung-Sun Lee, Hanwook Kim, Yungi Jung, Ki Joon Han

TEAM LOCATION
Seoul, South Korea

ENERGY TECHNOLOGIES
wind turbines

WATER TECHNOLOGIES
capacitive deionization (CDI) desalination

ANNUAL CAPACITY
3,000 MWh
160 million liters of drinking water

Connecting the Santa Monica Pier, the beach, and the breakwater, the promenade offers various programs and changing scenery along the way. Dynamic paths are connected and soar up in a spiral, which leads people to the top of the installation. At its peak, a towering fountain awaits, brimming over with fresh water to greet people as a new icon for Santa Monica.

SANTA MONICA

At the peak of the water tower, visitors can look down the walkway and the water rails, bringing everything together with an understanding of the importance of fresh water, renewable energy, and a truly sustainable Santa Monica.

Plan

Nozzle ....

Spiral drain ....

Inside section of the spiral drain

Water tower

Nozzle ....

Spiral drain ....

Water cascade ....

Water storage ....

Water pump ....

Structure section

CDI desalination rail ....

Seawater suction

Electronic wire ....
Steel structure ....
Suction pipe ....

Power supply

ETFE sheet ....

Power supply ....

Seawater ....

Foundation ....

CDI cell body

Electrode contact hole
Titanium sheet
Carbon acrogel
Rubber gasket
Polymer spacer mesh

Steel structure and
Suction pipe

Electronic wire
ETFE sheet

Each rail module includes two highly porous electrodes inside, which absorbs ions and desalinates seawater by applying an electrical potential difference.

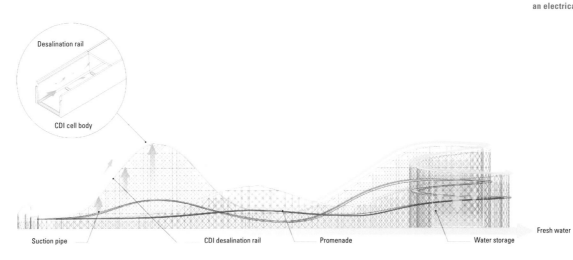

Desalination rail

CDI cell body

Brackish water

Suction pipe

CDI desalination rail

Promenade

Water storage

Fresh water

Light Drop

TEAM
Antonio Maccá, Flavio Masi

TEAM LOCATION
Padova, Italy

ENERGY TECHNOLOGIES
semitransparent photovoltaic
panels, tidal power pumps

WATER TECHNOLOGIES
reverse osmosis desalination

ANNUAL CAPACITY
3.5 billion liters of drinking water
from solar and tidal energy

Light Drop houses a public
panoramic space—a dome-shaped
observatory with a 360-degree view.

Light Drop is a sustainable artwork that expresses its unique profile over the ocean—a new point of reference for the people of Santa Monica.

A slender aerial arch raises a mirrored sphere over the line of the horizon. In the daylight, the artwork resembles a drop of water suspended over the skyline, with its reflective surface constantly changing with respect to the different light conditions of the surrounding environment. *Light Drop* houses a desalination plant that converts marine water into drinking water. Tidal-powered pumps convey the water through a pipe system incorporated in the main structure of the arch. The processed drinking water is distributed by gravitational flow from the artwork to the pier. The design implicitly focuses people's attention on the urgent need to solve California's water crisis.

During the sunset, the mirrored solar envelope captures the colors of the atmosphere and dazzles with a golden shimmer. While the new "photovoltaic sun" provides light and power to the desalination plant, the arch of the installation symbolizes the path of the sun across the sky of Santa Monica from sunrise to sunset.

During the night when the sphere lights up it creates the illusion of a second moon low in the sky. The artwork represents a welcoming beacon and an ideal continuation of the lights of the Santa Monica Pier.

In its essence, *Light Drop* reflects and projects light in continuous evolution over time. It explores the water theme in relation to both science and ecology, contributing to the development of environmental sustainability and artistically transforming the drought emergency into an optimistic message of beauty and hope.

Light Drop is a light-oriented artwork with different possible meanings. It is a design of reflected and projected light, with its reflective surface constantly changing with respect to the different light conditions of the surrounding environment.

During the day *Light Drop* resembles a drop of water suspended over the skyline.

During the night *Light Drop* becomes a sort of lighthouse with a computer-controlled display. At the right angle it can seem as if it is a second moon sitting on the horizon.

181

E-Yacht

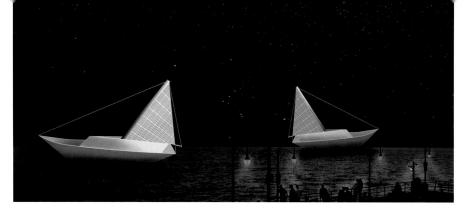

The form of the design is inspired by the history of the site as a yacht harbor.

E-Yacht is designed to build awareness of the severe water shortage in California while also contributing to the solution—producing energy and water from the abundant natural resources of the site. The structure is designed in the form of a yacht to recall the history of the Santa Monica Pier—creating a symbolic place for visitors to recall the past and look to the future.

The form is playful and friendly, using the familiar folding patterns of origami art. The shape is mutable at various times of the day, taking advantage of the folds to create movement.

The sail of *E-Yacht* is composed of multiple layers. The top waterproof layer functions as a seawater basin, with a luminescent panel below. A hybrid photovoltaic and thermal (PVT) system is incorporated into the sail to generate both electricity and heat energy. During the day, the sail is unfolded to hold seawater. The heat from the sun and the PVT system evaporates the seawater to extract fresh water distillate. When the sun has set, the sail is folded upward to emit light, providing visitors with an attractive nightscape.

The hull of *E-Yacht* acts as a drinking water basin, accumulating distilled water before it is conveyed to the shore. A mast adhered to the sail provides the guide for its folding and unfolding. A second mast fixes *E-Yacht* to the seabed and incorporates tidal stream turbines for additional electricity generation. *E-Yacht* can be manufactured and distributed at a variety of scales. This range makes it available for installation and use anywhere that seawater and sunlight exist.

At the *E-Yacht* installation visitors can experience seawater become drinking water by the power of the sun while understanding renewable energy as something that can be beautiful.

TEAM
Eunhi Kim, Koungjin Cho
([i:kei] office)

TEAM LOCATION
Seoul, South Korea

ENERGY TECHNOLOGIES
hybrid photovoltaic and thermal (PVT) system, tidal stream generator

WATER TECHNOLOGIES
solar distillation

ANNUAL CAPACITY
5,000 MWh
20 million liters of drinking water

E-Yacht uses distillation to produce drinking water from seawater.

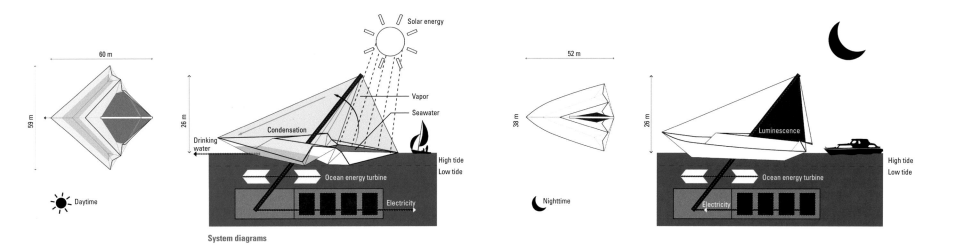

System diagrams

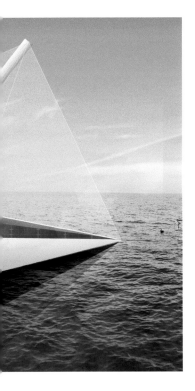

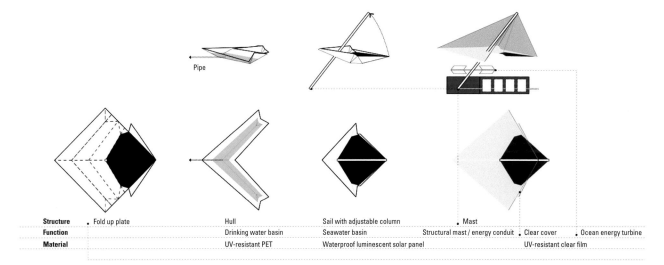

Structure	Fold up plate	Hull	Sail with adjustable column	Mast		
Function		Drinking water basin	Seawater basin	Structural mast / energy conduit	Clear cover	Ocean energy turbine
Material		UV-resistant PET	Waterproof luminescent solar panel		UV-resistant clear film	

Pipe

E-Yacht is a friendly and fun
installation with a form that
references the art of origami.

Water Hyacinth Crop

Green energy systems should be informed by natural systems. *Water Hyacinth Crop* is therefore a reflection of vegetative formations, their geometries, systems of growth, and how they adapt to the environment.

The natural water hyacinth provides a phytoremediative process to the water in which it lives. This new *Water Hyacinth* also understands the environment and the health of local ecosystems as a part of its functionality. There are two types of devices that comprise the artwork. Both challenge the relationship between function and aesthetics.

The main function of *Water Hyacinth* "A" is to generate green energy through two systems associated with the sea waves and the sunlight. The first system is submerged and anchored to the seabed, while the second one emerges from the sea and responds to the movement of sunlight. Buoy-type wave energy converters create electricity from the ocean waves, while solar cells add to the electrical power. The main function of *Water Hyacinth* "B" is to collect rainwater through funnels and translucent floating tanks and filter it for drinking water.

The buoys light up like contemplative lighthouses. This allows visitors to have a visual relation to the artwork along the beach. Rather than rely on electricity for illumination, the artwork uses chemiluminescence by incorporating phosphorescent materials.

The dance of *Water Hyacinth Crop* celebrates the clean energy process.

TEAM
Juan Pablo Giraldo (Relieve Arquitectura), Catalina Patiño, Juan Pablo Ramos (CAPA Arquitectura), Maria Paulina Vargas, Esteban Ramos, Sara Lugo

TEAM LOCATION
Medellin, Colombia

ENERGY TECHNOLOGIES
thin-film photovoltaic, point absorber wave energy converter

WATER TECHNOLOGIES
rainwater harvesting

ANNUAL CAPACITY
6,000 MWh
5 million liters of drinking water

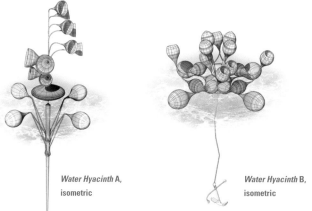

Water Hyacinth A, isometric

Water Hyacinth B, isometric

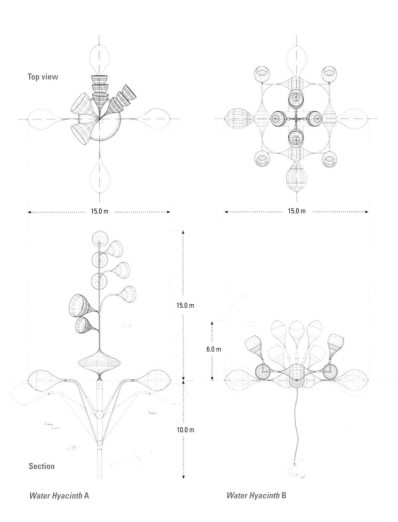

Top view

|← 15.0 m →|

|← 15.0 m →|

15.0 m

6.0 m

10.0 m

Section

Water Hyacinth A

Water Hyacinth B

A sand filter strains larger particles in the collected rainwater. The water is then stored in a transparent container that allows UV light from the sun to react with, and disinfect smaller particles.

Bubble in the Sea

View from the beach

Bubble in the Sea is of a hidden dimension. It engages with the seascape, enhancing the beauty of the horizon. At sunset it merges with the colors of the sky, and at night it mirrors the sunset as a seaside landscape attraction.

The construction is a transparent sphere containing a multistage flash desalination system with an activity space below. Under gradually reduced pressures, the seawater changes to vapor, which is then cooled to produce drinking water. Tidal power provides a steady stream of energy to run the system and provide illumination.

Through the *Bubble*, visitors can see the production of fresh water, reminding them of its value. This educational benefit of the artwork is as important as its infrastructural benefit.

Below the *Bubble* is an underwater aquarium—a public and hydrophilic space where people can learn about marine biology and watch the aquatic life—while on the upper decks visitors fish and enjoy the sunset.

TEAM
Junyi Leng, Rundong Lu

TEAM LOCATION
Shenzhen, China

ENERGY TECHNOLOGIES
tidal power (100% goes to on-site distillation)

WATER TECHNOLOGIES
multistage flash distillation (MFD)

ANNUAL CAPACITY
1.5 billion liters of drinking water

The view from underwater allows visitors to watch the fresh water recycling equipment.

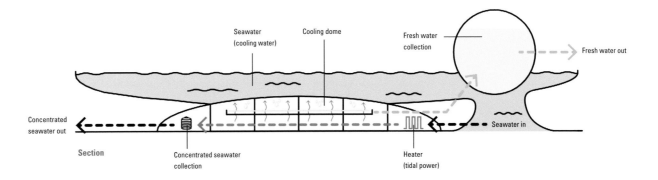

Seawater
(cooling water)

Cooling dome

Fresh water
collection

Fresh water out

Concentrated
seawater out

Section

Concentrated seawater
collection

Heater
(tidal power)

Seawater in

View from the axis

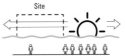

Site

As the sun's azimuth changes
throughout the year, the location
of the sunset shifts on the horizon.

Diagram of form generation

A transparent sphere will not block,
but merely distort the light of the
setting sun, magnifying its effect
when viewed from certain angles.

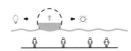

Fresh water is periodically
channeled to the *Bubble* following
desalination, adding to the
complexities of light refraction.

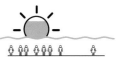

On the occasion when the sun
sets behind the water-filled
Bubble, the spectacular image
will remind beachgoers of the
importance of water conservation.

Chainsword

An aquatic forest emerges from the ocean.

Water is a precious resource. One way that we can be responsible for our destiny and live in harmony with nature is to develop systems capable of converting seawater to fresh water in a sustainable way.

Chainsword draws inspiration from the energetic and cheerful atmosphere of the Santa Monica Pier, preserving its personality and history.

Beyond the old pier a new object emerges from the ocean, an aquatic forest, which hosts a hidden footbridge system. It is on these pathways where the magic happens. Visitors can walk amid the forest and admire the breathless view. They can take a sunbath or enjoy the water slide.

The access areas to the sea are secured by a safety grid outlining the swimming boundaries. The "forest" is made up of 770 transparent polycarbonate masts (25 cm in diameter). Reminiscent of the aquatic chain sword plant, they rise out of the water to a height of 36 meters.

Each of these vertical masts contains a sustainable energy and potable water production system. Below the surface is a wave power buoy that pumps water up into the solar distillation chamber located at the top of each mast. There, sunlight is concentrated by a lens to evaporate the water. The now desalinated water flows back down through a filter to a collection point.

TEAM
Angelo Balducci, Umberto Di Tanna, Marco Lucchesi, Stefano Nesci, Aurora Sbrizzi (TWOSIX architecture)

TEAM LOCATION
Rome, Italy

ENERGY TECHNOLOGIES
point absorber wave energy converter (hydraulic pump powers distillation process)

WATER TECHNOLOGIES
micro solar distillation

ANNUAL CAPACITY
500 million liters of drinking water

Each vertical element produces energy using wave motion. At the first step, the spring is fully elongated and the hydraulic cylinder is in a neutral position. When the wave breaks on the structure, the spring is compressed and the hydraulic cylinder extends the float through the floating force. Next, the buoy moves down with the motion of the waves, compressing the hydraulic cylinder.

Within the same architectural element we propose a new desalination method based on a microdistillation. Salt water is desalinated to produce fresh water with evaporation and condensation. A spring-loaded piston brings seawater into the system with the power of the sea waves.

The sunset brings a beautiful glow to *Chainsword*.

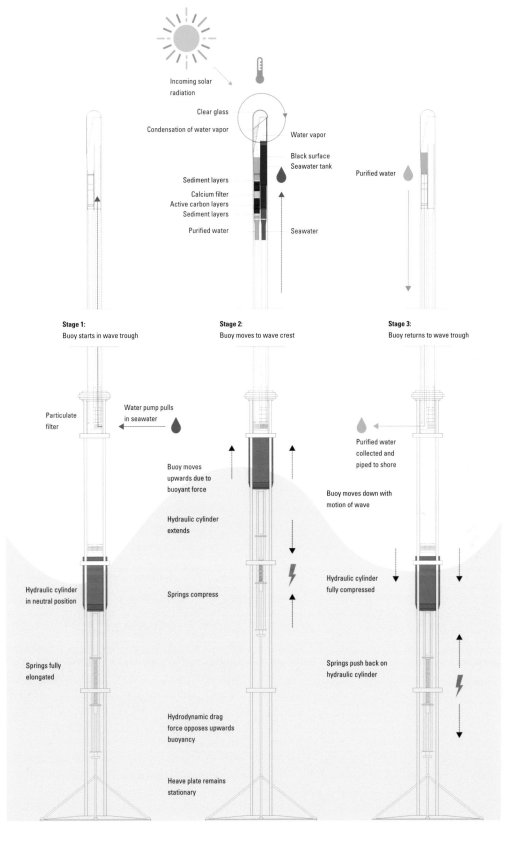

Incoming solar radiation

Clear glass

Condensation of water vapor

Water vapor

Black surface

Seawater tank

Sediment layers

Calcium filter

Active carbon layers

Sediment layers

Purified water

Seawater

Purified water

Stage 1:
Buoy starts in wave trough

Stage 2:
Buoy moves to wave crest

Stage 3:
Buoy returns to wave trough

Particulate filter

Water pump pulls in seawater

Purified water collected and piped to shore

Buoy moves upwards due to buoyant force

Buoy moves down with motion of wave

Hydraulic cylinder extends

Hydraulic cylinder in neutral position

Springs compress

Hydraulic cylinder fully compressed

Springs fully elongated

Springs push back on hydraulic cylinder

Hydrodynamic drag force opposes upwards buoyancy

Heave plate remains stationary

Power Leaves

View from the beach

Power Leaves is architecture in motion that breathes with nature. Floating on the surface of the water, like a yacht on the sea, it generates power and supplies its own energy.

The installation generates power by harnessing the flow of the wind and the waves. Each of the "leaves" moves up and down in response to force and velocity, encircling a tidal power pool. Stationary poles assist to balance the opposing forces.

The accumulation of overlapping "leaves" changes its appearance depending on the tide levels. The ebb and flow controls the presence of the pathway, as well as the sizes of the open spaces where people can experience the beauty of sustainable energy.

On some days, mist shrouds the silhouette, blending into the sky and the sea. Soft shadows cast down onto the water's surface during the day. At sunset the water glows orange, and at night the reflection of the moonlight brings a sense of serenity.

TEAM
Kohki Hiranuma (Kohki Hiranuma Architects & Associates)

TEAM LOCATION
Osaka, Japan

ENERGY TECHNOLOGIES
tidal power, kinetic energy harvesting

ANNUAL CAPACITY
7,500 MWh

Pathway traced by the ebb and flow

Silhouette form of the yacht

Power is generated by wind forces

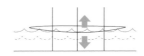

Power is generated by the movement of the water

Tidal power pool

Form in motion, changing from time to time

Open space by the sea constantly varies through time

Silhouette of the artwork covered by the mist

Kinetic
Manifesto

The kinetic structure is a floating sculpture in the sea, and a public space which invites, educates, and serves as a social platform to question, discuss, and experience water consumption. It is a tool to stimulate public awareness through the production of fresh water.

Southern California's thirst has led to the importation of water from rivers across the Western United States. These sources have helped to hydrate the urban metropolis for the past century, in turn taking a toll on the reciprocal landscapes. As the impacts of climate change increase, how can Los Angeles become less dependent on imported water, and sustain itself with its own local hydrological system?

As a way of provoking this question, *Kinetic Manifesto* harnesses energy from waves through a sculptural form floating on the sea. This energy is used to convert seawater into fresh water, which is then released at the top of the metronomic masts. At first site it appears that this valuable resource of fresh water is spilling into the sea. This visual expression of wastefulness is intended to encourage a sense of absurd loss in the hearts and minds of visitors, who will reflect upon how this experience relates to the daily activities of Los Angeles County residents.

In fact, the water spilled by the masts is harvested by the structure and collected in different recreational pools. Undersea hoses direct the overflow toward the beach, where it connects with people through small-scale interventions along the coast. A series of showers and drinking fountains emerge from the sand as the captured water continues its travel.

The structure is wave-powered and articulated in order to react to a succession of waves. It incorporates a pendulum action to assist with the kinetic energy. This motion powers a seawater piston that injects salt water at the base of the mast, which houses a reverse osmosis cylinder. The pressurized salt water gets filtered through a sequence of chambers and only fresh water reaches the very top part of the mast where it produces showers, rain, and fog by way of a series of jets.

TEAM
Gauthier Durey, Eric Reid
(Vagabond Atelier)

TEAM LOCATION
Oslo, Norway

ENERGY TECHNOLOGIES
kinetic wave energy converter,
thin-film photovoltaic

WATER TECHNOLOGIES
reverse osmosis desalination

ANNUAL CAPACITY
6 million liters of drinking water

During the day *Kinetic Manifesto* is a destination, a playful sculpture for visitors to roam and experience the fresh water atmosphere. By night it is a light sculpture powered by solar cells, emerging ghostly through the water stream.

Solar Cloud

Technological, medical, and social improvements have allowed humanity to develop at an unprecedented pace, with global population anticipated to reach more than 10 billion people in 2100. However, technological improvements are also increasing our energy demands, making us dependent on large amounts of terrain outside of our settlements. Land use optimization is therefore a key for our future cities.

Composed of modular solar balloons that use the combination of air and sun as the only lifting force, *Solar Cloud* is an answer to these challenges. The greenhouse effect produced by the absorption of solar radiation allows the cloud to lift up to great heights where solar energy is stronger, avoiding complex technological systems that would require external energy consumption.

Flexible thin-film solar cells form part of the skin of the *Solar Cloud*, sending electricity back to the ground via lightweight fiberglass tension cables. Additional electricity is generated from the waves by point absorbers built into a pedestrian walk that spans the length of the existing breakwater.

Evaporation is the first step in which nature transforms salt water into fresh water. *Solar Cloud* learns from the processes inherent within natural clouds with several fog-harvesting meshes. The water harvested is conducted through the main path and collected in the new stormwater holding tank on shore.

Instead of a direct pedestrian access, three docks allow for controlled maritime access. In this sense, *Solar Cloud* forms its own island that invites people to walk through its path and observe all of the energy streams constantly at work within and around the ocean.

Solar Cloud is modular and can be arranged at a variety of scales. An array of balloons is created by joining their corners in order to leave the faces of the units free for the sun to pass through.

TEAM
Gabriel Muñoz Moreno (Social Cooperation Architects)

TEAM LOCATION
Cambridge (MA), USA

ENERGY TECHNOLOGIES
thin-film photovoltaic (high altitude), point absorber wave energy converter

WATER TECHNOLOGIES
fog harvesting mesh

ANNUAL CAPACITY
3,600 MWh
73,000 liters of drinking water

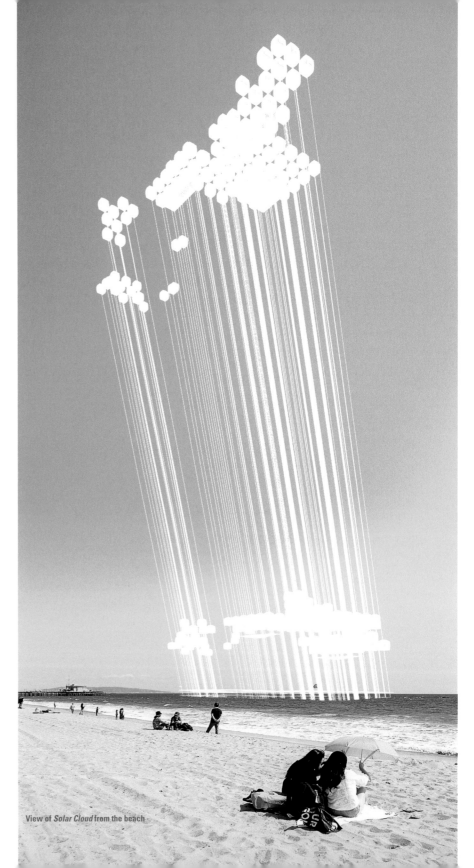

View of *Solar Cloud* from the beach

Solar Clouds are lighter-than-air
solar collectors.

The modularity of the design allows
it to expand to any scale.

Wharf
of Cloud

For people living in arid areas the rain and clouds can seem far away—like family members on ships out to sea for whose return they yearn. The white diamond-shaped vessels of *Wharf of Cloud* bring back the scent of rain and wind to berth in the wharf forever.

Wharf of Cloud incorporates the form of the old breakwater, creating an oblong pool, inside of which the vessels can move freely alone or in groups. Each vessel or boat functions independently as a seawater distilling system and solar power plant. The upper portion of the design is covered in solar panel plates that receive direct sunlight, while white aluminum plates act as cooling fins underneath. The electricity produced from sunlight is used to heat seawater and create steam, which condensates into water in the cooler inner chambers of the "cloud." The water is then conveyed by gravity to the cistern in the bottom of each boat.

When the boats berth in the wharf they automatically link to the system of pipes that transport the clean water to the wharf.

More than 600 Windbelt™ generators are installed atop the two mountain-shape seawalls on either long side of the oblong pool. During normal operation, this electricity is fed directly into the city grid. On especially cloudy days and at night the wind power is sent to the boats berthing by the wharf for lighting and to provide electricity for water purification.

The new circular wharf is not only a harbor for berthing the *Cloud* boats, but it also offers spaces for human activities on the sea. Visitors can take a walk, go jogging, ride bicycles, or just watch the "clouds" on the sea by idly lying on the gently cambered seawall.

At night, the "clouds" become softly illuminated by the Windbelts™ creating a dreamlike experience when viewed from shore.

TEAM
Beiming Liang

TEAM LOCATION
Changsha, China

ENERGY TECHNOLOGIES
aeroelastic vibration
(Windbelt™), thin-film
photovoltaic

WATER TECHNOLOGIES
distillation with electric heat

ANNUAL CAPACITY
580 MWh
17 million liters of drinking water

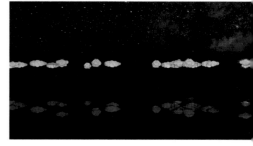

Wharf of Cloud at night

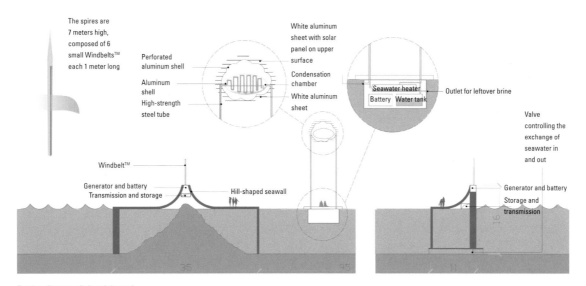

The spires are 7 meters high, composed of 6 small Windbelts™ each 1 meter long

Perforated aluminum shell

Aluminum shell

High-strength steel tube

White aluminum sheet with solar panel on upper surface

Condensation chamber

White aluminum sheet

Seawater heater

Battery   Water tank

Outlet for leftover brine

Valve controlling the exchange of seawater in and out

Windbelt™

Generator and battery
Transmission and storage

Hill-shaped seawall

Generator and battery
Storage and transmission

Section diagram of electricity and water generation

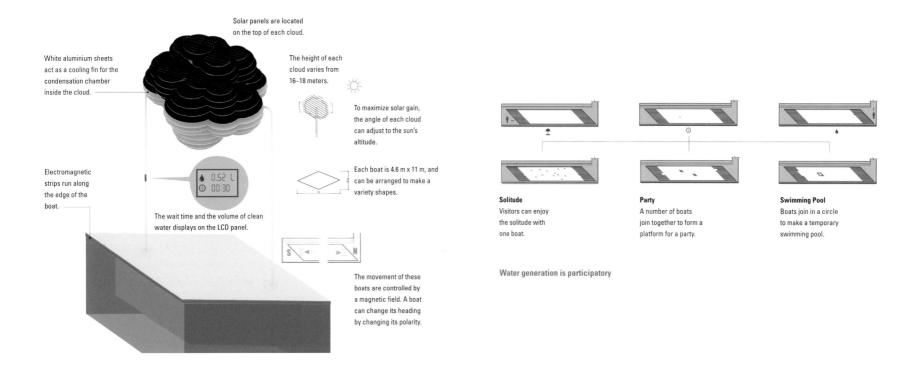

Solar panels are located on the top of each cloud.

White aluminium sheets act as a cooling fin for the condensation chamber inside the cloud.

Electromagnetic strips run along the edge of the boat.

The wait time and the volume of clean water displays on the LCD panel.

The height of each cloud varies from 16–18 meters.

To maximize solar gain, the angle of each cloud can adjust to the sun's altitude.

Each boat is 4.6 m x 11 m, and can be arranged to make a variety shapes.

0.52 L
00:30

S   N

The movement of these boats are controlled by a magnetic field. A boat can change its heading by changing its polarity.

Solitude
Visitors can enjoy the solitude with one boat.

Party
A number of boats join together to form a platform for a party.

Swimming Pool
Boats join in a circle to make a temporary swimming pool.

Water generation is participatory

197

Light Pyramids

People use the public barge parks on site while they are temporarily docked.

Barges with different water-related programs journey to *Light Pyramids* and recharge water. Depending on how much water they require their docking time will be varied.

On the horizon, barges make their way to and from softly glowing inverted pyramids standing in the sea. Inside *Light Pyramids* are gardens, wetlands, and public spaces.

Light Pyramids generates drinking water from the sea and electricity in excess of that required to sustain itself. The project is also a harbor for barges, each of them with a different water-related public program. Visitors can ride the barges from the pier and sail into the structures.

On top of some of these structures Fresnel lenses are installed to heat up and desalinate seawater, while on others solar panels are installed in two rows at an optimum angle to the sun's path.

During the daytime, people on the beach can see the semitransparent structures in the sea, rising subtly and elegantly to a height of about 10 meters. At night, visitors will experience the beautiful light beams projected into the sky.

The barges are for both on-site and off-site visitors. Inspired by local culture, environment, and water systems, six designated programs are located on the barges: wetlands, vineyards, sanctuary islands, swimming pools, water play and water art, formal garden, and mangrove.

TEAM
Liu Liu, Bo Lu, Guangyu Zhao

TEAM LOCATION
Toronto, Canada

ENERGY TECHNOLOGIES
photovoltaic panels

WATER TECHNOLOGIES
solar distillation

ANNUAL CAPACITY
2,000 MWh
450,000 liters of drinking water

Formal Garden
While in the formal garden visitors can appreciate the art of gardening. The barge can be used to host small ceremonies and exhibitions.

Mangrove
The mangrove provides biodiversity for local environments and enhances fish and bird habitat. The main species include red mangrove and white mangrove.

Wildlife Sanctuary
The wildlife sanctuary is designed for wildlife protection and habitat restoration. Endangered amphibians such as the California red-legged frog, salamander, birds, and other species can find a safe habitat on the barge.

Vineyard
California is famous for its beautiful vineyards. Utilizing the desalinated water generated from *Light Pyramids* structure for irrigation, this barge celebrates the wine culture of California.

Wetland
The barge designated for wetland restoration can benefit the local environment. Native California plants such as rushes, sedges, bulrush, cattail, spike rush, and alders are planted in a modular box that can be easily transplanted.

Water Play and Water Art
Children can enjoy the water entertainment facilitated by the desalination plants, and temporary water art can attract tourists.

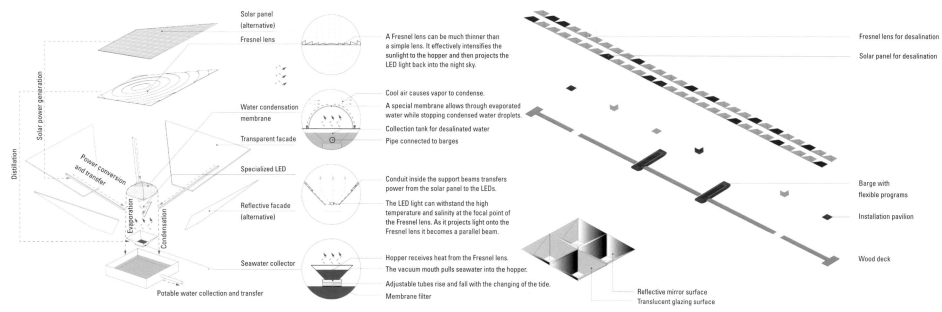

Solar panel
(alternative)

Fresnel lens

A Fresnel lens can be much thinner than
a simple lens. It effectively intensifies the
sunlight to the hopper and then projects the
LED light back into the night sky.

Cool air causes vapor to condense.

A special membrane allows through evaporated
water while stopping condensed water droplets.

Water condensation
membrane

Collection tank for desalinated water

Transparent facade

Pipe connected to barges

Specialized LED

Conduit inside the support beams transfers
power from the solar panel to the LEDs.

The LED light can withstand the high
temperature and salinity at the focal point of
the Fresnel lens. As it projects light onto the
Fresnel lens it becomes a parallel beam.

Reflective facade
(alternative)

Hopper receives heat from the Fresnel lens.

Seawater collector

The vacuum mouth pulls seawater into the hopper.

Adjustable tubes rise and fall with the changing of the tide.

Potable water collection and transfer

Membrane filter

Solar power generation

Distillation

Power conversion
and transfer

Evaporation

Condensation

Fresnel lens for desalination

Solar panel for desalination

Barge with
flexible programs

Installation pavilion

Wood deck

Reflective mirror surface

Translucent glazing surface

The Forest

Aerial view of *The Forest*

The Forest is a green Eden built on the water—an artistic addition to the coastal landscape of Santa Monica that invites people to live in peace with the natural world. It is an amplification of the atmospheric, visual, and auditory phenomena that define our relationship with nature. The presence of the Pacific Ocean is contrasted by the insertion of this new forested island.

The design is framed in the boundaries between landscape, architecture, engineering, and Land Art. It is intended to replace the current breakwater—now eroded by the ocean—with a rectangular structure to absorb the impact of waves while generating electricity and absorbing carbon dioxide and other atmospheric pollutants.

The oscillating water column (OWC) wave energy converter involves the construction of a system of air chambers located on the seabed with an opening at the bottom. Each chamber is equipped with a Wells turbine that spins continuously with airflow in either direction and is connected to a generator. The turbine is activated by the pressure force that each wave exerts on the body of air located within the chamber, and likewise by the suction of air when the wave recedes. The system is in continuous production of electricity due to the constant movement of the waves.

The arrangement of 32 OWCs off the coast of Santa Monica and the current breakwater acts as a new resilient infrastructure for erosion control, while channeling the energy of the waves into more productive use.

With 99,000 m² of indigenous plants thriving within the framework of the OWC breakwater, *The Forest* will annually produce 120 tons of O_2 while absorbing 180 tons of CO_2.

TEAM
Christian Durango

TEAM LOCATION
Bogotá, Colombia

ENERGY TECHNOLOGIES
oscillating water column (OWC) wave energy

CARBON SEQUESTRATION TECHNOLOGY
new forest (life)

ANNUAL CAPACITY
7,920 MWh
120 tons of O_2 while absorbing
180 tons of CO_2

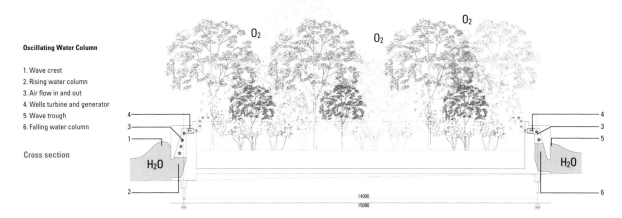

Oscillating Water Column

1. Wave crest
2. Rising water column
3. Air flow in and out
4. Wells turbine and generator
5. Wave trough
6. Falling water column

Cross section

View from the beach

Coralscape

Seawater pool at 8:30 p.m.

Coralscape begins with an understanding of the local environment and habitats and brings advanced sustainable technology to address the issues of climate change and drought conditions in Southern California.

The artwork connects many different layers in the environment. Inspired by coral reefs, the installation creates resources that give back to the ecosystem surrounding it. Using artificial photosynthesis, *Coralscape* takes CO_2 from the atmosphere and combines it with sunlight and water to create a solar fuel. The fuel can be utilized in various forms, but for the purpose of this installation, energy is used to power the Santa Monica Pier and local shops and residences.

The process of artificial photosynthesis begins with harvesting solar energy through solar cells located along the visible surface of the towers. Large extractors, placed behind the photovoltaic cells, pull carbon dioxide and humidity from the air. The energy harvested from the photovoltaic skin then creates an electric current that separates hydrogen, carbon, and oxygen. Solar fuel is created and stored, and oxygen is returned into the atmosphere as the only by-product of production.

TEAM
Jonathan Wang, Hector Bello,
Manh Tran, Zhihang Zhou

TEAM LOCATION
Los Angeles (CA), USA

ENERGY TECHNOLOGIES
photovoltaic panels, electrolysis,
artificial photosynthesis for
solar fuel

WATER TECHNOLOGIES
atmospheric water generation

ANNUAL CAPACITY
5,000 MWhe
100,000 liters of drinking water

Beach view at 11:45 a.m.

Main entry at 7:00 p.m.

Seawater pool at 6:30 p.m.

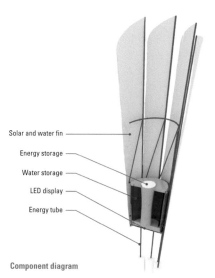

Solar and water fin

Energy storage

Water storage

LED display

Energy tube

Component diagram

RODS
(Radian Oceanic Data Sensors)

Radiant Oceanic Data Sensors (RODS) provides sophisticated oceanic data collection that encourages further exploration of tidal and wave power technologies. A matrix of rods provides real-time data to visitors on land. The artwork moves with the waves while visually dissolving into the sea. This optimistic place requires a solution that is playful, sustainable, and informative. *RODS* continuously monitors conditions beneath the surface of Santa Monica Bay. These conditions are reflected in a radiant display of data-informed hues (DIH). The design increases community awareness, responsibility, participation, and education toward a more sustainable future through the collection and display of relevant data trends. As the waves pass, the generator within each buoy converts kinetic energy into electricity. Greater waves provide a stronger "glow" from *RODS*. Electricity is transmitted to the local grid through a series of underwater cables.

TEAM
Seung K. Ra, Minwoo Hahm,
Blake Mitchell, Bailey Brown,
Austin Mitchell

TEAM LOCATION
Stillwater (OK), USA

ENERGY TECHNOLOGIES
point absorber wave energy
converter

ANNUAL CAPACITY
4,000 MWh (less the energy
required for illuminated data
display)

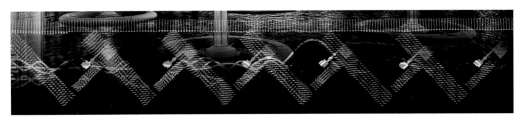

As each wave passes, the generator first speeds up, then slows down again, generating electricity from 0 to 500 volts. On more tumultuous days the amount of energy increases allowing for a stronger "glow" from the *RODS*. Underutilized electricity is then moved into the *RODS* integration nodes and transferred to the local grid through a series of cables.

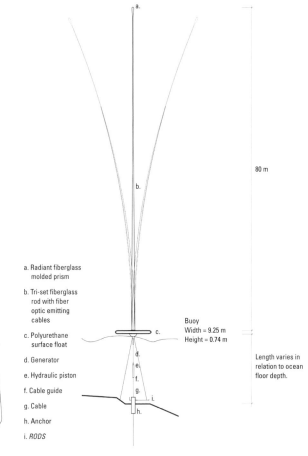

80 m

a. Radiant fiberglass molded prism

b. Tri-set fiberglass rod with fiber optic emitting cables

c. Polyurethane surface float

d. Generator

e. Hydraulic piston

f. Cable guide

g. Cable

h. Anchor

i. *RODS*

Buoy
Width = 9.25 m
Height = 0.74 m

Length varies in relation to ocean floor depth.

a. Polyurethane surface float

b. Generator

c. Hydraulic piston

d. Cable guide

e. Cable

a. Cable

b. Anchor

c. *RODS* integration node

a. Radiant fiberglass molded orb

b. Tri-set fiberglass rod with fiber-optic emitting cable tapering from 100 mm to 900 mm

a. Tri-set fiberglass rods 144 mm diameter

b. Cast polymer water retentive coating

c. Fiber-optic threads

d. Fiberglass single-walled tube: 450 mm diameter with 11 mm thickness

The Ocean Still
Lagrimas de Santa Monica

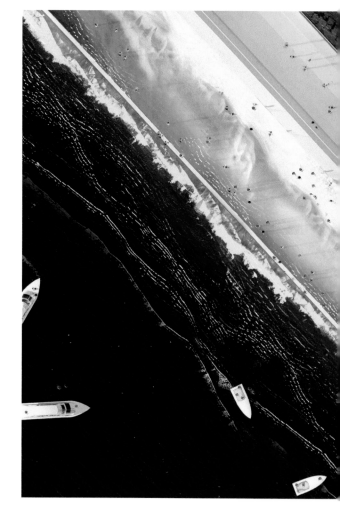

The twin springs that inspired Santa Monica's name were fabled to be the tears of a saint. At a time of growing thirst in California, *The Ocean Still* augments this sacred source of water by transforming seawater into fresh water, using only the energy of the sun. A large, transparent enclosure—a solar still perched on the old breakwater—makes a surface for collecting the saint's pure tears once again. This simple, premodern technology concentrates sunlight, distills salt water, and condenses fresh water on a glass shell. The entire breakwater structure, including the passive solar still and its complex of pools, celebrates the many forms of water as well as the residue of desalination.

Fusing urban needs and pleasure, the expanded breakwater complex recalls the history of the Santa Monica Pier as municipal sewage utility and its vital role in urban metabolism. Now, as before, the processes that make city life possible are tied to entertainment and destination—water production as spectacle.

Inside *The Ocean Still* solar radiant heat is absorbed and concentrated. The seawater evaporates. As it condenses on the glass shell, a collection channel diverts the pure distillate into a cistern and to the pier. The angled glass walls face due south, absorbing maximum solar heat and exploiting the flow of prevailing westerly and southwesterly winds.

The concentrated saline brine that results from desalination exits from a low point into the "brine pool"—a long, deep swimming pool that induces the body to float. Swimmers churn the brine water with their movements, maintaining the water at a consistent density.

When the brine waters approach the pool's capacity they flow onto the "mixing beach." Here, short walls allow for waves to crash and stir the concentrate—brine mixing with seawater. This slow reclamation of diluted brine back to the Pacific Ocean prevents the dead zones associated with industrial desalination. The shallow slope of sand and gravel at the "mixing beach" creates a protected habitat for marine fauna, and an idyllic floating coast for California sunbathers.

The Ocean Still encourages hope in simple technologies that will not readily become obsolete. Drought and thirst cannot be easily solved at the push of a button. Thoughtful interventions in our lives and landscapes, beyond providing solutions, have the capacity to engage the desires and delights of the senses.

TEAM
Nuith Morales, Stephanie Hsia, Courtney A. Goode, Michelle Arevalos Franco, Helen E. Kongsgaard

TEAM LOCATION
Boston (MA), USA

WATER TECHNOLOGIES
solar distillation

ANNUAL CAPACITY
9 million liters of drinking water

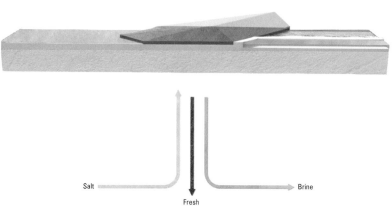

Salt · Fresh · Brine

The Ocean Still's axis is aligned due west. At dusk, especially during the equinox, *The Ocean Still* refracts sunlight, creating an optical spectacle.

Suspended in brine

Seawater Warming

1. Wave action charges the warming pool with seawater.
2. The warm, salty water is pumped into the still.

Making Fresh Water

3. The salt water evaporates, condenses, and is collected in a distillate channel.
4. Fresh water is harvested from breakwater cisterns into pier-bound fresh water ferries.
5. *The Ocean Still* provides drinking water for visitors to the Santa Monica Pier.

Brine Collection

6. Brine is released into the brine pool once salinity has increased three-fold.
7. As brine reaches the upper weep holes it moves into the mixing pool for dilution.

Brine Slowly Released

8. Wave action dilutes and recaptures brine back to the Pacific Ocean.

Enveloped between sky and sea

Tidal 94

TEAM
Alex Collins, Ben Llewellyn,
Dylan Tiss, Kyle Pollack

TEAM LOCATION
Eugene (OR), USA

ENERGY TECHNOLOGIES
tidal energy (used to drive water
movement)

WATER TECHNOLOGIES
reverse osmosis desalination,
Fresnel-assisted solar distillation

ANNUAL CAPACITY
1.3 billion liters of drinking water
100 million kilograms of sea salt

Tidal 94 is an extension of the axis
created by Santa Monica Boulevard
and the pier.

Inspired by the form of a water droplet and designed for efficiency, *Tidal 94* represents a beautiful convergence of form and function. These drops in the ocean off the Santa Monica Pier represent a revolution in water production. If enough drops fall along the coastline, they could flood Southern California with fresh water!

Conventional technologies to create fresh drinking water from seawater are prohibitively energy-intensive and damaging to surrounding ecosystems.

Powered by the gravitational pull of the Moon and focused solar heat, *Tidal 94* separates seawater into fresh drinking water and crystallized sea salt. The localization of the system engages the public in the spectacle of infrastructure and lowers the environmental footprint of water production.

The tidal pump and cylinder system act as a large syringe. When the tide goes out and the floats drop, suction is created in the cylinders on the deck. This suction pulls water from the sub-sand seawater intake to fill the cylinders until the tide slacks. As the tide comes in, pressure is created as the ocean pushes up on the large buoyant floats. This immense pressure forces the water that has filled the cylinders through a reverse osmosis filtration system. The resulting fresh water is directed toward the storage tank. The force utilized in this system is slow, methodical, and incredibly powerful.

One negative externality of modern desalination plants is the disposal of the high salt brine, which can result in the destruction of marine ecosystems. Rather than disposing of excess salt brine into the sea, *Tidal 94* harvests sea salt from the ocean. The salty brine that results from the reverse osmosis process is directed to the evaporation tents, filling a large shallow dish. Fresnel lenses focus the suns' rays throughout the day to heat the brine and bring it to a boil. Salt is left in the dish while water vapor condenses and collects.

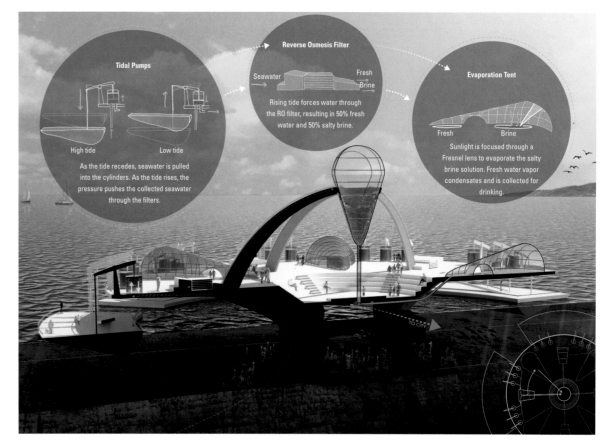

The platforms are sized to supply specific neighborhoods of Santa Monica with their fresh drinking water needs. Views from the decks and water-level floats offer an experience unique to

Santa Monica. By bringing water generation into the city and integrating it into daily life, *Tidal 94* increases public awareness of energy and water generation and consumption.

Tidal 94 separates ocean seawater into fresh drinking water and crystallized sea salt. The localization of drinking water and salt production engages the public in the spectacle of infrastructure.

Flight Energy

It seems as though the general public is split on the aesthetics of renewable energy. It's either beautiful or an eyesore. This controversy informs the design process for *Energy Flight*. Here a typical wind farm is transformed into something that everyone can react to and enjoy.

The artwork celebrates the ecosystem of the maritime birds that exhibit grace and beauty, soaring down to the water's surface and taking off again. The view of a bird or group of birds flying off into the sunset can be majestic and serene. This is the feeling captured in the form of *Energy Flight*.

A wind farm off of the Santa Monica Pier becomes four energy birds taking off into the sky. Each of the four birds is made up of approximately 85 wind turbines with a rotor diameter of six meters and mounting heights ranging from three to 44 meters. Each wind turbine is offset from the one ahead and set back by four meters. Turbulence created from one turbine can affect the performance of another in its wake. Each of these small wind turbines is placed in a diagonal pattern and at varying heights in order to reduce the "wake effect."

The foundations are made from eco-concrete that contains aggregates to allow for attachment of organisms such as oysters, coral, or barnacles. This will create a new reef system to attract life to the area. The tower of the wind turbine is meant to blend into the surroundings so that they do not obstruct the view of the "birds in flight." The column is chrome-finished stainless steel, making it almost invisible from shore. The rotor blades are made of white-coated steel to stand out against the landscape and give visual form to the installation.

Flight Energy birds take off into the sunset.

Eco-concrete foundations will create a new reef.

TEAM
Paige Collins

TEAM LOCATION
Boulder (CO), USA

ENERGY TECHNOLOGIES
horizontal axis wind turbine (HAWT)

ANNUAL CAPACITY
500 MWh

The height of the wind turbines range from 3 to 44 meters. Each bird formation has a wingspan of 50 meters from above. The birds each take up an area of 2,000 m².

The Beacon

TEAM
Timothy Tay, Lance Hassani, Ted Pan

TEAM LOCATION
Pomona (CA), USA

ENERGY TECHNOLOGIES
concentrated solar thermal power (CSP), point absorber wave energy converter (similar to Carnegie Wave Energy CETO™), rotating mass wave energy converter (similar to Wello Penguin™)

WATER TECHNOLOGIES
reverse osmosis desalination, oyster bed biofiltration

ANNUAL CAPACITY
11,000 MWh (less energy used for on-site desalination)

The Beacon points us to a near future in which humans have forged a bond with marine life—a parallel convergence of species in balance with the environment and with recognition of our mutual dependency.

The design categorizes the site into three layers: land, sea, and sky. The artwork incorporates symbols to represent these layers and binds them together through their interactions.

Inspired by the form of a jellyfish, a monumental structure stands tall as a new symbol for the City of Santa Monica. Spiral "tentacles" emerging from the top region of the tower convey the unity between all living things both on land and in the water.

A field of heliostats focuses sunlight onto the solar tower receiver, producing electricity for the city, and providing shade for visitors on the tessellated patterned walkways below.

The central tower extends its reach underwater where low-temperature thermal desalination (LTTD) creates fresh water from seawater. In addition, a biofilter habitat incorporates large quantities of oysters along the breakwater and helps to keep the Santa Monica Bay free from pollution.

Two types of wave power buoys provide additional electricity from wave action. The rotating mass type devices are incorporated into the pattern of the walkway, while the point absorber buoys are scattered throughout, barely visible below the surface of the water.

These advancements in energy technology on display here will mold a thriving and more sustainable future.

Section Legend

1. Central tower
2. Heliostats
3. Moving landscape (play area)
4. Transparent platform
5. Kelp forest / wildlife habitat
6. Buoy wave actuators
7. Rotating mass

Section

Conspicuous Habitat

TEAM
Andres Raygada, Kevin Lei,
Antonio De Jesus

TEAM LOCATION
Pomona (CA), USA

ENERGY TECHNOLOGIES
point absorber wave energy
converter

ANNUAL CAPACITY
5,000 MWh

Conspicuous Habitat serves both the aquatic environment and the urban grid. Its form is composed of overlapping linear elements emerging from the ocean and into the atmosphere where their expressive structure reminds visitors of the complex ecology beneath the waves.

Attached to the buoyant pillars, a system of nets creates a new marine habitat for mussels and oysters. Each of these species at their mature stage can sift up to 5 liters of water per hour—a biological filtration system for a cleaner Santa Monica Bay.

The piles gradually start descending, and floating beams begin to emerge. These buoyant pillars express the energy of the ocean through their movement, while harnessing the kinetic energy provided by the ocean waves to generate electricity for the urban grid. Each buoyant pillar has a peak capacity of 300 kWh per day. With 223 buoyant configurations deployed throughout the site, *Conspicuous Habitat* can generate electricity for more than 500 homes in Santa Monica. A small portion of the electricity generated is used to illuminate the artwork at night.

A visual density is created by various overlapping linear, stainless steel elements. This compact mesh becomes an underwater marine habitat with an artificial reef—a safe and protective environment for a variety of fauna. Within the gaps created by the artificial reef are more buoyant luminosities bobbing perpendicular to the ocean waves.

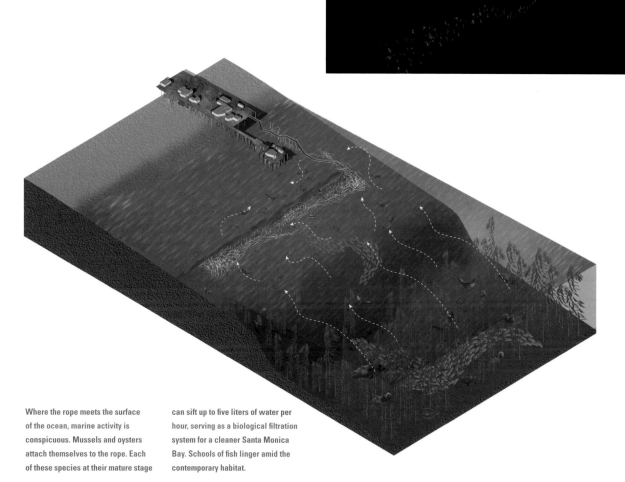

Where the rope meets the surface of the ocean, marine activity is conspicuous. Mussels and oysters attach themselves to the rope. Each of these species at their mature stage can sift up to five liters of water per hour, serving as a biological filtration system for a cleaner Santa Monica Bay. Schools of fish linger amid the contemporary habitat.

Plant Drinking Water

TEAM
Wilhelm Scherübl, Philippe Jans,
Charles Rauchs, Therese Leick
(TAB)

TEAM LOCATION
Vienna, Austria

WATER TECHNOLOGIES
reverse osmosis desalination,
living forest

ANNUAL CAPACITY
10 million liters of drinking water

An oasis of green in the middle of the ocean seems simply like a forest surrounded by water. During high tide it is unreachable, but during low tide visitors are welcome to walk out to this oversized pot of plants along an exposed path.

Fresh water is created from fog and rainfall. Plants and vegetation play an important role in filtering and capturing this water. One hectare of drinking water forest provides the water demand of 20 people. *Plant Drinking Water* therefore creates a long-term effect on Santa Monica and the region by adding more vegetation to affect the hydrological cycle without the need for highly technical solutions.

During high tide, a semipermeable membrane on the outside of the platform reduces the percentage of salt in the water for natural irrigation. From the perimeter area of the sculpture to the middle area, a zoning into four categories of plant groups creates a transition from salt-tolerant to salt-intolerant plants. The outer plants act as an additional filter for interior plants. The vegetation transpires and induces water vapor and precipitation into the hydrological cycle.

Plant Drinking Water is a living sculpture of vegetation that invites people to accept responsibility for the environment by carrying home plants from the oversized pot. This participation with the ever-changing artwork will help to green each individual garden and the City of Santa Monica in its entirety.

This oasis of green in the middle of the ocean seems like a forest surrounded by water. During high tide it is not reachable.

At low tide the oasis of green can be approached.

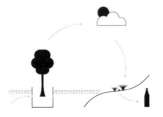

Section

Santa Monica Regatta
Race toward Sustainability

TEAM
Jordi Barba (BC Estudio Architects), Beatriz Yuste, Zuzana Prochazkova (Onda Studio), Melissa Prieto

TEAM LOCATION
Barcelona, Spain

ENERGY TECHNOLOGIES
thin-film photovoltaic

WATER TECHNOLOGIES
fog harvesting

ANNUAL CAPACITY
5,800 MWh
1 million liters of drinking water

The useful surface area can hold more than 16,000 solar panels. Behind the solar array there is an efficient membrane designed to capture the water vapor from air.

Sails remind us of the origins of the Santa Monica Pier. From a distance *Santa Monica Regatta* appears as if fourteen vessels have arrived to port from far beyond. Something about the scale is intriguing. Fourteen gracious silhouettes emerge from the sea, 50 and 80 meters tall, facing the sun and the wind silently.

Visitors to the Santa Monica Pier can now continue their journey further to the sea. Catwalks descend closer to the water where the jingle of boat sounds once again fills the Santa Monica Harbor. Just beyond the "green island" a sustainability race is on!

Santa Monica Regatta is a photovoltaic installation and water harvester. Taking advantage of the climate, *Santa Monica Regatta* produces solar energy with high efficiency when the sun is shining. When the weather is foggy or rainy, water collection is at its peak.

Behind the array of PV panels there is an efficient membrane, a synthetic surface employing chemistry and structural engineering. The surface consists of two polymer layers: the top is hydrophilic, while the bottom is hydrophobic, making water droplets detach as soon as they become large enough.

Drops of water are collected on the membrane and gravity makes them flow along the surface. They are gathered in channels situated at the base of the membrane section. Each section covers two rows of PV panels. Water is pumped from sails to the island with a system of buoys that also serve as navigational guides protecting the artwork.

The "green island" is made of a mix of recycled materials. The envelope of recycled concrete creates a new habitat and helps to purify the seawater of Santa Monica Bay. The center of the island protects the balance of the electrical systems and water collection facilities. The "green island" becomes an educational and relaxing spot where people can acquire knowledge about the importance of conservation, while observing how much water and electricity are produced in real time.

Underground connections transmit the energy and water collected by the sails to the "green island" storage area, and from there to the inhabitants of Santa Monica.

Energy Funnel

TEAM
Akira Sogo, Mami Sogo, Akane Hattori (SOGO AUD)

TEAM LOCATION
Tokyo, Japan

ENERGY TECHNOLOGIES
solar updraft tower, point absorber wave energy converter

WATER TECHNOLOGIES
reverse osmosis desalination

ANNUAL CAPACITY
15,000 MWh
20 million liters of drinking water

Each of the 23 *Energy Funnels* rises 17 meters above the fluctuating sea level and is 32 meters in diameter.

Energy Funnel works to channel the natural energy of the coastline of Santa Monica. Rather than a power plant, it is a translator of resources—solar energy and ocean waves are translated into electricity and fresh water.

The design collects fresh water from moisture by taking advantage of the thermal difference between sun-heated air and cold ocean current. The shape is abstract and simple to fit in with the beautiful coastal landscape of Santa Monica.

Global climate change requires society to develop redundant systems in many respects. *Energy Funnel* utilizes multiple energy sources—a reflection of Santa Monica's natural diversity and our need for resiliency.

Energy Funnel is composed of two different energy generators and a fresh water collector. One of the energy generators is an updraft tower, which uses solar power and sea breeze. The air beneath the ETFE skin is heated by the sun. The temperature differential between the warmer air within the greenhouse and the cool ambient breezes above stimulates an updraft effect—constant airflow through the tower—which is captured by a turbine.

The other energy generator is the buoy-type wave energy converter. The float of the *Energy Funnel* moves up and down in response to the motion of the waves. This linear motion produces electricity, and the float system enables the energy funnel to adjust to the tidal fluctuations.

Finally, *Energy Funnel* works as a fresh water collector by stimulating the condensation of moisture from the air. Within the process of the updraft tower, heated humid air rises and touches the cooled dew condenser. The dew condenser is made of cast aluminum alloy having high thermal conductivity, and is cooled by the cold ocean currents of the Pacific Ocean.

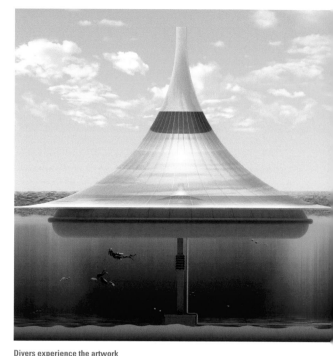

Divers experience the artwork from beneath.

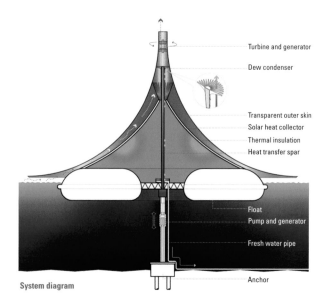

Turbine and generator

Dew condenser

Transparent outer skin
Solar heat collector
Thermal insulation
Heat transfer spar

Float
Pump and generator

Fresh water pipe

Anchor

System diagram

A Field in Motion

TEAM
Maëlle Bodet, Maxime Bonnefoy, Serge Akopian

TEAM LOCATION
Paris, France

ENERGY TECHNOLOGIES
point absorber wave energy converter with linear alternators (similar to Seabased™)

ANNUAL CAPACITY
3,000 MWh

| Take wave motion | shift it up | in a kinetic roof. | Connect the two seas | to produce electricity | through a public space. |

Sculpted by the sea breeze, waves are tirelessly reaching the coast and spreading their energy on the shore. Sculpted by the Moon, tides are a manifestation of the rotation of the Moon around the Earth.

The artificial landscape of *A Field in Motion* emerges from the sea to harness its energy and bring people closer to the process. As an interface between two worlds, the kinetic installation brings natural forces together with human activities. The infinite renewable energy of water motion links poetry to the subtle power of celestial mechanics.

An extension of the Santa Monica Pier, *A Field in Motion* is a park raised on stilts, a playful area where pleasure and awareness meet each other.

This landscape is modulated in order to propose spaces with climatic and functional variations. While rising and ebbing, tides are covering or revealing this landscape, changing the atmosphere. When the tide is low, the entirety of the surface is accessible and areas for sports activities emerge. When the tide is high, half of the surface is under the water. However, all paths remain dry and accessible. The topographic platform is connected to the pier at its elevation and slowly reaches the sea level, taking into consideration the breakwater volume.

The roof level varies following the tide. It is not only imitating waves in its form, but also transferring their motion to electricity instantaneously in its function. The columns are linear coil generators. The up-and-down movement of a permanent magnet generates a voltage in the copper wire by induction. Each module is 1.5 meters high, the average of wave oscillations. One column is made from five to eight modules and linked to one buoy. At night, a small amount of the produced electricity is used to light the project with LED lights shining with intensity according to the waves.

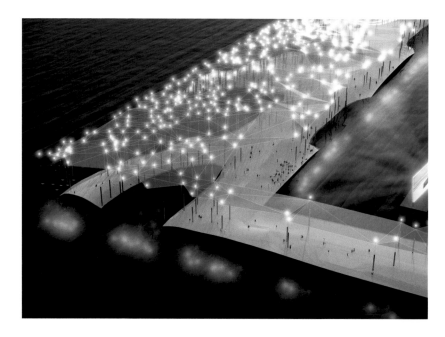

Mounting plate and steel bars
Copper coil and glass protection
Permanent magnet
Rubber
Magnet guide line
Steel rod

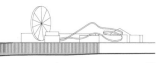

Ocean Spring

TEAM
Radic Gojko, Natasa Stefanovic

TEAM LOCATION
Belgrade, Serbia

ENERGY TECHNOLOGIES
oscillating water column wave energy converter, point absorber wave energy converters

WATER TECHNOLOGIES
reverse osmosis desalination

ANNUAL CAPACITY
1,200 MWh
500 million liters of drinking water

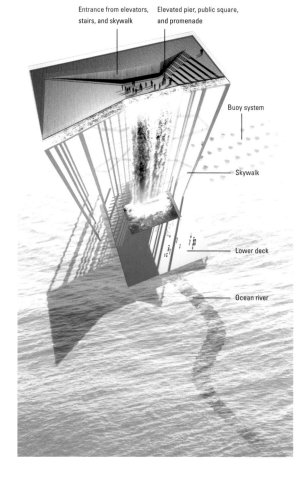

Entrance from elevators, stairs, and skywalk

Elevated pier, public square, and promenade

Buoy system

Skywalk

Lower deck

Ocean river

Ocean Spring is an extension of the Santa Monica Pier, a promenade, a place for gatherings, and a unique landmark for Santa Monica symbolizing the power of nature. Using the latest technology it is also a factory for desalination of seawater and a facility for the production of clean, renewable energy.

The structure is composed of two platform-terraces—one at the height of the old pier and the other raised 80 meters in height. Taking a walk through a Skywalk Trail provides a unique experience of Santa Monica Bay and an education in the latest sustainable technologies. The lower platform has the Waterfall Mist Adventure, which can provide relief on hot days. The upper deck is public space for gathering and special events. *Ocean Spring* is not only visually connected with the old pier but it is also connected by an underwater walking trail. Underwater River is both a pipeline for fresh water and a scenic trail that connects the Santa Monica Pier Aquarium with its latest extension, *Ocean Spring*.

In order to create a transparent structure that will not obstruct the view to the open sea, the Whale Tail Terraces are supported with a forest of thin columns and slabs through which the Skywalk Trail winds.

Oscillating water columns in the lower structure and an array of buoy-type wave energy converters provide the power to pump the water through the desalination process and to the reservoirs at the top of the tower.

The central part of the structure is a water treatment plant organized vertically. Reservoirs with desalinated water and brine located at the very top present a large kinetic energy potential (a battery storing the energy used to pump the water to the top). These also serve structurally as a fluid seismic damper.

The energy of the water falling from such a great height is captured by turbines integrated into downspout pipes and water wheels under the open waterfall to provide excess electricity to the city grid. Fresh water goes into the pool, situated on the lower platform and flows through Underwater River to the mainland for further processing and use.

When the wind speed adversely affects the operation of the waterfall, water is diverted to the turbine in the downspout pipe and Underwater River to prevent waste.

Visitors enjoy the spectacle of
Ocean Spring.

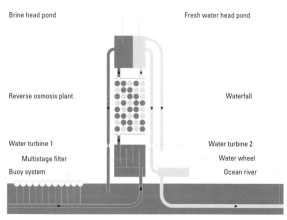

Brine head pond

Fresh water head pond

Reverse osmosis plant

Waterfall

Water turbine 1

Water turbine 2

Multistage filter

Water wheel

Buoy system

Ocean river

Onda de la Luz

Shrouded tidal turbines can operate in a variety of sites and in a range of low and high water flow environments.

Thin-film dye-sensitized panels are semitransparent, flexible, durable, and colorful. The design includes 18,290 m² of panels.

From a distance, *Onda de la Luz* is experienced as a ribbon of bright pink dye-sensitized solar material emerging as a curving plane from the extended wooden pier. At the end of the day, as the ribbon absorbs the last rays of solar radiation, energy from the waves turns the ribbon into an illuminated path, guiding visitors along the ocean surface.

Onda de la Luz utilizes two complementary renewable energy sources—thin-film dye-sensitized photovoltaic panels and shrouded tidal turbines—to achieve maximum energy output and to provide more consistent power on cloudy days or days with small tidal differentials. With this dual approach, the artwork will contribute significantly to California's Renewable Portfolio Standard of 50% renewable energy by 2030. Because no tidal energy projects have yet been installed in California, *Onda de la Luz* will also be a pilot project to demonstrate the technology's efficacy in the Pacific Ocean to meet state goals.

Thirty-three shrouded vertical axis tidal turbines of three different sizes spin below the ocean surface, harnessing the incredible power of the ocean to provide energy throughout the night. Shrouded tidal turbines concentrate the flow of water, allowing the turbine to harvest three times the amount of energy of an unshrouded turbine. Marine species are also protected from the tidal turbines by the shroud barrier isolating the blades.

Mirrors rise vertically from the turbine structure above the pier, slowly spinning with the shrouded tidal turbines below. Visitors will be attracted to the reflections of themselves and the surroundings, and come to learn more about renewable energy and the life beneath the ocean surface.

Lower deck

TEAM
Sheena Zhang, Meghan Lewis, Emily Wier, Lynsey Gaudioso

TEAM LOCATION
New Haven (CT), USA

ENERGY TECHNOLOGIES
dye-sensitized solar cells (DSSC), shrouded vertical axis hydro turbine (VAHT) similar to the Davidson-Hill Venturi Turbine™

ANNUAL CAPACITY
4,200 MWh (DSSC)
15,000 MWh (VAHT)

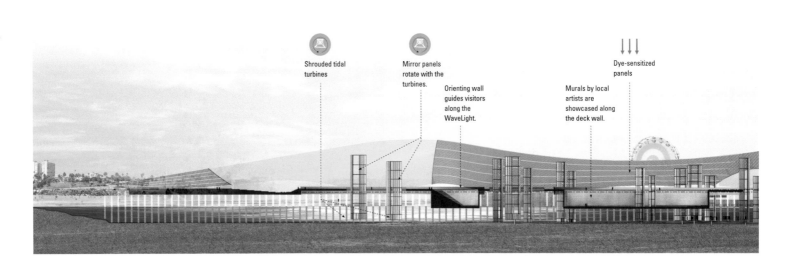

Shrouded tidal turbines

Mirror panels rotate with the turbines.

Orienting wall guides visitors along the WaveLight.

Murals by local artists are showcased along the deck wall.

Dye-sensitized panels

Swell

Swell as seen at low tide.

Two looming arches float above the surface of the water. From afar the structure appears to be static, with only slight movement from the rolling waves. As the Ferris wheel turns and the roller coaster glides, the structure begins to transform. What was once two arches sitting above the water is now two thin bands sitting on the horizon.

Swell is a dynamic installation located on the far side of the breakwater that is constantly manipulated by the tides and the waves of Santa Monica Bay. The structure resembles the wave-like shape of the West Coaster that winds through Pacific Park. The large arches of the structure highlight the tension between man and the natural environment.

Swell uses buoy wave power technology, an uninterrupted power supply. The buoy shafts and the generator are located below the surface of the water, leaving only the two arches visible from shore. The structure is a sheet of aluminum coated in a clear zinc-phosphate paint that measures 20 meters long and 3 meters wide. The four points of the arch are connected to the buoys, which keep the structure afloat. A hinge allows the structure to fold and release based on the tides.

There are two main movements of *Swell:* the bending or flattening of the structure in response to the tides, and the more rapid oscillations created by the waves as it generates electricity.

TEAM
Stephanie Koenig, Paul Grawitz

TEAM LOCATION
Vancouver, Canada

ENERGY TECHNOLOGIES
PowerBuoy™ 3 (PB3) point absorber wave energy converter by Ocean Power Technologies

ANNUAL CAPACITY
5,280 MWh

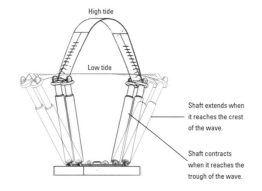

High tide

Low tide

Shaft extends when it reaches the crest of the wave.

Shaft contracts when it reaches the trough of the wave.

Swell as seen at high tide.

Melody of the Ocean

TEAM
Xie Xinye, Xiong Enwei, Yang Jinwen, Sheng Jing, Chen Xi

TEAM LOCATION
Wuhan, China

ENERGY TECHNOLOGIES
thin-film photovoltaic, submerged pressure differential wave energy converter

(Archimedes Wave Swing™), point absorber wave energy converter, overtopping wave energy converter

ANNUAL CAPACITY
10,000 MWh

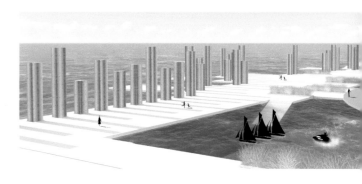

Melody of the Ocean emphasizes the importance of sustainable development by combining energy exploration with landscape design. It makes visible the rhythm of the sea waves.

Several types of flat planes constitute an uneven boundary symbolizing the wandering coastline. Some of the planes remain fixed in their position, concealing power buoys underneath. Others are secured to Archimedes Wave Swings™ and move along with the waves through horizontal movements.

At the center of the composition is an overtopping wave energy converter that visitors can experience up close. Wave water is allowed to rush over the edges and into the landscape reservoir, creating a waterfall-like experience. Once full, the water is allowed to flow back into the sea through turbines near the bottom of the reservoir. Wind and gravity combine to create useful energy.

Vertical solar panel boxes also move up and down along with the waves. The path they trace is similar to a sound wave of music. After sunset, the LED lights installed on the boxes create a beautiful scene like a sound wave dancing over the sea.

As an educational amenity for Santa Monica, *Melody of the Ocean* will demonstrate three types of wave energy conversion technologies in a way that visitors can observe in real time and at a close distance—building a sense of responsibility and empathy to protect the natural world.

Melody of the Ocean serves as a multifunctional scenic destination for Santa Monica. Several of the horizontal planes can work together to create an activity for exhibitions, music festivals, and other events. Some planes also function as docks so that visitors can take small boats to reach the artwork.

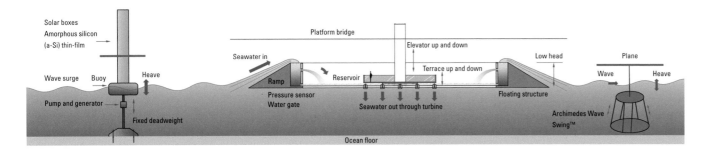

Dew Screen

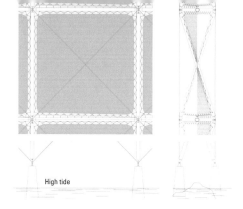

Detail elevation and section of one structural bay

In sensitive environments like Santa Monica Bay it is important to consider light and soft infrastructures, as opposed to highly technical and synthetic systems, the externalities and risks of which we can no longer afford. The more our economy and ecology are unstable, the more we have to be creative. Great advances in computer science show us how important it is to develop agile responses to contemporary challenges.

Infrastructures are often thought of as heavy elements that aggressively shape land. Highways, dams, dikes, and embankments tend to disrupt the landscape with imported materials (aggregates, sand, concrete) and aesthetics. But how can these heavy materials be resilient?

There are no human creations heavy and strong enough to forever resist nature. We need to redefine infrastructure from a planning perspective. Thus, when we think of infrastructure that supports urban life and economy we have to shift our views and think of a lightweight, evolving, and lean structure.

There is an opportunity to think of infrastructures as landscape projects. They shape the earth and our relationship to the environment. More than simply providing water to a group of people, *Dew Screen* creates a symbol that binds us. Can the immensity of the ocean be the symbol that assembles us around fresh water?

The Santa Monica shore is influenced by the creation of an advection fog above the sea. It is known as the marine atmospheric boundary layer (MABL), and consists of a thousand-meter-thick layer of cool and moist maritime air immediately below a temperature inversion.

The water that fog contains can be harvested. It is possible with lean/low technologies to collect that water and transport it to the coast for use as drinking water or to support the leisure activities on the beach.

TEAM
Guillaume de Morsier, Valentin Kuník, Angélique Kuenzle (Kuník de Morsier architectes)

TEAM LOCATION
Lausanne, Switzerland

WATER TECHNOLOGIES
fog harvesting

ANNUAL CAPACITY
114 million liters of drinking water

A soft landscape infrastructure

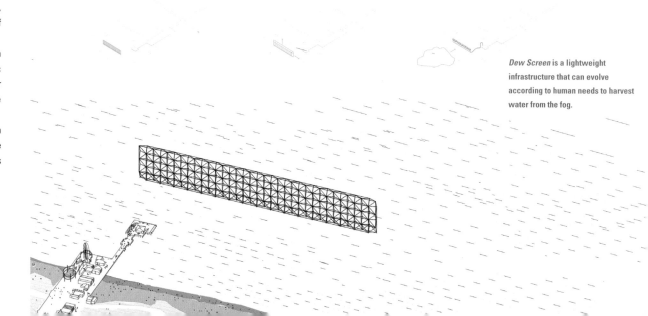

Dew Screen is a lightweight infrastructure that can evolve according to human needs to harvest water from the fog.

Solar Reef

Enhancing the existing breakwater while using it to provide structural support, *Solar Reef* simulates a natural coral reef with 75 half-spheres that capture solar energy with concentrated photovoltaic (CPV) technology. CPV uses a Fresnel lens that concentrates sunlight and routes it to a high-efficiency multijunction photovoltaic cell.

In good weather, a new wooden deck provides access to the hemispheres. Visitors can get an entirely new perspective on the Santa Monica Pier, the city, and the sea.

Three different sizes of solar concentrators are proposed to simulate scale variability within natural reefs, and are distributed throughout the breakwater at random.

All of the hemispheres face south with an inclination of 56°. Inside each module, the internal Fresnel lens tracks the sun in its path across the sky.

Solar Reef encourages the healing of natural reefs by providing carbon-free electricity for generations to come.

TEAM
Alberto Fernández Gonzalez,
Benjamin Fernández Gonzalez

TEAM LOCATION
Santiago, Chile

ENERGY TECHNOLOGIES
concentrated photovoltaic (CPV)

ANNUAL CAPACITY
600 MWh

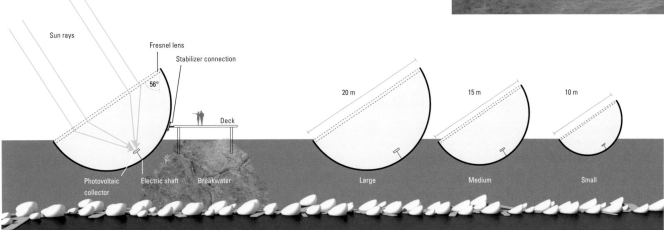

Longitudinal elevation

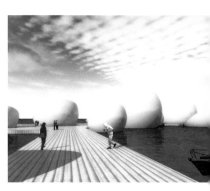

LAGI 2016 YOUTH PRIZE

[1] Joe Myers, "What New Jobs Will Exist in 2035?" (World Economic Forum, February 29, 2016). See http://www.weforum.org/agenda/2016/02/these-scienctists-have-predicted-which-jobs-will-be-human-only-in-2035. The online article cites: Stefan Hajkowicz, Andrew Reeson, Lachlan Rudd, Alexandra Bratanova, Leonie Hodgers, Claire Mason, and Naomi Boughen, "Tomorrow's Digitally Enabled Workforce," (Commonwealth Scientific and Industrial Research Organization, January 2016).

According to a recent report highlighted by the World Economic Forum[1], as automation continues to change the workplace, the highest valued skills are increasingly dominated by creativity, critical thinking, complex problem solving, cognitive flexibility, and emotional intelligence—all qualities that require the arts to be integrally interwoven into the fabric of our lives.

Providing STEAM education to high school students using the Arts as the delivery vehicle is an engaging way to instill an early interest in the scientific method, provide useful technical skills, and introduce systems thinking. Project-based learning can help students think creatively about design challenges in order to find innovative solutions.

With these thoughts in mind, and building off of the educational materials from past LAGI competitions, we launched a Youth Prize to coincide with the LAGI 2016 professional competition.

In addition to a custom Youth Prize design brief, we provided a 13-step Toolkit of activities that teachers and students could use to take them through the entire design process for the development of a land art generator for a site next to the Santa Monica Pier.

Entering a world already grappling with the issue of climate change, the high school students of today will be leading the design of our energy solutions of tomorrow. Through LAGI, we want to nurture a global community of young people equipped to design our new energy landscapes. The process of imagining renewable energy as artwork for public spaces is a great way to inspire young people to want to learn more about energy science and engineering.

The Youth Prize was open throughout the 2015–2016 school year, allowing classrooms to integrate the project into their curriculum. We were delighted by the embrace of the Toolkit by teachers and administrators, and the way that cross-disciplinary collaborations within schools brought teachers from many different subjects together for the challenge.

It was a pleasure to be able to speak in person at schools or video conference into classrooms to provide feedback and answer questions about the design brief. We're looking forward to continuing and expanding on the Youth Prize Toolkit in the years to come. For more information, see http://youth.landartgenerator.org.

"LAGI is building a global community of young people who are inspired and equipped to design the landscape of our clean energy future."

—Elizabeth Monoian and Robert Ferry
Founding Directors, Land Art Generator Initiative

LAGI 2016
YOUTH PRIZE

LAGI 2016 Youth Prize Design Site

LAGI 2016 YOUTH PRIZE DESIGN GUIDELINES

1. Your proposal for an artwork must be designed as a three-dimensional form that includes at least one kind of renewable energy technology. In your written description tell us what technology you've integrated and why.

2. How will your artwork fit onto the existing design site? How will people interact with it? Make sure that you show how big your artwork is (is it at the right scale?). In your sketches, write down some of the dimensions in feet or meters. Make sure that you haven't gone outside of the site boundary line!

3. Develop a message that you want to communicate to the people who will come to see your artwork (this is sometimes called the concept). Your message or concept can be absolutely anything you can imagine. Tell us about it in your written description.

4. How will your artwork relate to the natural world? Think about where the materials came from that you would use to build your full-scale artwork. Does your artwork disturb habitat of any animals, birds, or insects? Or does it provide new homes for wild creatures? Put some of these thoughts down in your written description.

LAGI 2016 STEAM TOOLKIT

The activities and presentations in the Toolkit were developed in collaboration with educators and follow the design process.

Activities in the Toolkit include:

Learn about Art Outside of the Gallery
Introduction to LAGI
Discover Design I
Discover Design II
Energy Fundamentals
Imagining Energy
LAGI Idea Generator
Sketching in Context
Make a Prototype
LAGI Youth Jury
Good Ideas Get Better
Your Creative Statement
Tell the World

LAGI 2016 YOUTH PRIZE JURY TEAM

Katie Henry
STEAM Educator, Ohio Public Schools

Sandra Preiss
STEM Consultant

Shaun Tomaszewski, MEd, BPhil
Coordinator of STEAM Education,
Pittsburgh Public Schools

LAGI 2016 YOUTH PRIZE

Youth Winning Submission

The Octopus's Garden

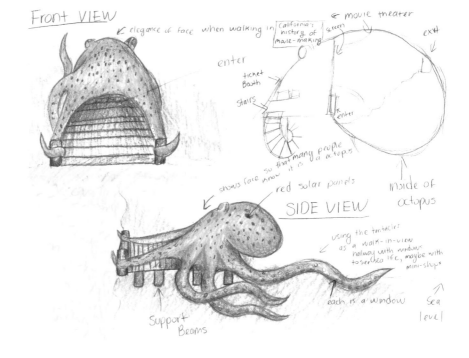

TEAM
Marina Heredia, Leo Mei, Raul Chavez, Michael Wood, Shanti Davis

TEAM LOCATION
Lancaster (CA), USA

ENERGY TECHNOLOGIES
flexible solar thin-film, wind turbine, solar pond, point absorber wave energy, converter

ANNUAL CAPACITY
2,600 MWh

HIGH SCHOOL
Quartz Hill High School, Antelope Valley Union High School District

TEACHER
Deepak Dhillonn

The Octopus's Garden is inspired by the California two-spot octopus. Around the artwork four unique habitats house eleven species that are indigenous to the Santa Monica Bay.

As visitors make their way from the beach and into the geodesic dome (the octopus's mantle) they are greeted with two cephalopod arms, each wrapped around a conch shell with a wind turbine inside. Once in the dome, the visitors discover a museum with information about local marine life. From there, they make their way to a viewing deck where they can look out to the horizon beyond the six other arms of the octopus.

On the surface of the octopus and along the boardwalk, translucent solar panels convert sunlight into electricity. The skin of the structure also heats up water that is fed into a solar pond. A Rankine cycle turbine uses the difference in temperature between the cold ocean water and the warm solar-heated water to generate additional electricity. Along the free-floating arms of the octopus, wave energy converting buoys also make electricity while the waves appear to give life to the creature.

Most of the energy from these systems is fed into the city's grid, but some is used to illuminate the land-side end of the octopus, mimicking the natural bioluminescence of some cephalopod species.

The end curls of the sea-side arms create micro-environments ideal for various species. Four arms contain rocks, kelp forests, and coral reefs. The last two arms house a rocky environment with eight species: two-spot octopus, round stingrays, California mussels, Norris top snail, bat star, ochre sea snail, sea urchin, and sand dollar. The furthest arm contains a kelp bed for kelp crab, club tipped anemone, and tube dwelling anemone. The curl of the closest arm contains a coral reef for sea stars such as the brittle star.

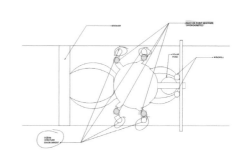

Fields of Golden Sun
The Eco Poppies

Youth Second Place Winner

TEAM
Austyn Adams, Jandy Alegre, Steven Aguilar, Ricardo Guzman, Blanca Zepeda, Fernando Martinez, Savannah Fournier, Daniel Ramirez, Lucas Lescano, Alexis Lorenana, Genesis Aquino, Jonathan Pinedo

TEAM LOCATION
Palmdale (CA), USA

ENERGY TECHNOLOGIES
thin-film solar, kinetic wind harvesting, point absorber wave energy converter

ANNUAL CAPACITY
2,500 MWh

HIGH SCHOOL
Palmdale High School, Antelope Valley Union High School District

TEACHER
Steven R. Calzada

Fields of Golden Sun is an expanse of California poppy flowers, a symbolic representation of Southern California and a familiar, recognizable, and playful form. This land art generator harnesses solar, kinetic, and tidal energy to help power existing needs such as the adjacent Santa Monica Pier. The flowers on the beach transform into water lilies as they work their way out into the surf. A walkway leads visitors through this transitional space and out into the ocean. The land-side poppies incorporate solar panels into their petals and generate additional energy by harvesting the back-and-forth movement of the stalk as it sways gently in the wind. The water lily generators utilize wave energy, taking advantage of the never-ending motion within the Pacific Ocean waters.

Along the walkway are places for visitors to rest and relax, and enjoy the shade and movement created by the poppy structures. At night the poppies are illuminated by LED lights placed along the stem and leaves.

Process note: The design began with drawings and sketches in various mediums created by the art department students. The ideas were then re-created in large sheets of cardboard, which were used as a platform for placing small solar panel cells so that we could learn what type would make the best choice for our design. Design and engineering students took the sketches and models and made the designs come to life using computer graphics and 3-D modeling programs to create digital renderings. Along the way, math, geometry, and physics students challenged the design while taking care to understand the correct incident angles for solar panel energy capturing.

Oasis

Youth Third Place Winner

TEAM
Hanna Wells, Sagar Kamath, Gabriel Tobias

TEAM LOCATION
Pittsburgh (PA), USA

ENERGY TECHNOLOGIES
flexible solar thin-film, piezoelectric stacked actuators (similar to *Windstalk* from LAGI 2010), point absorber wave energy converter

ANNUAL CAPACITY
2,000 MWh

HIGH SCHOOL
Creative and Performing Arts (CAPA) Magnet, Pittsburgh Public Schools

TEACHER
Allan Finch

Imagine spending a day by the ocean—walking along a boardwalk, engulfed in the morning mist of the salty air, and seagulls above. The boardwalk leads to a garden. Stepping into this wonderland, the atmosphere becomes more serene, with blossoming flowers and swaying grass. The path continues to weave through the hazy field of colors, as the flowers become increasingly monumental. At the end of the path lies an open flower, a gigantic blossom.

Oasis is a garden on the beach, inspired by nature and the beauty of Santa Monica. Reflecting the natural world, it invites visitors to question their own relationship with nature and the environment. The largest flowers along the boardwalk and the flower floating at the terminus are California poppies. The crocus is the model for the smaller flowers and the medium-sized petals mimic the anemone. An arrangement of benches and a central platform creates a "flower pavilion" for street performers or family picnics.

The petals of the flowers slant toward the south in order to create maximum energy from their flexible thin-film solar panel surfaces. The "grass" of *Oasis* is constructed from Windstalks—modeled from the design of a 2010 LAGI competition submission by Dario Nuñez Ameni and Thomas Siegl. The largest flower at the end of the boardwalk is designed to float up and down with the waves, constantly converting hydrokinetic energy into electricity.

Beginning at dusk, the flowers of this energy bouquet glow gently to create a perfect nightlife atmosphere.

Music of
the Wind

Visitors to this art installation adjacent to the Santa Monica Pier delight in the magical wonder of this energy landscape. There is an equalizing effect on the people walking through the artwork—everyone is dwarfed by the scale of the flowers, which call to mind scenes from a Lewis Carroll story.

Each flower is made using colorful thin-film solar materials that feed electricity into the city grid. With some of the stored energy collected during the day, the flowers come to life at night, illuminating the beach with a rotating array of colors and sounds. The sound and light reflect the direction and the strength of the wind. The central wind turbines have the dual benefit of generating electricity while also desalinating ocean water for use in fountains on site.

TEAM
Edly Reyes, Daniel Estrada,
Dylan Cabanlit

TEAM LOCATION
Lancaster (CA), USA

ENERGY TECHNOLOGIES
thin-film photovoltaic,
wind turbine

ANNUAL CAPACITY
1,200 MWh

HIGH SCHOOL
Eastside High School, Antelope
Valley Union High School District

TEACHER
Evelyn Rivas

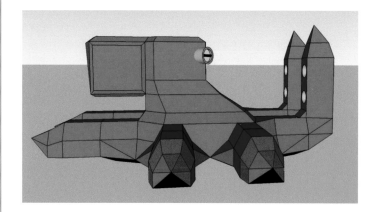

Solar Octopus

Solar Octopus is a larger-than-life sculpture of the California two-spot octopus set close to the shore and best viewed from the Santa Monica Pier. The artwork is roughly ten feet tall and almost completely covered in orange solar panels, with the exception of the bottom and the eyes of the octopus. Additional electricity is generated by four small wind turbines, which are placed within the two front arms of the octopus, resembling suckers.

The message of the artwork is that nature is important and a key part of our survival. The actual two-spot octopus along with other sea creatures help sustain the environment just as the sculpture will provide sustainable energy to help power the pier.

TEAM
Aidan Ray

TEAM LOCATION
Pittsburgh (PA), USA

ENERGY TECHNOLOGIES
tinted solar panels,
wind turbines

ANNUAL CAPACITY
500 MWh

HIGH SCHOOL
City Charter High School, City
Charter High School District

MENTOR
Trina Heimbach

BIOGRAPHIES,
GLOSSARY,
AND INDEX

BIOGRAPHIES

SHANNON DAUT

Shannon Daut leads the Cultural Affairs Division for the City of Santa Monica, where she works to integrate the arts into all aspects of life in the community. She was previously the Executive Director of the Alaska State Council on the Arts (ASCA). While there, she reimagined and reinvigorated the leadership role that the agency plays in the policies of the state, from tourism and economic development to education and Alaska Native cultural advancement. Prior to moving to Alaska, Daut was Deputy Director of the Western States Arts Federation (WESTAF), where she oversaw the organization's work in the areas of cultural policy and technology. Daut serves on the board of the National Performance Network/Visual Arts Network and has also served on the boards of the Association of Performing Arts Presenters and WESTAF. Daut received her bachelor's degree in communication arts/film from the University of Wisconsin, Madison, and her graduate degree in communication/rhetoric from the University of Colorado, Denver.

ROBERT FERRY

Robert Ferry is the co-founder of the Land Art Generator Initiative and Studied Impact Design. His focus is on designing places that achieve complete harmony with their local and global environments and with the people that use them. His "positive-impact" buildings that double as renewable energy power-plants have been featured in *Superlative Emirates* (Daab Publishing), several *Popular Science* magazine articles, and have been shown at international exhibitions.

With roots in new urbanism and environmental design, Robert has had the privilege to work on a wide range of net-zero and LEED certified developments, from single-family residential through $500 million mixed-use projects including Project 1 at Masdar City, Abu Dhabi. Robert is a graduate of Carnegie Mellon University and a LEED-accredited licensed architect.

His publications include *Regenerative Infrastructures, The Time Is Now: Public Art of the Sustainable City, New Energies, Powering Places,* and *A Field Guide to Renewable Energy Technologies.*

JAMES HARRIS

James Harris is the Deputy Director of the Santa Monica Pier Corporation and has been an active, regular part of the everyday life at the Pier since 1989. Known by many as the "Pier Historian," he is the author of *Santa Monica Pier: A Century on the Last Great Pleasure Pier* (2009) and the stage play *Save the Pier* (2015). He is also the founder and chair of the pop-up "Waterman Museum for a Day" committee, which annually exhibits Santa Monica's rich water sports history during the Santa Monica Pier Paddleboard Race & Ocean Festival.

BARRY LEHRMAN

A licensed landscape architect and Assistant Professor of Landscape Architecture at California State Polytechnic University, Pomona, Lehrman teaches the poetic expression of urban metabolic systems and used the 2016 LAGI competition for his winter 2016 landscape design studios.

Through the Aqueduct Futures Project (2012–2015), Lehrman addressed the century of antagonism and disenfranchisement wrought by the City of Los Angeles upon the Owens Valley by mapping the influence of the Los Angeles Aqueduct and defining future scenarios to empower the local community. The Aqueduct Futures Project was exhibited at Los Angeles Contemporary Exhibitions in the *After the Aqueduct* show (2015) and at Los Angeles City Hall (2013). His scholarship into the Los Angeles Aqueduct began with his 2005 MLA/MArch thesis (University of Pennsylvania) that proposed an alternative dust control landscape for Owens Lake. His writings on Owens Valley and the Aqueduct are included in *The Infrastructural City* (ACTAR 2008), *Arid Journal* (2013), and *Water Index* (ACTAR 2016).

GLEN LOWRY

Glen Lowry is a researcher, writer, editor, and publisher whose work investigates new forms of critical and creative practice, most often from the perspective of collaborative investigation. Trained as a cultural theorist (PhD English), Lowry works with artists and collectives on projects that look at questions of social justice and emergent publics. From 2007 to 2015, he worked with Henry Tsang and M. Simon Levin as a lead artist-researcher on Maraya (marayaprojects.com), a project that links urban waterfront developments in Vancouver and Dubai. Increasingly, his studies look at questions of spatial justice and social engagement. As an editor/publishing consultant with the Aboriginal Healing Foundation (2011–2014), Lowry traveled across Canada participating in discussions about truth and reconciliation among Aboriginal and non-Aboriginal communities. Lowry also edited the literary and cultural journal *West Coast LINE* (2001–2012).

Lowry is an Assistant Dean in the Faculty of Culture and Community and Chair of the Research Ethics Board at Emily Carr University of Art + Design. He is also an Affiliate Professor in the Faculty of Creative and Critical Studies at the University of British Columbia.

ELIZABETH MONOIAN

Elizabeth Monoian is the founder and director of Society for Cultural Exchange (SCE), an organization that is developing global partnerships between private and public entities around interdisciplinary projects that address issues of climate and sustainability through the lens of creativity. Under SCE she cofounded the Land Art Generator Initiative (LAGI) and works closely with cities, universities, arts organizations, and community groups around the world to develop customized approaches to renewable energy installations that are both aesthetically and culturally responsive.

Through LAGI Elizabeth has published, exhibited, and presented globally on the aesthetics of renewable energy and the role of art in providing solutions to climate change. She holds an MFA from Carnegie Mellon University.

Her publications include *Regenerative Infrastructures, The Time Is Now: Public Art of the Sustainable City, New Energies, Powering Places,* and *A Field Guide to Renewable Energy Technologies.*

PAUL SCHIFINO

Paul received his degree in graphic design from the Art Institute of Pittsburgh in 1979. His work has been published in design publications including *Communication Arts* (CA), *Graphis, Print, How,* and *ReadyMade* magazine. His art has been included in shows at The Andy Warhol Museum (*AMP*), the Mattress Factory (*Gestures #4* and *#14*), TRAF Gallery (*By Design*), and the TRAF (*Best of Pittsburgh Show*).

He has served as president of the Pittsburgh chapter of the American Institute of Graphic Arts (AIGA), and is a former Advisory Board member of the American Shorts Reading Series, and the Art Institute of Pittsburgh. Paul currently serves on the board of Society for Cultural Exchange, and the advisory board of AIGA Pgh.

CRAIG WATSON

Craig Watson is the Director of the California Arts Council, a position he has held since August 2011 when he was selected by the Council after a nationwide search. Watson started his career in the arts field at local arts agencies and arts services organizations, and later built a career in the telecommunications industry before returning to the arts as Executive Director of the Arts Council for Long Beach. The California Arts Council is the official state arts agency for California, the state with the largest number of artists and creative-industry workers in the nation. Learn more at www.arts.ca.gov.

PATRICIA WATTS

Patricia Watts is founder and West Coast curator of ecoartspace, providing a platform for artists addressing environmental issues since 1997. Watts lived in the Los Angeles Basin from 1982 to 2005 and was the Topanga Creek Watershed Coordinator in the Santa Monica Mountains from 2001 to 2004. She curated one of the first temporal site-based art-in-nature exhibitions in Los Angeles County, in Escondido Canyon, Malibu, in 1999, and has recently worked with the National Park Service to install site-based works at Peter Strauss Ranch in Agoura Hills in the summer 2016. Watts has curated more than thirty art and nature exhibitions for multiple arts institutions. In 2015 she curated and project managed a permanent public art work in the Midwest titled *Cloud House* by Matthew Mazzotta, a living sculpture that rains on a tin roof, watering food in the windowsills, exploring the water cycle and our interdependence with the natural world. Watts has served as an Eco Art panelist for several public art departments in California including the cities of Los Angeles, San Jose, San Francisco, Sacramento, and Napa. She served as juror for LAGI 2012 NYC.

GLOSSARY

AEROLASTIC FLUTTER

A self-feeding regular vibration that occurs when wind passes by an object and stimulates the object's natural frequency, creating a positive feedback loop. This often destructive effect is avoided in airplane wing and bridge engineering, but it can be intentionally utilized for wind energy power generation often in combination with piezoelectronics.

ADVECTION FOG

When relatively warm moist air passes over a cool surface the water vapor condenses into water droplets suspended in the air. Advection refers to the movement of the air by the wind, and is common at coastal sites such as Santa Monica when moist air encounters cooler waters.

AEROPONICS

Combining the Greek words *aero* (air) and *ponos* (labor), *aeroponics* refers to the process of growing plants in a humid air or mist environment. By comparison, growing plants in soils is referred to as *geoponics* and growing plants in water is referred to as *hydroponics*, or *aquaponics* when fish provide nutrients. In aeroponics, plant roots and lower stems are periodically sprayed with an atomized nutrient-rich water solution.

ALGAE BIOFUEL

Algae can be grown and harvested (algaculture) as a feed stock for the production of alternatives to fossil fuels. Naturally occurring oils within algae (lipids) can be used directly (similar to straight vegetable oil), or they can be refined to burn more cleanly. Different production methods can result in biodiesel, biobutanol, biogasoline, methane, ethanol, or even jet fuel. The uptake of CO_2 by the algae during cultivation offsets the CO_2 that is emitted during the combustion of the algae-generated fuel.

ANTHROPOCENE

The geological epoch that began when human activity started to have a significant global impact on the geochemical signatures that can be traced through ice and sediment cores. As of 2016, the epoch is in the process of being officially recognized, and is in common use among scientists. If approved it would either replace or immediately follow the Holocene. Used within the humanities, the term is a reference to the detrimental impact that human activity is having on the environment.

ARTIFICIAL PHOTOSYNTHESIS (SOLAR FUEL)

Any number of chemical processes that create useful energy from the similar natural inputs that plants use to create sugars (air, water, and sunlight). The term is also applied to photocatalytic water splitting, which results in hydrogen fuel.

ATMOSPHERIC WATER GENERATION

Air contains water vapor. This vapor can be converted into liquid water by reducing the temperature or increasing the pressure of the air so that it passes the saturation point (dew point). Other methods of AWG include wet desiccation, which extracts water from air through absorption using a dry brine solution.

BI-FACIAL SILICON SOLAR PANEL

Any solar panel that has solar cells on both sides. These can benefit from environments with reflected light to produce more electricity than a panel with solar cells on only one side.

BIOFILTRATION OR BIOREMEDIATION

Living material can be used to take pollution from water, soil, or air. Through chemical processes inside plants or microorganisms, pollutants become biologically degraded or less harmful.

CARBON DIOXIDE (CO₂)

A naturally occurring chemical compound critical to life on earth, carbon dioxide also functions as a greenhouse gas (GHG) in the Earth's atmosphere (contributing to anthropogenic climate change and global warming). The emission of CO_2 through fossil fuel combustion by humans has, since modern industrialization, created an increase of 40% in the parts per million (ppm) concentration of the gas in the Earth's atmosphere. Since 1960, its concentration has risen from 320 ppm to 407 ppm (as of 2016) and further increases threaten rapid shifts upward in global temperature and sea levels. In order to avoid a temperature rise beyond 2° Celsius, between two-thirds and four-fifths of the known reserves of fossil fuel will need to remain unused. Increased atmospheric concentrations of CO_2 also have effects on the chemical composition of the oceans, as surface-level carbon dioxide dissolves forming other carbon compounds and leading to acidification.

CARBON FIBER REINFORCED RESIN POLES

A material that displays great strength in both tension and compression, but that is ductile along its length. Similar to the material used in pole vaulting poles or tent structures.

COMPACT WIND ACCELERATION TURBINE (CWAT)

This type of horizontal axis wind turbine uses a cone or series of cones to concentrate the wind, increase the velocity of the wind as it passes through the rotor's swept area, and thus increase the efficiency of the overall system. They are also known as *ducted turbines* or *lens wind turbines*.

CONCENTRATOR PHOTOVOLTAIC (CPV)

Typically using Fresnel lenses, CPV systems concentrate sunlight onto high-efficiency multijunction photovoltaic solar cells that can reach conversion efficiencies of 44% (standard solar modules are around 20%). CPV systems most often (with the exception of low-concentration, or LCPV) require dual-axis sun tracking to maintain the lens orientation perpendicular to the rays of the sun.

CONCENTRATED SOLAR POWER (CSP)

Describes a variety of systems that use mirrors or lenses (see *heliostatic*) to concentrate the power of the sun in order to create heat energy that can then be converted into electricity.

CONVECTION LOOP

In the dynamics of fluids or gas, the tendency of higher pressure and lower pressure to equalize causes warm to migrate toward cool, thus creating a flow of gas or liquid. In closed systems with heat input in one area, a continuous loop is created as warm material flows to cool areas.

DYE-SENSITIZED SOLAR CELL (DSSC)

The DSSC is alternatively known as the *Grätzel* cell. They have the characteristic of being semitransparent, flexible, and very durable. They also function comparatively better than other PV technologies in low light levels and indirect light.

ELECTROACTIVE POLYMERS (EAP)

Electroactive polymers are very complex and large molecules that alter their physical form when exposed to an electrical field. These polymers can be used to create materials that expand and contract in ways similar to that of animal muscle. There is some similarity between EAPs and piezoelectric materials, but EAPs can withstand far greater deformation and forces of strain. EPAM is an acronym for Electroactive Polymer Artificial Muscle and most closely relates to a product that can be licensed from SRI International.

ELECTRODIALYSIS AND CAPACITIVE DEIONIZATION

These are techniques for converting brine or salt water into drinking water by applying electrical potential difference to the fluid, which causes the adsorption of salt ions from the water.

EMISSIVITY

This is a quality of a material that refers to its effectiveness at emitting energy as thermal radiation (can include visible light and infrared radiation).

ETFE

Ethylene tetrafluoroethylene is a fluorine-based plastic designed for high strength. It is popular as a building facade material where light transmission is desired through curved forms. Examples include the Eden Project in Cornwall, United Kingdom, and the Beijing National Aquatics Centre.

FOG HARVESTING

A mesh material suspended across open areas commonly subjected to fog conditions can be used to collect tiny water droplets (through condensation) that then coalesce and flow down channels to storage cisterns. The technique has been successfully implemented in various parts of the world, most notably in the Atacama Desert of Chile. For other methods of collecting water from the atmosphere, see *atmospheric water generation*.

FRESNEL LENS

A magnifying lens that takes the sectional geometry of a simple convex lens and flattens it by slicing it in concentric circles and shifting the sliced segment profiles to create a flattened, corrugated surface. The optical effect of the lens is very similar to that of the original convex lens. Fresnel lenses are used to focus sunlight.

HELIOSTATIC (HELIOTROPIC)

The ability to follow the location of the sun in the sky and maintain an object's consistent relationship to it throughout the diurnal and seasonal shift. In solar energy technology, heliostatic mechanisms can maintain a solar cell perpendicular to the sunlight for ideal absorption and conversion, or mirrors can maintain an angle-of-incidence relationship to the sun so as to consistently reflect sunlight to a central collector.

HOLOGRAPHIC PLANAR CONCENTRATOR (HPC)

A holographic thin-film material channels direct and reflected light onto photovoltaic cells interspersed across the face of the collector. HPC panels can use 50% less silicon to generate the same amount of power. The optical technique is similar to luminescent solar concentrators, except that the solar cells are not relegated to the edges, but appear periodically across the face. HPC is well-suited to bi-facial panel design.

HYBRID PHOTOVOLTAIC THERMAL (PVT)

Any system that converts solar energy into both electrical and heat energy simultaneously. Because photovoltaic panels operate at approximately 20% conversion efficiency, much of the potential solar energy is lost to heat. This heat build-up has a detrimental impact on the performance of the solar cell due to increased electrical resistance within the circuitry. PVT systems can operate at 75% total conversion efficiency (electricity + heat).

HYDRAULIC TURBINE

A rotary engine that is driven by the force of passing water.

HYDROELECTRIC STORAGE

Excess capacity electricity is used to pump water temporarily into an upstream reservoir. The water can then later be released when there is demand for electricity. The force of gravity on the water drives generators just like at a conventional hydroelectric dam (which instead relies on natural precipitation cycles to provide its water source).

KILOWATT (KW)

Equal to 1,000 watts. See *watt*.

KILOWATT-HOUR (kWh)

Equal to 1,000 watt-hours. See *watt-hour*.

LED

Light-emitting diode, a semiconductor light source. An OLED is a LED that is fabricated using organic materials.

LINEAR ALTERNATOR

A linear motor used as a power generator for alternating current. Linear motors do not rely on torque and rotation but rather on simple linear motion.

LOW-TEMPERATURE THERMAL DESALINATION (LTTD)

Water can evaporate at low temperatures (even ambient air temperature) if the pressure is low enough. *Low-temperature thermal desalination* is a process that takes advantage of this by using vacuum pumps to make water vapor from surface seawater without the addition of heat energy. Much colder water from the deep sea is then used to condense the evaporated water into distilled drinking water.

LUMINESCENT SOLAR CONCENTRATORS

Using special optics, a large flat plane can create internal reflections that concentrate light hitting the surface of the plane out to the edges of the material where it is then converted into electricity with solar cells. Some versions of the technology can maintain transparency for certain wavelengths of light, while capturing others for conversion at the edge.

MARINE ATMOSPHERIC BOUNDARY LAYER (MABL)

The atmospheric boundary layer is the lowest part of the earth's atmosphere. When in contact with the ocean, the layer exchanges large quantities of heat and moisture. An "MABL inversion" refers to the times when this layer is trapped below an upper layer of higher temperature (typically atmospheric temperatures tend to decrease with altitude). These are common in the Los Angeles Basin due to the prevalence of warm continental air drifting out over the ocean over coastal mountain ranges. During an inversion, fog often forms as the ocean moisture is trapped within the ABL. Inversions can also trap pollutants in the lower atmosphere, contributing to smog effects.

MEGAWATT (MW)

Equal to 1,000,000 watts. See *watt*.

MEGAWATT-HOUR (MWh)

Equal to 1,000,000 watt-hours. See *watt-hour*.

MULTISTAGE FLASH DISTILLATION (MFD)

The most common type of commercial desalination technology, MFD operates by flash-heating a portion of water into steam through multiple stages, each containing a heat exchanger and a condensate collector. MFD plants typically require between 23–27 kWh to produce one cubic meter (1,000 liters) of distilled water. As with most types of desalination, the environmentally safe disposal or discharge of the resulting high-concentration brine is a difficult problem to overcome.

MWhe

Megawatt-hour equivalent. This unit of measurement for energy is often used when quantifying liquid fuel in comparison to electricity.

OMNIDIRECTIONAL PHOTOVOLTAIC

Able to convert sunlight into electricity at any angle in relation to the sun. Most PV technologies either require or work best at an angle perpendicular to the sun's position in the sky.

ORGANIC PHOTOVOLTAIC (OPV)

Organic PV can be manufactured in solutions that can be painted or rolled onto proper substrate materials. They have a lower conversion efficiency (8–10%), but can be produced at very low cost in comparison with other PV technologies because they can take advantage of roll-to-roll production techniques in which the organic photovoltaic system is "printed" onto a long, continuous sheet of substrate material.

PARABOLIC TROUGH

A type of concentrated solar power that uses a long, mirrored surface with the cross-sectional shape of a parabola. Sunlight that hits the mirror surface (at an angle parallel to the central axis of the parabola) is directed to the focal point of the parabola, thus providing energy to a heat transfer fluid that runs continuously along its length. The heated transfer fluid can be used to generate the steam required for turbine generators.

PHOTOVOLTAIC (PV)

The photovoltaic effect, first recognized by A. E. Becquerel in 1839, is the ability of a material to produce direct current electricity when exposed to solar radiation. Silicon (Si) is a semiconductor material that displays the photovoltaic effect. It was the first material to be employed in solar cells and is still the most prevalent. It can be applied for use in either a crystalline (wafer) form, or in a noncrystalline (amorphous) form. There are two types of crystalline silicon: monocrystalline and polycrystalline (aka multicrystalline). Monocrystalline is expensive to manufacture (because it requires cutting slices from cylindrical ingots of silicon crystals that are grown with the Czochralski process) but it displays a high conversion efficiency (around 23%). Polycrystalline is easier to manufacture than monocrystalline silicon and is more versatile, but has lower conversion (around 18%).

PHYTOREMEDIATION

In land areas that have experienced contamination (such as toxic heavy metals and organic pollutants), certain types of plants can be effective at transferring contaminates into the plant cells. The type of plants that excel at this are referred to as hyperaccumulators. Because the process occurs in-situ, the cost can be lower than other kinds of soil remediation techniques. Limitations of the technique include soil depth (plant roots only extend so deep), time (multiple seasons of growth are usually required for results), and safe disposal of affected plant material. See *biofiltration*.

PIEZOELECTRIC FIBER COMPOSITES (PFC)

An array of piezoelectric ceramic fibers arranged on a flexible substrate and protected by a resin film. PFCs provide higher performance, greater flexibility, and higher strength than monolithic piezoelectric materials.

PIEZOELECTRIC GENERATOR

A device that generates electrical power from pressure force. Common application of a piezoelectric device is as the ignition source for gas range and grill "push starters." Piezoelectric discs or torriods can be stacked within a flexible pole to generate electrical current from the bending of the pole (piezoelectric stacked actuators).

PTFE-WOVEN TEXTILE

A fabric made by weaving PTFE (Polytetrafluoroethylene) fibers. PTFE is a synthetic resin most commonly known by the trademark Teflon® owned by Chemours (formerly DuPont).

PVB FOIL

Polyvinyl butyral is a resin that provides strong binding, optical clarity, adhesion, toughness, and flexibility. Its most prevalent use is in lamination safety glass for automobile windshields, and it has found wide use in solar module manufacturing.

RECIPROCATING

Operating with a repetitive back-and-forth or up-and-down linear motion.

REVERSE OSMOSIS DESALINATION

This is an increasingly popular method of converting salt water into drinking water, used in nearly all new plants. The energy input (approximately 3 kWh per cubic meter) is far less than multistage flash distillation. RO desalination relies on semipermeable membranes that let water pass through while removing ions, molecules, and larger particles. Water passing through the membrane must be pressurized to the osmotic pressure in order to pass through the membrane. As with most types of desalination, the environmentally safe disposal or discharge of the resulting high-concentration brine is a difficult problem to overcome.

SANTA MONICA URBAN RUNOFF RECYCLING FACILITY (SMURRF)

Opened in 2001, the SMURRF facility treats an average of 500,000 gallons per day of urban runoff generated in parts of the cities of Santa Monica and Los Angeles. The runoff water is diverted from the city's two main storm drains into the SMURRF and treated to remove pollutants such as trash, sediment, oil, grease, and pathogens. Once treated, the water is safe for all landscape irrigation and dual-plumbed systems.

SOLAR DISTILLATION FOR DESALINATION (SOLAR STILL)

The solar humidification-dehumidification method (HDH) is a thermal water desalination technique based on evaporation of salt water and condensation of the humid air that results. The process is very similar to the natural water cycle, but accelerated by the greenhouse effect of the enclosure.

SOLAR POND

The heat that is trapped at the bottom of a saltwater pond can be harnessed to power an organic Rankine cycle turbine or a Stirling engine, both of which convert heat into electricity without steam (does not require temperatures in excess of H_2O boiling point). Via the Organic Rankine Cycle (ORC), water is piped to an evaporator coil that heats a low-boiling-point fluid to pressurized vapor, driving a turbine. The vapor then passes to a condenser, where water from the top layer of the pond is used to cool the fluid back into liquid form.

SOLAR THERMAL

Solar radiation used to heat a medium such as water or air.

SOLAR UPDRAFT (SOLAR CHIMNEY)

Combines the chimney/stack effect and greenhouse effect with wind turbines located at the base of a tall tower. The tower is surrounded by a greenhouse which serves to create superheated air at the ground level. With a sufficiently tall chimney structure, the air temperature at the top of the tower will be cool enough to provide pressure differential convection movement of air through the turbines.

STIRLING HEAT ENGINE

Device that converts heat into mechanical energy with high efficiency. This mechanical energy can then be used to power an electrical generator.

TENSEGRITY

Individual structural members (usually metal bars) working in compression are suspended away from each other by means of a continuous tension net (usually comprised of metal cables). The term was coined by Buckminster Fuller as a portmanteau of "tensional" and "integrity." The structural system has been used in many works of public art, including those by Kenneth Snelson.

THIN-FILM

As applied to photovoltaics, any of a variety of non-crystalline solar cell technologies that can be applied in very thin layers, thus reducing material costs. Sometimes referred to as *second-generation photovoltaic cells*.

TIDAL TURBINE / TIDAL STREAM GENERATOR

Similar in appearance to a wind turbine (either vertical or horizontal in orientation), these machines extract energy from moving masses of water, such as tides. They are relatively environmentally benign as they operate in open waters and do not require the construction of a tidal barrage or lagoon.

TRANSPARENT OR TRANSLUCENT PHOTOVOLTAICS

Solar cells that are laminated in a transparent or translucent material in such a way that allows light to pass through at least partially. The solar cell technology itself can be transparent/translucent or opaque with gaps between. The pattern of the photovoltaic material placement can be dense or sparse, ordered dense or sparse, ordered or irregular. See *luminescent solar concentrators*.

TURBINE ROTOR

The moving part of a turbine engine which consists of a drum or a shaft with blades attached to it.

UTILITY-SCALE

Significant enough power generation so as to warrant the distribution of the energy to the utility grid (as opposed to on-site power generation for local use).

VENTURI EFFECT

When a fluid body, such as air, is in motion and is constricted in its path, such as by a funnel, the velocity of the fluid will increase and its static pressure will be reduced. The effect can be felt in urban areas when standing between two tall buildings, which together act as a funnel. This principle is incorporated into the design of compact wind acceleration turbines (CWAT).

VERTICAL AXIS WIND TURBINE

Any wind turbine in which the rotational axis is vertical in orientation (perpendicular to the ground plane). Types of vertical axis wind turbines include Savonius, Darrieus (eggbeater), and Giromills.

VORTEX BLADELESS™ WIND TURBINE

A wind energy conversion device that does not require rotating blades or other moving parts. It instead makes use of resonance within a system that is vibrated by the force of wind across the body of the device.

WATT (W)

Unit of measure of electrical power equivalent to 1/746 horsepower.
W = Volts x Amperes

WATT-HOUR

A measure of electrical energy equivalent to one watt of power used or produced for a one-hour duration.

WAVE ENERGY CONVERTER

Any device that uses the kinetic force of waves to generate electricity or some other useful energy.

Types of wave energy converters include:
- point absorber wave energy converter
- oscillating water column
- overtopping
- oscillating wave surge
- attenuator (surface following)
- submerged pressure differential
- rotating mass

WELLS TURBINE

Developed by Alan Wells in the late 1970s, the Wells Turbine incorporates symmetrical airfoil blades that provide continuous rotation regardless of the direction of air movement through the device. It is most typically used within oscillating water column wave power devices where the up and down movement creates compression of air into a chamber followed by the release of pressure from the chamber.

WIND MICROTURBINE

A small wind turbine with less than 3,000 watt peak capacity. Pico wind turbines are even smaller with peak capacity of less than 500 watts.

WIND TURBINE

A rotary engine driven by the force of passing wind that can convert rotational force into electrical power.

"Imagine the majestic beauty of the massive infrastructures that will power our prosperity for the next hundred years, regeneratively designed with input from creatives, that will allow the planet to heal."

—Elizabeth Monoian and Robert Ferry
Founding Directors, Land Art Generator Initiative

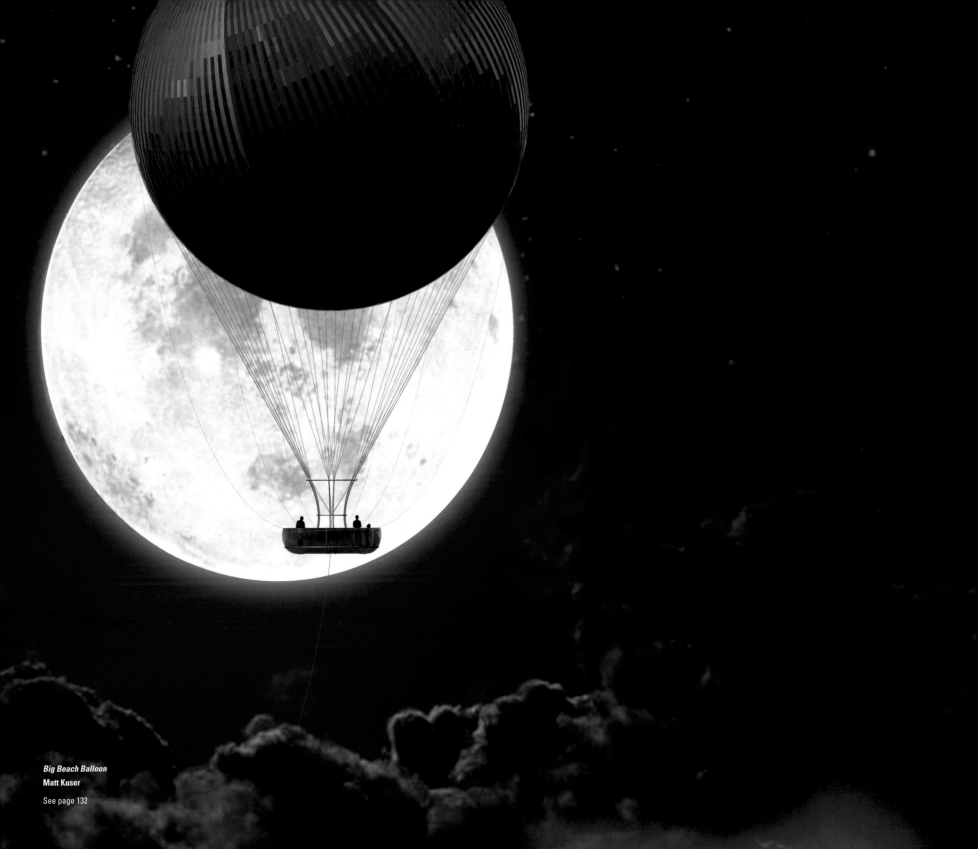

Big Beach Balloon
Matt Kuser

See page 132

INDEX

ACKNOWLEDGMENTS

The LAGI competitions are always a testament to the importance of partnerships, and LAGI 2016 is no exception. The competition would not have happened if it were not for Rebecca Ehemann of Green Public Art who contacted us in 2014 asking what we thought about bringing the next competition to Los Angeles County. We didn't hesitate for a minute to say yes. Her tremendous skills at project development helped to bring LAGI 2016 to life as she connected us with almost everyone to whom we express further thanks below.

Thanks to Dean Kubani, Jessica Cusick, Andrew Basmajian, and many others with the City of Santa Monica who provided us with the canvas on which our teams could design.

Our project partners and the institutions that provided us with critical support: the Los Angeles Chapter of the US Green Building Council (USGBC-LA), Los Angeles County Arts Commission, County of Los Angeles Department of Public Works, the Annenberg Community Beach House, The Bay Foundation, Santa Monica Pier Foundation, the Santa Monica Library, and the California Arts Council.

Those who helped to make the LAGI 2016 Youth Prize a success: the Museum of Art & History (MOAH), the City of Lancaster, Monica Mahoney, Devora Orantes, the Antelope Valley School District, Donita Winn, Robyn Young, Pittsburgh Public Schools, and the many students and teachers who participated.

Our media partner Shawati', the bilingual (Arabic/English) arts and culture publication based in Abu Dhabi, whose gorgeous design and thoughtful journalism is setting a new standard of excellence in socially-conscious print media.

A special thanks to Paul Schifino of Schifino Design who designed the LAGI 2016 identity and this very book that you are reading. Paul is a member of our Board of Directors, and we would like to thank him in that capacity along with fellow Board member Deborah Hosking.

Thank you to the shortlist committee and the jurors who so graciously gave their time to the 2016 LAGI competition.

We are also thankful for the support of the J.M. Kaplan Fund. We are honored to be among the awardees of the J.M.K. Innovation Prize, which has made it possible for us to successfully deliver LAGI 2016 while we grow our organization in a sustainable way.

The Elizabeth Firestone Graham Foundation for providing financial support for this publication.

Thanks also goes out to Rhonda Hauff for her support, to Lance Diernback who found inspiration to support LAGI through his great niece Mia Wavrek, to Geoffrey Glick for his sound advice and support, to Peter Coombe, and to Michael Ferry and Susie Boucher for their continued support. They have been sharing the LAGI publications with their children, John and Eleanor, who we are certain will go on to help change the world in wonderful ways.

All of the individuals who have helped us throughout LAGI 2016 development, including, Sen. Ben Allen, Julie Du Brow, Jim Harris, Brian Kern, Lauren Pizer Mains, Andi Campognone, Camilla Griggers and Marni Borek of the Healist, Matthew Rosenberg, Tafline Laylin, Sara Neff, Dominique Hargreaves, Malina Moore, Jennifer Lieu, Vanessa Olivas, Patrick Holland, Craig Watson, John and Jennifer Ferry, and Anita Monoian whose commitment to social justice continues to inspire us.

And of course there is no LAGI competition without those who spend their time dedicated to the creation of the ideas contained in this book. Thank you to all of the LAGI 2016 design teams.

This book is dedicated to Col. Pearl E. Tucker (Ret.), who founded the field of aerospace nursing in the 1950s and dared to imagine a space age in which human health was prioritized, and also to Marian Pearl Nicholas, one of our newest fellow travelers on spaceship Earth. Her future depends on the actions we take today.

Robert Ferry and Elizabeth Monoian
Land Art Generator Initiative

© Prestel Verlag, Munich · London · New York, and
Society for Cultural Exchange, 2016

All text © the authors or their estates unless
otherwise noted. All works © the artists, artist teams,
or their estates unless otherwise noted. All project
descriptions © the artists, artist teams, or their estates
unless otherwise noted.

Front cover: *Regatta H2O*, Christopher Sjoberg,
Ryo Saito
Title page: *Misty(Cal) Fog Catchers*, Rafael Fernandez,
Marie-Adelaide Mol (Maria Design Studio)
Back cover: *The Clear Orb*, Jaesik Lim, Ahyoung Lee,
Jaeyeol Kim, Taegu Lim

Prestel Verlag, Munich
A member of Verlagsgruppe Random House GmbH
Neumarkter Strasse 28, 81673 Munich
Tel. +49 (0)89 4136-0
Fax +49 (0)89 4136-2335

Prestel Publishing Ltd.
14-17 Wells Street
London W1T 3PD

Prestel Publishing
900 Broadway, Suite 603
New York, NY 10003

www.prestel.com

Library of Congress Control Number 2016952033;
A CIP catalogue record for this book is available from
the British Library.

Editorial direction: Robert Ferry, Elizabeth Monoian
Project management Prestel: Constanze Holler,
Juliane Eisele
Production Prestel: Andrea Cobré
Design: Paul Schifino, schifinodesign.com
Printing and binding: GCC Cuno, Calbe
Printed in Ultra HD Print®

Printed in Germany

ISBN 978-3-7913-5550-4

Verlagsgruppe Random House FSC® N001967
The FSC®-certified paper *Condat Perigord*
was supplied by Papier-Union

FSC
www.fsc.org

MIX
Paper from
responsible sources
FSC® C043106

Funding for this publication came from:
Elizabeth Firestone Graham Foundation

The Land Art Generator Initiative is a
project of Society for Cultural Exchange

www.landartgenerator.org